MACROENVIRONMENTAL ANALYSIS FOR STRATEGIC MANAGEMENT

THE WEST SERIES IN STRATEGIC MANAGEMENT

Consulting Editor
Charles W. Hofer

MACROENVIRONMENTAL ANALYSIS FOR STRATEGIC MANAGEMENT

Liam Fahey
BOSTON UNIVERSITY

V.K. Narayanan
UNIVERSITY OF KANSAS

WEST PUBLISHING COMPANY
St. Paul   New York   Los Angeles   San Francisco

Acknowledgment: The diagram on page 21 is reprinted with permission of The Free Press, a division of MacMillan, from RENEWING AMERICAN INDUSTRY, by Paul R. Lawrence and Davis Dyer. Copyright © 1983, by The Free Press.

Copyediting by Joan Torkildson

Interior art by Alice B. Thiede, Carto-Graphics

Cover design by Peter Thiel, Kim Rafferty

Index prepared by Virginia Hobbs

Library of Congress Cataloging-in-Publication Data

Fahey, Liam, 1951–
  Macroenvironmental analysis for strategic management.

  (West series in strategic management)
  Bibliography: p.
  Includes index.
  1. Strategic planning. 2. Business and politics.
3. Industry—Social aspects. I. Narayanan, V.K.
II. Title. III. Series.
HD30.28.F34 1986   658.4′012   86–15682
ISBN 0–314–85233–6

CONTENTS

1

Introduction   *1*

2

Conceptual Overview   *10*

3

The Process of Environmental Analysis   *36*

4

Demographics   *58*

5

Life-Styles   *73*

6

Social Values   *90*

7

The Economic Environment   *105*

8

Technology   *119*

13

Environmental Analysis Techniques   *206*

14

Managing Environmental Analysis   *222*

FOREWORD

This series is a response to the rapid and significant changes that have occurred in the strategic management/business policy area over the past twenty-five years. Although strategic management/business policy is a subject of long standing in management schools, it was traditionally viewed as a capstone course whose primary purpose was to *integrate* the knowledge and skills students had gained in the functional disciplines. During the past fifteen years, however, strategic management/business policy has developed a substantive content of its own. Originally, this content focused on the concepts of corporate and business strategies and on the processes by which such strategies were formulated and implemented within organizations. More recently, as Figure 1 and Table 1 illustrate, the scope of the field has broadened to include the study of both the functions and responsibilities of top management and the organizational systems and processes used to establish overall organizational goals and objectives and to formulate, implement, and control the strategies and policies necessary to achieve these goals and objectives.

When the *West Series in Business Policy and Planning* was originally published, most of the texts in the field did not yet reflect this extension in scope. The principal purpose of the original series was, therefore, to fill this void by incorporating the latest research findings and conceptual thought in the field into each of the texts in the series. In the intervening seven years, the series has succeeded to a far greater degree than we could have ever hoped.

However, the pace of research in strategic management/business policy has, if anything, increased since the publication of the original series. Some changes are, thus, clearly in order. It is the purpose of the *West Series in Strategic Management* to continue the tradition of innovative, state-of-the-art coverage of the field of strategic management started by the *West Series in Business Policy and Planning* both through revisions to all the books in the original series, and through the addition of two new titles. In making such revisions, care has been taken to ensure not only that the

ix

Figure 1 The Evolution of
Business Policy/Strategic Management as a Field of Study

The Traditional Boundary of Business Policy

The Current Boundaries of Strategic Management

Some Major Contributors to the Redefinition of the Field

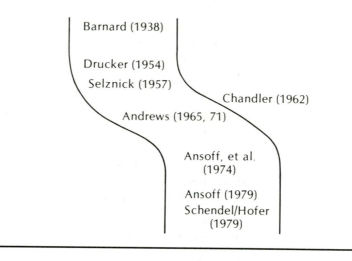

various texts fit together as a series, but also that each is self-contained and addresses a major topic in the field. In addition, the series has been designed so that it covers almost all the major topics that form the heartland of strategic management, as Figure 2 illustrates. The individual texts in the series are

Setting Strategic Goals and Objectives, 2d ed.
Max D. Richards

Strategy Formulation: Issues and Concepts
Charles W. Hofer

Table 1   The Major Subfields of Business Policy/Strategic Management

1. Boards of Directors
2. The Nature of General Management Work
3. Middle-Level General Management
* 4. Stakeholder Analysis
* 5. Organizational Goal Formulation
6. Corporate Social Policy and Management Ethics
↙ 7. Macroenvironmental Analysis
* 8. Strategy Formulation and Strategic Decision Making
9. Corporate-Level Strategy (including Mergers, Acquisitions, and Divestitures)
10. Business-Level Strategy
* 11. Strategic Planning and Information Systems
12. The Strategy-Structure-Performance Linkage
13. The Design of Macroorganizational Structure and Systems
14. Strategic Control Systems
15. Organizational Culture
16. Leadership Style for General Managers
17. The Strategic Management of Small Businesses and New Ventures
18. The Strategic Management of High Tech Organizations
19. The Strategic Management of Not-for-Profit Organizations

↙ Indicates subfields that are covered extensively by this text
* Indicates other subfields that are discussed in this text

Strategy Formulation: Power and Politics, 2d ed.
Ian C. MacMillan and Patricia E. Jones

Strategy Implementation: Structure, Systems, and Process, 2d ed.
Jay R. Galbraith and Robert K. Kazanjian

Strategic Control
Peter Lorange, Michael F. Scott Morton, and Sumantra Ghoshal

Macroenvironmental Analysis for Strategic Management
Liam Fahey and V.K. Narayanan

The series has also been designed so that the texts within it can be used in several ways. First, the entire series can be used as a set to provide an advanced conceptual overview of the field of strategic management. Second, selected texts in the series can be combined with cases drawn from the Harvard Case Services, the Case Teaching Association and/or the Case Research Association to create a course customized to particular instructor needs. Third, individual texts in the series can be used to

Figure 2 The Strategic Management Process

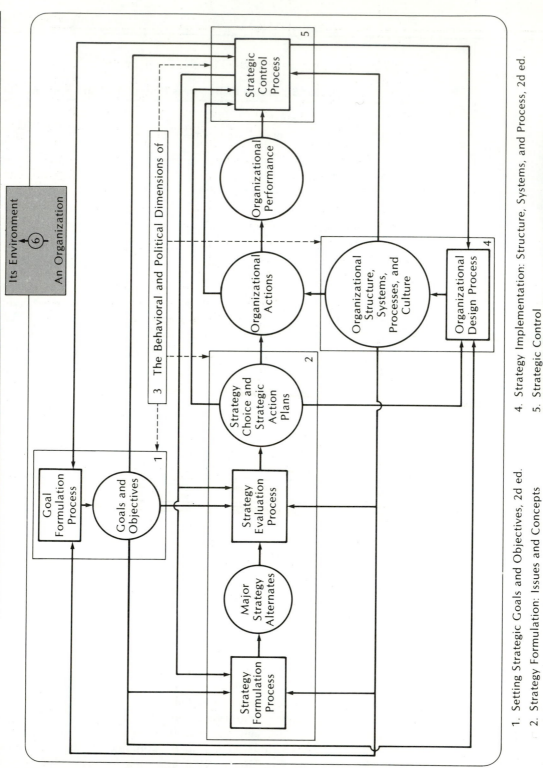

1. Setting Strategic Goals and Objectives, 2d ed.
2. Strategy Formulation: Issues and Concepts
3. Strategy Formulation: Power and Politics, 2d ed.
4. Strategy Implementation: Structure, Systems, and Process, 2d ed.
5. Strategic Control
6. Macroenvironmental Analysis for Strategic Management

supplement the conceptual materials contained in the existing text and casebooks in the field. The series thus offers the individual instructor great flexibility in designing the required business policy/strategic management course. Fourth, because of their self-contained nature, each of the texts can be used either individually or in combination with other materials as the basis for an advanced specialized course in strategic management. For instance, the text on *Strategic Control* could be used to create a state-of-the-art course on "Strategic Control Systems." Likewise, the *Macroenvironmental Analysis for Strategic Management* and *Strategy Formulation: Power and Politics* texts could be combined to create an innovative course on "Stakeholder Management." Or the text on *Setting Strategic Goals and Objectives* could be combined with a text on boards of directors to create an advanced course on the latter topic.

Finally, in concluding this Common Foreword I would like to thank my co-editor on the original series, Dan Schendel of Purdue University, for his efforts on that series. They were both substantial and valuable. Indeed, the series could not have been established as effectively as it was without him.

Charles W. Hofer
Editor
October 1985

PREFACE

This textbook is an introduction to macroenvironmental analysis and its role in strategic decision making. By the word *macroenvironment* we mean the total environment outside the industry: the social, economic, technological, political, and regulatory environments. The book provides a framework for analyzing the macroenvironment and incorporating the analysis into the broader terrain of strategic decision making. The thrust of the argument is that managers, as strategists, must take into account macroenvironmental forces, as they shape and reformulate their organizations' strategies.

The book is intended for both practicing managers and business management students. It is presented with the macroenvironmental analyst in mind—that is, the person who must confront the task of analyzing the macroenvironment and make use of the analysis in the process of strategic decision making.

The intent of the textbook is to provide a comprehensive and systematic approach to macroenvironmental analysis that is applicable to any type of organization. The emphasis is upon application—the development of an analytical framework that can be adapted to meet each organization's macroenvironmental analysis needs.

Acknowledgments

In writing this book we have benefited greatly from the comments of colleagues, students, practitioners, and reviewers. A number of former and current colleagues read and critiqued large segments of the book: Don Haider and Gene Lavengood (Northwestern University), George Kanatas (Indiana University), John Mahon (Boston University), and John Garland (University of Kansas). Two of our students, Larry Goldstein and Richard Oxandale, deserve special mention for their background research and assistance. We were also fortunate in being able to subject various chapters to the demanding and stern criticism of a number of practitioners of macroenvironmental analysis: Michael Adams (Burson-Marsteller),

Michael Broad (National Gas Pipeline), John Gaffney (the American Medical Association), Susan Schmidt (Northern Trust Company), Richard Smith (Loretto Hospital), Glen Seretan (Allstate Insurance), Tom Stock (Ameritech), and Paul Weininger (Washington National Insurance Company). We particularly thank the following five reviewers, whose comments and insights compelled us to rethink many segments of our first draft: John Grant (University of Pittsburgh), John R. Montanari (Arizona State University), Gary B. Roberts (Kennesaw College), Warren Keith Schilit (University of South Florida), and Robert Sobek (University of Pittsburgh). Finally, we thank Julia Taylor for her patience in turning some roughly scribbled notes into readable manuscript during the early stages of writing this book.

MACROENVIRONMENTAL ANALYSIS FOR STRATEGIC MANAGEMENT

1

Introduction

In the last two decades, there has been a growing recognition of the need to understand environments of organizations in order to devise successful strategies. This recognition is manifest on several fronts: in the shift in conception of organizations from one of closed to one of open systems, in increased awareness of environmental turbulence, in the advancement of the notion that environments should be understood and studied in their own right, independent of the immediate context of an organization, and in efforts to include environmental analysis in the ongoing strategy formulation processes in organizations.

The first of these shifts toward the open systems view can be traced to the increasing acceptance of general systems theory (Bertalanffy 1968) as a valid epistemological platform for inquiry into the affairs of organizations. This shift is illustrated in the volume of research generated in organizational theory and in strategic management (Hofer and Schendel 1978). Indeed, Hofer and Schendel define strategy as the characteristics of the match that an organization achieves with its environment.

This shift is joined by a growing recognition of the increased turbulence displayed by environments. As early as 1965, Emery and Trist provided a glimpse of the characteristics of turbulent environments. More currently, Ansoff (1981), describing the U.S. environment from a historical perspective, sharply notes the characteristics of turbulence in the postindustrial society: growth in the novelty and intensity in the environment, and the increase in the rate and complexity of environmental change. The critical implication flowing from this recognition of turbulence is the need to institutionalize environmental analysis in large organizations.

Along with these, a number of attempts have been made to understand environments in their own right. The school of futures studies

1

specifically addresses issues pertaining to the future evolution of environments. In addition, several futurists (e.g., Toffler 1980) have discussed possible scenarios of the evolution of postindustrial societies, whereas social observors such as Naisbitt (1982) have provided portraits of current trends in society.

Efforts to include environmental analysis efforts in strategy formulation have always been present in business organizations. Consider the following:

■ Market researchers have long monitored the activity of competitors, changes in demographic patterns, and consumer tastes. A traditional role of R and D specialists has been to follow developments in science and technology taking place in universities, research institutes, other industries, and government facilities. The job of the corporate economist is largely to track and forecast key macroeconomic data and relate them to company markets and products. The Washington offices of major companies are established to keep tabs on—and to influence—what is happening (or is likely to happen) in Congress, the independent agencies, and the Executive Branch. When the Corporate legal staff acts in an advisory (as against a litigious or contract-drawing) capacity, it is, in effect, probing the legal environment. Institutional advertising campaigns, speeches to outside groups, efforts to anticipate questions that will be asked at the annual shareholders' meeting and the preparation of suitable responses for the presiding executives—these familiar phenomena all manifest corporate involvement with issues and trends in one or another of the company's environments. (James Brown. *The Business of Issues: Coping with Company's Environment*, 1979, The Conference Board, Inc.)

In the seventies, these efforts, which had till then been sporadic, began to receive increased attention because of the turbulence noted earlier, and environmental analysis as an integrated, unified effort began to be undertaken in large organizations.

Taken together, these four shifts signal a change in the practice of strategic management. The organization was once considered primary, but in the seventies and eighties, environment is being regarded as the focal point and the central problem of strategic management: the latter is viewed as orchestrating organizational activities to meet the challenges that environment poses. Thus, understanding the environment is a critical task of strategic management. With the experience gained in the last decade, detailing the contours of the domain sketched by environmental analysis is now possible. This book attempts to do so.

This text is designed to help students and practitioners of strategic management develop an understanding of macroenvironmental analysis and its linkages to strategy formulation. Because the book's focus is the macroenvironment, applying the concepts of the book to contexts outside of the business firm is possible. Indeed, these concepts have been found useful for nonprofit organizations, government agencies, and social entities such as churches.

The text addresses environmental analysis concepts from an applications perspective; it tries to present ideas and models useful for managers in their efforts to formulate strategies to confront macroenvironmental challenges. It is intended as a complement to the writings of other authors in the *West Series in Strategic Management* and avoids repetitions of the work that they present. Thus, issues related to industry and competition analysis are not detailed here, though linkages of macroenvironmental analysis to these are clearly pointed out.

MACROENVIRONMENTAL ANALYSIS

The focus of this book is the macroenvironment—that is, the environment external to an industry. Concern with the macroenvironment is predicated upon the assumption that the forces in the macroenvironment affect industries and destinies of the firms within them. We conceive of the macroenvironment as consisting of four segments or sets of forces: social, economic, technological, and political. Macroenvironmental analysis is thus the analysis of current and potential change in these segments and the assessment of their implications for strategic management.

To place the treatment here in perspective, a useful approach is to consider the goals, value, and limitations inherent in environmental analysis.

Goals of Environmental Analysis

Environmental analysis has three basic goals.

First, the analysis should provide an understanding of *current* and *potential* changes taking place in the environment. These words are emphasized to highlight that (1) understanding changes taking place currently is an important guide to anticipating the future, and that (2) the analysis should cover a time frame from short run to long run.

Second, environmental analysis should provide *important intelligence* for strategic decision makers. The analysis is often intrinsically interesting, but the primary goal is not the generation of information for its own sake but information that is of use in determining and managing a firm's strategies.

Third, environmental analysis should facilitate and foster *strategic thinking* in organizations—typically a rich source of ideas and understanding of the context within which a firm operates. It should challenge the current wisdom by bringing fresh viewpoints into the organization.

Value of Environmental Analysis

The value of environmental analysis inheres in the *product* of the analysis as well as the *process* of engaging in it.

At the product level, the outputs of environmental analysis generally consist of (1) descriptions of changes *currently* taking place, (2) harbingers of *potential* changes in the future, and (3) alternative descriptions of *future* change. Together they provide descriptions of alternative futures. Such descriptions provide organizations with *lead time* to identify, understand, and adapt to external issues, to anticipate the consequences of environmental trends, and to develop well thought out positions and policies. In addition, lead time enables organizations to convert emerging issues from threats to opportunities.

At the level of process, environmental analysis underscores the notion that organizations are incessantly pervious to the influence of outside forces. When conducted properly, this leads to enhanced capacity and commitment to understanding, anticipating, and responding to external changes on the part of the firm's key strategic managers. Responsiveness is achieved by inducing managers to think beyond their task or industry environments, often forcing them to reflect upon their cognitive biases. In short, at the process level, environmental analysis offers one basis for *organizational learning*.

Limitations of Environmental Analysis

Despite its potential value, environmental analysis should be placed in proper perspective: as with any other type of analysis, it has its limitations.

First, environmental analysis does not foretell the future, nor does it eliminate uncertainty for any organization. Thus, organizations that practice environmental analysis sometimes confront unexpected events—events not anticipated during environmental analysis. Environmental analysis, however, should reduce the frequency and extent of surprises that may confront the firm.

Second, environmental analysis in and of itself is not a sufficient guarantor of organizational effectiveness. It forms only one input for strategy development and testing. Environmental analysis should be used in conjunction with other forms of analysis such as industry, competitor, and organizational analysis.

Third, the potential of environmental analysis is often not realized because of how it is practiced. It is sometimes used as a crutch for post hoc reflection; at times managers place uncritical faith in the data without thinking about the data's variability or accuracy.

The primary value of environmental analysis lies in its use for strategic decision making and strategic thinking. However, these benefits do not evolve automatically; they must be created and sustained. Hence, issues of how to manage environmental analysis in organizations beyond those of analytical routines are important. These issues related to the management of environmental analysis are considered in addition to the techniques and frameworks available for engaging in analysis.

ORGANIZATION OF THE BOOK

The organization of the book is presented pictorially in Figure 1.1. The figure identifies four key considerations in environmental analysis: (1) conception of the macroenvironment, (2) process of analysis, (3) linkage to strategy analysis, and (4) organizational prerequisites. The central themes advanced here are that one's vision of macroenvironment (content) and approaches to analyzing it (process) are inextricably *intertwined;* that environmental analysis should *precede* strategy analysis, though the latter may induce the former for short-run purposes; and that analysis as carried out in organizations needs to be *supported* by organizational prerequisites that should reflect the structural differentiation implicit in the conception of environment. These themes are elaborated in the ensuing chapters.

Chapter 2 outlines some theoretical notions and a framework for thinking about the environment. A conception of macroenvironment, built around four segments—social, economic, political and technological—is presented, and various linkages to strategy formulation are pointed out.

In Chapter 3, an analytical framework for engaging in environmental analysis is developed. The four critical activities in environmental analysis—scanning, monitoring, forecasting, and assessment—are described in detail. The analytical process involved in doing environmental analysis is also detailed.

Chapters 4–10 focus upon individual segments of the macroenvironment and illustrate how the analytical framework developed in Chapter 3 can be utilized to analyze each segment. The

Figure 1.1   Organization of the Book: A Pictorial Representation

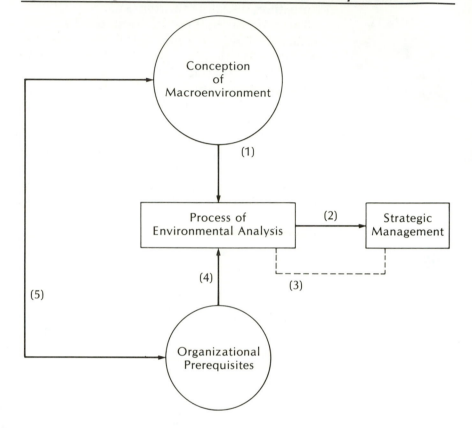

(1) Content/Process Interplay

(2) Precedence of Environmental Analysis to Strategic Management

(3) Induced Environmental Analysis ("Inside-out" Approach)

(4) Organizational Support: Strong link

(5) Structural Differentiation in Organizational Prerequisites

segments are discussed separately to highlight their distinctive features. Scanning, monitoring, and forecasting in each segment are then considered, and key implications of each for strategy development are pointed out.

The *social* environment is discussed in chapters on demographics (Chapter 4), life-styles (Chapter 5), and values (Chapter 6). The *economic* and *technological* environments are dealt with separately in two chapters (Chapters 7 and 8). Finally, the *political* environment is covered in the chapters on the political milieu (Chapter 9) and the regulatory environment (Chapter 10).

In Chapter 11, the focus is on integrating analysis of the individual environmental segments. The intent is to provide a conceptual framework that permits consideration of linkages across the individual segments. Thus, the chapter emphasizes the importance of going beyond trends and patterns to identify and analyze issues—that is, those aspects of the environment that the organization considers vital to its future.

Chapter 12 is devoted to the process of linking environmental analysis to strategic management. Critical areas of linkages are discussed, and a set of guiding questions for each area of linkage is presented to facilitate strategy development and implementation.

Chapter 13 discusses an overview of various techniques and methodologies that can be employed to structure and facilitate scanning, monitoring, and forecasting efforts. Our intent is not to provide an exhaustive treatment of these techniques but rather to illustrate their value and scope in environmental analysis as well as their strengths and limitations.

Finally, Chapter 14 deals with issues related to managing environmental analysis. As noted earlier, managing the process is crucial to realizing the full potential of environmental analysis. The structural, cultural, political and managerial prerequisites that are necessary for supporting environmental analysis in organizations are described, and the advantages and disadvantages of various environmental analysis mechanisms are outlined.

OPERATING ASSUMPTIONS

A number of operating assumptions underlie the treatment of environmental analysis in this text. Four of the key assumptions need to be highlighted to place the text in perspective.

First, the text is oriented toward practice more than toward theory. Environmental analysis is still more of an art than a science. Though the last two decades have witnessed a proliferation of techniques, many of them have not been subjected to scientific scrutiny. The data that form the grist to the analyst's mill are ambiguous, conflicting, and filled with "noise." The art element comes into play in weaving through the data and reaching meaningful and useful inferences. Techniques are useful, but a lot depends on the skill of the analyst. The text attempts to underscore this by highlighting the key questions to be raised during various stages of analysis rather than providing a catalog of sophisticated techniques or ready-made answers.

Second, the text is slanted toward practice in large organizations. Although small organizations need some form of environmental analysis, only in large organizations is the analysis necessary in its full breadth. The choice has been to focus on large organizations, as the text attempts broad coverage of environmental-analysis-related issues.

Third, discussion of environmental segments—social, economic, political, and technological, detailed in Chapters 4–10—assumes that readers have some basic familiarity with these topics. Volumes of literature are available on each of these segments, and covering these in detail is beyond the scope of a single text. Hence, the treatment in this text is interpretive in nature and is oriented to the key ideas that analysts need to keep in mind as they engage in analysis of particular segments.

Finally, the text is primarily oriented to the domestic U.S. economy as far as the content of the segment chapters is concerned. Although the process of analysis is likely to be useful on a global basis, issues related to content of environment are likely to be different among clusters of countries, depending on their sociocultural heritage and nature and level of economic development. Attention to these cross-country differences is beyond the scope of the text.

KEY TERMS: SOME DEFINITIONS

Conceptual development in any area of academic pursuit is dependent upon concept development and the definition of terms. Unfortunately, in the area of macroenvironmental analysis, much confusion exists with regard to isolating and defining the relevant concepts. Concepts such as scanning, monitoring, forecasting, trends, patterns, and issues are variously defined. In an effort to avoid such confusion, the following are the key concepts covered in this book, with a brief definition of each:

Indicators: operational measures of environmental variables
Trends: systematic variation of indicators over time
Patterns: meaningful clusters of trends
Segments: sections of the macroenvironment, such as social or political, created conceptually to facilitate analysis
Change: change in indicators, trends, or patterns in one or more segments

Forces: the causes underlying changes or factors that cause such changes

Issues: environmental changes considered important in their implications for an organization

Projections/forecasts: future states of trends or patterns

Prediction: projections or forecasts accepted for strategic purposes

Analyst: an individual engaged in environmental analysis

SUMMARY

This chapter presented an overview of macroenvironmental analysis as detailed in the text. It pointed out the goals, values, and limitations of macroenvironmental analysis to keep the discussion in perspective. The central themes around which the book is organized were presented, and the operating assumptions that have guided the treatment were noted. Finally, the definitions of some of the key terms that are employed in this book were provided.

2

Conceptual Overview

This chapter presents the conceptual overview of the macroenvironment that underlies the process of analysis described in the book. The scheme of the chapter is as follows. First, we provide a brief and selective review of theories dealing with environment. This section is primarily intended to point out the intellectual indebtedness of this book; since it is theory focused, it may be skipped by those interested only in applications. Second, we provide a conceptual framework for analyzing the macroenvironment. Third, we indicate key areas of linkage between environmental analysis and strategic management.

THEORETICAL OVERVIEW

Over the last three decades, a wide range of theorists and researchers have been concerned with the organization-environment interface. Broadly, these theoretical streams can be classified into three according to the primary focus of inquiry: (1) those attempting to conceptualize environments and how these change, (2) those dealing with how environments affect organizations, and (3) those dealing with how organizations go about understanding or analyzing environments.

Despite their primary focus, almost all theories dealing with organization-environment relationships have underlying them a conception of environments: how to describe them, how to identify their relevant features, and how to assess their influence on organizations. Note that not much consensus exists with respect to underlying conceptions of environment. Differences exist in (1) level of analysis and (2) dimensions of environment attended to (Scott 1981). We discuss these differences before summarizing the theories noted previously, in order to place the various theories in context and to anchor the conceptual framework presented in the next section.

Level of Analysis.   Environmental conceptions vary according to the theoretical level of analysis selected. Identifying three levels is helpful: (1) ecological community, (2) populations or organizations, and (3) organization-set.

■ At the most general level, we have the *ecological community,* or the *interorganizational field.* At this level, the theories focus on relationships linking a collection of organizations and other types of social units in a delineated geographical area. Emphasis is not on the individual organizational units but on the pattern or network of relationships connecting them and other social entities.

■ A second level is referred to as the *population* of organizations. This concept refers to aggregates of organizations that are alike in some respect—for example, firms in a single industry.

■ The third level is that of the *organization-set.* A given organization participates in a variety of relations depending on the identity of its specific partners. For example, a small grocery store will relate in one manner with its suppliers, in another with its customers, in yet another with its regulating bodies, and so on (Scott 1981).

Dimensions of Environments.   Theories often differ along the general and *abstract* features of the environment that are addressed. Two widely employed approaches are (1) to conceive of environment as a source of information and (2) to view the environment as a stock of resources (Aldrich and Mindlin 1978). Information-based theories focus primary attention on the degree of *uncertainty* confronting organizations, whereas resource-based theories focus on the degree to which the organization is *dependent* on others for vital resources. Several dimensions have been proposed as affecting uncertainty or dependence:

■ *Degree of homogeneity-heterogeneity* refers to the degree of similarity or differentiation between elements or entities within and across environmental segments—for example, the number of different types of customers in a market.

■ *Degree of stability-instability* refers to the degree and extent to which the various entities in the environment are undergoing change—for example, the rate of introduction of new products, change of regulation, or growth rate of the market.

- *Degree of connectedness* refers to the number of interconnections among various entities in the environment—for example, the number of different suppliers from whom a manufacturing company must buy its inputs.
- *Degree of munificence-scarcity* refers to the extent to which resources required by the organization are available in its environment—for example, the availability of crude oil for petroleum refiners.
- *Degree of concentration-dispersion* refers to the extent to which resources required are evenly spread throughout the environment—for example, the degree of concentration of the population in various geographical areas.
- *Degree of turbulence* refers to the extent to which individual entities in the environment and linkages among them are disturbed by increasing connectedness and an increasing rate of connectedness. Turbulence refers not to chaos in the environment but to increasing causal connections that may render the environment obscure to local observers (Aldrich 1979).

These dimensions have been utilized to assess the uncertainty or dependence presented by environments to organizations. As Scott (1981) notes, dimensions of homogeneity-heterogeneity, stability-instability, connectedness, and turbulence capture *uncertainty,* whereas munificence-scarcity, concentration-dispersion, and turbulence influence the *dependence* of organizations on environment.

As noted, various theories differ not only in levels of analysis or dimensions of environment attended to (or both) but also in their primary focus. We now turn to a selective review of these theories, classifying them according to their primary focus.

Theories of Environments and Their Evolution

A number of theorists have attempted to provide typologies of environments and to formulate some general theories of their evolution. Three of them are Emery and Trist (1965), Ansoff (1981), and international business scholars. Emery and Trist's work is a classic, early effort, Ansoff's is a more recent work, and the international business scholars have been concerned with global environment for two decades.

Emery and Trist.   In a seminal piece on environment, Emery and Trist (1965) identified four types of environment based on a case study of a firm in the food canning market in the United Kingdom.

They called these ideal types of environments "causal textures," approximations to which may be thought of as existing in the real world of most organizations. The four causal textures are as follows:

1. *Placid, randomized environment.* In this environment, the resources are distributed to the point of being randomly distributed, and therefore no causal laws connect the elements of the environment. The environment is stable and unchanging. The economists' classic market corresponds to this type. A critical property of organizational response is that there is no distinction between strategy and tactics. The best tactic is one of attempting to do one's best, and this tactic can be learned only by trial and error.

2. *Placid, clustered environment.* In this environment, resources are no longer randomly distributed but rather are concentrated. Thus, some positions in the environment are richer than others. The environment is still stable, but because of resource concentration, location becomes an important factor in the survival of organizations. Survival becomes critically linked with what an organization knows of its environment. In this environment, "optimal location" becomes a key objective.

3. *Disturbed-reactive environment.* Here, the resources are concentrated, but the environment becomes unstable because there is more than one kind of organization. The existence of a number of similar organizations now becomes a dominant characteristic of the environment. Further, these organizations are competing with each other. Now necessary is defining the organizational objective not so much in terms of location as in the power to be able to make and meet competitive challenges.

4. *Turbulent environment.* This is a dynamic environment in which relations among entities in the environment are changing and the rate at which these relationships are changing is high. Three trends contribute to the emergence of dynamic field forces: (a) the growth in number of organizations to meet disturbed-reactive environment, and linkages among them; (b) the deepening of interconnectedness between the economic factor and other factors of society; and (c) the increasing reliance on research and development to meet competitive challenges. An implication here is that in these environments, survival depends on efficient environmental scanning and monitoring.

Emery and Trist note that the tendency of all environments is to become turbulent. Thus, the general thrust of environmental evolution is toward increasing levels of uncertainty and complexity. This typology primarily addresses the level of ecological community, and includes dimensions from both informational and resource views of environment (stability, connectedness, concentration, and turbulence).

Ansoff.   More recently, and working from an understanding of changes taking place in various industries over the twentieth century, Ansoff notes that the environment confronting firms in the eighties is turbulent. It is characterized by increasing complexity and rate of change, rendering important events confronting firms disconnected from past experience, and necessitating a growing percentage of strategic resources to be allocated to maintaining links with environment. Ansoff provides a characterization of five distinct levels of "environmental turbulence" or complexity that characterize an industry. He anchors his levels in seven factors:

1. Strategic budget intensity, defined as the percentage of the total budget of the firms in an industry that is spent on strategic activity (roughly corresponding to percentage of sales spent on R&D)
2. Predictability, which refers to the degree to which events can be predicted
3. Frequency of changes
4. Response time, the time required by firms to respond
5. Novelty, or the degree to which the historical capabilities of firms are inapplicable for handling change
6. Turbulence level, which refers to the state of knowledge for successful response
7. Applicable forecasting technologies

Based on these factors, Ansoff identifies five levels of environmental turbulence: stable, reactive, anticipatory, exploring, and creative. Ansoff's classification is reproduced in Table 2.1.

Ansoff notes that during the past seventy years, turbulence has been increasing, though not all industries move in step. Further, a structural change in the markets or political discontinuity may rapidly escalate turbulence in a stable industry or send a growing industry into decline.

Three comments are in order. First, the factors provided by Ansoff as contributing to turbulence are highly interrelated; therefore, they should be viewed only as a device for assessing a general level of turbulence. Second, Ansoff addresses the level of environment roughly corresponding to population of organizations (industry).

Table 2.1 Ansoff's Framework of Environmental Turbulence in an Industry

LEVEL OF TURBULENCE / CHARACTERISTICS OF CHANGE	STABLE	REACTIVE	ANTICIPATORY	EXPLORING	CREATIVE
STRATEGIC BUDGET INTENSITY (% of total budget)	LOW		→		HIGH
PREDICTABILITY	Most changes fully predictable		→		Frequent surprises
FREQUENCY	LOW		→		HIGH
RESPONSE TIME	SHORT		→		LONG
NOVELTY (applicability of historical capability)	Capability applies	Incremental adjustment	Incremental expansion	Novel combination of existing capabilities	Novel capabilities needed
TURBULENCE LEVEL (State of knowledge for successful response)	Full impact (7)	First impact (6)	Outcome estimated (5)	Response determined or impact determined (4) or (3)	Source identified or sense of turbulence (2) or (1)
APPLICABLE FORECASTING TECHNOLOGY	Use of precedents	Management control	Extrapolation	Threat opportunity analysis or weak signal detection	Weak signal detection

Source: Igor Ansoff, *Strategic Management.*
By permission of Macmillan, London and Basingstoke.

Third, his focus is primarily on information dimensions of environment.

International Business Scholars.   Spanning a wide spectrum of perspectives, international business scholars have been concerned with the environment of international business. Their earlier focus on the environment of multinational corporations has been transcended in recent years by a focus on global and cultural environments. A wide array of perspectives is represented in this stream.

- Vernon and Wells (1981), in an update of their classic work, focus on the economic-technological aspects of international environment. They concern themselves with factors such as product life cycle extensions, technology transfer, and government economic policies.

- Terpstra and David (1985) delineate global environment in abstract dimensions: cultural environment, consisting of educational, religious, and value spheres; and interorganizational environment, consisting of technological, social, and political spheres.

- Kolde (1985) provides a characterization of environments at two levels: national and supranational. At the national level, he classifies nation-states into three: (a) the advanced, capitalistic countries, (b) the communistic countries, and (c) the less developed countries. At the supranational levels, he identifies several key issues related to North-South dialogue, East-West relations, and problems of European Economic Community as well as those pertaining to global institutions such as the International Monetary Fund.

Despite the pluralism in perspective, these scholars focus attention squarely on the environment at the ecological level. Their most important contribution to environmental analysis is the hierarchic differentiation of ecological level into global and national environmental levels. Although they address the abstract dimensions only implicitly, they address details of environment much more elaborately than either Ansoff or Emery and Trist.

Emery and Trist imply that environmental evolution tends to progress sequentially from lower levels of complexity to higher levels. Unlike Emery and Trist, Ansoff allows for the probability that under certain conditions, environmental evolution can skip stages and progress faster or even regress to a lower level of turbulence. International business scholars comment on the elaboration of environmental levels with the emergence of global interdependence. All sets of authors concur on the general tendency of the environment to be turbulent. They further concur on the increasing importance of environmental monitoring at higher levels of complexity in the environment. That is, the environments in these cases should be studied and analyzed in *their own right,* irrespective of the location of a specific organization.

Theories of Organization-Environment Relations

A second stream of theorists has focused on relationships between organizations and environments; indeed, most of the research activity in the last two decades has focused on this area. Four of the more recent types of models are (1) natural selection models, (2) resource dependence models, (3) industrial organization models, and (4) readaptation models. These models are discussed only briefly here, as they address issues in strategic management other than environment—issues such as strategy, structure, and processes.

Natural Selection Models. The best-known natural selection model of organization-environment interface is the population ecology model. As postulated by Hannan and Freeman (1977) and later elaborated by Aldrich (1979), the model is based on the natural selection model of biological ecology. It explains organizational change by examining the nature and distribution of resources in organizations' environments. Environmental pressures make competition for resources the central force in organizational activities. Ecologists refer to organizational forms—specific configurations of strategic and structural attributes—as the elements selected by environmental criteria. Change may occur either through new forms eliminating old ones or through the modification of existing forms. A three-stage model—variation, selection, and retention—is developed to explain changes in organizations.

- *Variation* between organizations is the first requirement for organizational change. Some variations arise through members' active attempts to generate alternatives and seek solutions to problems (e.g., strategic choices). The population ecology model is, however, indifferent to the ultimate source of variation, as planned and unplanned variation both provide raw material from which selection can be made. Thus, error, chance, luck, and conflict are also likely sources of variation.
- *Selection* of organizational forms is perhaps the critical stage in this model and occurs as a result of environmental constraints. Organizations fitting environmental criteria are positively selected and survive, while others either fail or change to match environmental requirements. Selection occurs through relative rather than absolute superiority in *acquiring information or resources* (or both). An effective organization is one that has achieved a relative-

ly better position in an environment it shares with others rather than a hypothetical "best" position.

■ *Retention* is the persistence of selected organizational forms over time. These forms provide transmission of knowledge. The forms are retained when no new variations are introduced, or because the environmental selection criteria continue to favor the form over the others.

The population ecology model focuses the analysis primarily at the level of population of organizations, and implicitly addresses both informational and resource characteristics of the environment. For our purposes, the model is useful in two respects. First, the model specifies that chance factors could play a role in survival of organizations, thus suggesting the notions of surprises (for a specific organization) presented by the environment. Second, it suggests that a key output of environmental analysis is an understanding of the variations and selection criteria operating in the environment. Beyond such general prescriptions, some of the key notions of the model need to be further refined; at this stage of development, it offers only a retrospective explanation of organizational survival.

Resource Dependence Models.   Resource dependence models view organizations as dependent on environment for resources, and an organization's continued ability to acquire and maintain resources is the key to its effectiveness. Typically, suppliers, customers, competitors, and regulators are treated as vital input and output resources of the organization (Pfeffer and Salancik 1978).

In the face of multiple resource dependencies, each with potentially different characteristics, an organization's response to a particular resource dependence is partly determined by the extent of its dependency and its relative criticalness compared with other dependencies. An organization's response strategies may assume two forms: (1) individual (firm) action and (2) collective action.

■ *Individual action* refers to the strategic and structural responses of a firm. These include seeking a dominant position in environments with little or no competition and plenty of suppliers and customers, negotiating long-term contracts, formation of mergers, altering organizational goals, or adopting technological innovation.

■ *Collective action* refers to responses undertaken by an organization in conjunction with others to ameliorate resource dependencies. These include co-optation of key environmental elements through mechanisms such as interlocking directorates, lobbying of governmental agencies, or participation in trade associations to influence informal industry norms.

As can be seen, individual action strategies roughly correspond to business unit strategies (Hofer and Schendel 1978) and collective action to political strategies (MacMillan and Jones 1986). Resource dependence models focus primarily on the level of organization-set and address the dependence dimensions of the environment.

Industrial Organization (I–O) Models. Porter's (1980) competitive strategy model is perhaps the most popular I–O model in strategic management. Building on the works of economists such as Bain, Mason, and Caves, Porter (1980) presents a framework for analyzing industry and competitive environment and deriving firm-specific strategies. This framework consists of five variables: (1) entry barriers, (2) threat of substitutes, (3) bargaining power of suppliers, (4) bargaining power of customers, and (5) intensity of rivalry among competitors.

- *Entry barriers* refers to the ease with which firms can enter an industry. Such factors as patents, economies of scale, high capital requirements, and inaccessibility of distribution channels serve as strong barriers to entry.
- *Threat of substitutes* refers to the extent to which other products that are substitutes to the focal one exist. These serve to constrain the level of prices that can be imposed by a firm in the industry.
- *Bargaining power of suppliers* refers to the factors that enhance the power suppliers can exert on firms in an industry. Such factors as few suppliers or lack of alternatives can enhance bargaining power.
- *Bargaining power of customers* refers to the factors that enhance the power customers exert on firms in an industry. Such factors as volume of purchases, importance of products to customers, and alternative sources impact bargaining power.
- *Intensity of rivalry* refers to the intensity of competition among firms within an industry. Intensity of rivalry drives down the profits that can reasonably be realized by a firm in the industry.

Porter suggests that these factors together determine the profitability of an industry and point up the feasible strategies that a firm can adopt if it decides to stay in or enter the industry. The analysis is focused roughly at the level of population of organizations, and the model primarily addresses the resource dimensions of environment.

Readaptation Models. Building on the earlier work of scholars dealing with organization-environment relations, and working with case studies of firms in several industries, Lawrence and Dyer (1983) explain the readaptive processes in organization, and suggest the relationships between environments, organizational strategies and forms, and outcomes. Lawrence and Dyer focus on two dimensions of environment: strategy and organizational forms.

- *Resource scarcity:* Defined as a composite of (1) availability of raw materials, human resources, and capital, (2) customer impact on resource availability, (3) competitor impact on resource availability, and (4) governmental impact on resource availability.
- *Information complexity:* Operationalized as in (1) competitive, (2) technical, (3) customer, (4) product, and (5) government regulatory variations.
- *Strategy:* Organizations are classified as prospectors, defenders, reactors (Miles and Snow 1978), or readaptive.
- *Form:* Organizations are classified as simple, adhocracy, machine bureaucracy, professional bureaucracy (Mintzberg 1979), entrepreneurial, or readaptive.

Lawrence and Dyer utilize two outcome measures: innovation and efficiency. The model is complex; a simplified version is presented in Figure 2.1.

The readaption model is focused primarily at the level of organization-set and addresses both uncertainty and dependence dimensions of the environment. This is perhaps the most fully developed and comprehensive model of organization-environment relations.

For our purposes, the significant contribution of these models is that they provide a map of the kinds of linkages between environment and organizations that need to be stressed. Environment is linked to (1) strategies, both product-market and political, (2) structure, and (3) processes in organizations.

Models of Understanding Environment

A third stream of work has addressed issues related to how organizations understand their environments. This stream of work is particularly important because it informs the key analytical and managerial tasks involved in engaging in environmental analysis. Three strands of work of this genre deserve mention: enactment theorists, scanning models, and systemic models.

Figure 2.1 Lawrence and Dyer's Model of Environmental Relationships

INFORMATION DOMAIN

INFORMATION COMPLEXITY — High / Intermediate / Low

RESOURCE SCARCITY — Low / Intermediate / High

	Low R.S.	Intermediate R.S.	High R.S.
High I.C.	**1.** High I.C., Low R.S. Strategy: Prospector Form: Adhocracy Structure: High Differentiation Low Integration Power: Professional Domination HRP: Clan High Innovation Low Efficiency Moderate Involvement Example: Hospitals 1945–1982	**2.**	**3.** High I.C., R.S. Strategy: Defender Form: Simple Structure: Low Differentiation High Integration Power: Owner/Manager Domination HRP: Market Low Innovation Moderate to High Efficiency Moderate to High Involvement Example: Agriculture 1920–1935
Intermediate I.C.	**4.** Intermediate I.C., Low R.S. Strategy: Prospector Form: Entrepreneurial Group Structure: Mod. Differentiation Mod. Integration Power: Founding Group HRP: Clan High Innovation, Involvement Low Efficiency Example: Early Auto Firms	**5.** Intermediate I.C. and R.S. Strategy: Readaptive Form: Readaptive Structure: High Differentiation High Integration Power: Balanced HRP: Clan/Market/Bureaucratic High Efficiency, Innovation and Involvement Example: General Motors 1920–1935	**6.** Intermediate I.C., High R.S. Strategy: Defender Form: Machine Bureaucracy Structure: Low Differentiation High Integration Power: Top Dominant HRP: Market/Bureaucratic Low Innovation Low to Moderate Involvement Moderate to High Efficiency Example: Steel 1960–1980 Coal 1920–1970
Low I.C.	**7.** Low I.C. and R.S. Strategy: Reactor Form: Professional Bureaucracy Structure: Low Differentiation Low Integration Power: Dominant Clique HRP: Bureaucratic Low Efficiency, Innovation and Involvement Example: Western Union	**8.**	**9.** (Unstudied) Local Monopoly Cottage and Handicraft Industry

COMPETITIVE VARIATIONS
TECHNICAL VARIATIONS
CUSTOMER VARIATIONS
PRODUCT VARIATIONS
GOVERNMENT REGULATORY VARIATIONS

RESOURCE DOMAIN

AVAILABILITY OF RAW MATERIALS, HUMAN RESOURCES, CAPITAL
CUSTOMER IMPACT ON RESOURCE AVAILABILITY
COMPETITOR IMPACT ON RESOURCE AVAILABILITY
GOVERNMENT IMPACT ON RESOURCE AVAILABILITY
ORGANIZED LABOR IMPACT ON RESOURCE AVAILABILITY

Enactment. Working from cognitive psychology, Karl Weick (1979, 1974) develops the notion of enactment as the active process that organizational participants carry out in defining their environments. Individual information processors in an organization enact the environment to which the system then adapts (Weick 1979, 147–69). The process of enactment introduces information into the system, which is dealt with according to organizational rules and routines. Weick emphasizes the importance of "attention" processes, as they determine what kinds of information get selected and what kinds get neglected from the available cues. These processes are highly variable, as they take into account a wide range of situational factors.

Weick's imaginative ideas cannot be done justice here, but four comments should help to place the enactment process in perspective. First, the notion of enacted environment states than an organization or the key decision makers in it generate a socially shared way of envisioning the complex world of environment beyond their borders, Weick's model thus draws attention to the tendencies to develop cognitive distortions. A key implication here is that the image of environment, in which organizational strategies and structures are anchored, may be incomplete or distorted. Second, we suggest that systematic environmental analysis is one mechanism of enactment that may reduce such distortions. Third, and anticipating our discussion in the next section and in the ensuing chapter, the notion of "relevant" environment is squarely anchored in this view, as it highlights the judgmental processes involved in analysts' focusing on one or more segments of the environment rather than others. Finally, no one to date has searched for systematic tendencies of distortion in the enactment process. As such, specific prescriptions for enhancing the quality of environmental analysis must be treated with caution.

Scanning Models. Scanning models focus on the key modes of exposure and perception of information about environment. The classic description of these modes was provided by Aguilar (1967) as a result of his field study of information-gathering practices of managers. Aguilar identifies four modes of information collection:

- *Undirected viewing* refers to a manager's exposure and perception of information that has no specific purpose. The sources and substance of information are highly varied, and typically much information is dropped from attention. Undirected viewing can, however, be valuable as a means of reducing the natural tendency to perceive and digest only information of immediate relevance.

- *Conditioned viewing* involves a degree of purposefulness by the manager as he or she receives information inputs. The individual is receptive to information and to assessing its significance. The natural tendency is to *react* or respond under this mode.

- *In informal search,* the individual moves on to a proactive orientation toward searching for information. However, there is a limited and relatively unstructured effort to seek out information for a specific purpose.

- *Formal search* is a highly proactive mode deliberately undertaken to obtain information for specific purposes. Here the emphasis is on formal procedures and methodologies for obtaining informational inputs.

Aguilar also notes the now-classic distinction between personal and impersonal sources of information about environment, and highlights the importance of the role of personal sources to managers. A number of other authors have addressed how to analyze various parts of environments; these are selectively referred to in the various segment chapters (4–10).

Two comments are in order with respect to this stream of work. First, the focus is primarily on the kinds of analytical activities involved in understanding environment. Relatively little attention is paid to systems for environmental analysis. Second, given the key role played by individuals, the work offers a framework for studying analytical activities. The activities involved in environmental analysis—detailed in the ensuing chapters—are anchored in this stream of research.

Systemic Models.   In recent years, a growing number of studies have described the systems for environmental analysis found in organizations. Unlike the scanning models, the focus of the studies is not analysis-related activities but systems of management found in organizations. In an early study, Fahey, King, and Narayanan (1981) provided a typology of such systems: irregular, periodic, and continuous.

- *Irregular* systems are found in organizations primarily on an ad hoc basis and tend to be crisis initiated. These systems focus on specific events and deal with retrospective data for decisions in current and near-term future. At best, the structure for analysis may consist of ad hoc teams that engage in simplistic data and budgeting projections. Environmental analysis in these cases is not integrated into the mainstream of activity.

- *Periodic* systems are guided by the need for environmental information for problem solving or decision making. They focus on selected events and deal with current, retrospective, and somewhat prospective data for decisions in near-term future. They engage various staff agencies for periodically updated studies of economic and market environment. They allocate a relatively low level of resources for this and employ statistical forecasting-oriented techniques. These systems are partially integrated into strategic planning processes.

- *Continuous* systems focus on finding opportunities and avoiding problems in addition to information for decision making. The breadth of environmental analysis is wide; these systems collect data on social, political, technological, and economic trends of both a current and prospective nature. They are utilized for decisions of a long-term nature, involve structured data collection and processing units, and employ sophisticated futuristic methodologies. Scanning units with a relatively high level of resources are the norm. These systems are fully integrated into strategic planning systems.

Studies of this genre (Fahey, King, and Narayanan 1981; Diffenbach 1982; Stubbardt 1982; Lenz and Engeldow 1986) point up three issues related to environmental analysis. First, managerial/organizational factors influence the analytical activities in the process. Second, great variability exists among organizations as to how analysis is performed. Third, these systems are in flux; they will need to be developed and studied further. These studies form the basis of our concluding chapter on managing environmental analysis.

A CONCEPTUAL FRAMEWORK FOR ANALYSIS

This section lays out the conceptual framework that informs the analysis of the macroenvironment detailed in this book. It presents the constructs necessary for understanding the various elements of macroenvironment, the linkages among these, and their evolution. It does not specify the kinds of linkages or paths of evolution; these are deemed to be the outputs of the process of analysis. In this sense, it is a framework rather than a theory.

Three key assumptions underlie this framework. First, the macroenvironment needs to be analyzed in its own right, irrespective of the immediate context of an organization—a position we share with Ansoff and Emery and Trist. Second, specific implications of environmental evolution for a *firm* need to be discerned by the analysts described in strategy formulation models (Hofer and Schendel 1978). Finally, action responses that are chosen should be anchored in these implications.

The framework is composed of four constructs: (1) levels of environment, (2) a model of macroenvironment, (3) constructs for describing environmental evolution, and (4) linkages to a firm. Each of these constructs provides the lenses through which analysts can begin to understand the environment. This framework thus addresses the *content* of macroenvironmental analysis; the *process* of analysis is detailed in the next chapter.

Levels of Environment

The framework posits three levels of environment: task environment, competitive or industry environment, and general environment.

The *task environment* refers to the set of customers, suppliers, competitors, and other environmental agencies such as trade associations directly related to the firm. Much of the day-to-day operations of a firm involve activities or concerns dealing with its task environment. Thus, a firm negotiating a loan with a bank, requesting supplies from a supplier, or dealing with customer service are examples of operating within a task environment. The task environment is more or less specific to a firm and not necessarily shared by its competitors. Customers are often loyal to a firm's brand; suppliers may have granted preferred customer status to a firm. Such factors as brand loyalty or preferred customer status ensure that the task environment of a firm is generally distinct from that of its competitors.

Beyond the task environment lies the *competitive or industry environment*, which comprises a firm or a business unit and its competitors functioning in the same industry. At this level, environmental factors directly affect all competitors in the same industry. As previously noted, Porter (1980) suggests that (1) new entrants, (2) substitutes, (3) suppliers, (4) buyers, and (5) rivalry among competitors influence what happens in an industry. The analyst here is concerned with the competitive environment to assess the attractiveness of an industry and the feasibility of alternative competitive strategies for a specific firm.

At the broadest level lies the *general environment,* or *macroenvironment,* sometimes referred to as the political economy. Factors in the general environment influence all the industries functioning within it. Although their influence may be experienced differently by different industries, such issues as inflation or interest rates—factors in the general economic environment—affect a host of industries from automobiles to financial services to restaurants. Consider the following examples:

■ General Motors and Ford Motor have both committed extensive resources to improving their manufacturing efficiency, to creating joint ventures with foreign firms, and to enhancing their marketing capability in order to reach and satisfy different customers' needs.

■ As a result of deregulation in the passenger airline industry, a drastic price war erupted among airlines, causing most firms to experience a reduction in profits.

■ After the 1982 recession, inflation was reduced, consumer purchasing power rose, and many firms experienced an upsurge in sales relative to the recession era.

In the case of the auto firms, we refer primarily to the task environment and the operating problems posed by it. In the case of the airline industry, we highlight how the regulatory environment influences the industry in general. In the third case, the reference is to the economic segment of the macroenvironment and its impact on many industries.

The various levels of environment can be presented schematically as in Figure 2.2. Here, the general environment affects the specific industry environment, and the industry environment in turn affects the task environment of the firm. In addition, in Figure 2.2 we note a concept called *relevant environment*. Relevant environment refers to the boundaries of general environment drawn for analytical purposes. Note that general environment, in its broadest sense, includes almost everything outside the firm's task and competitive/industry environments. Such a broad definition, however, makes the analysis task well-nigh impossible because of the multiplicity of factors involved. For the purpose of analysis, then, the analyst needs to focus on aspects of the environment deemed relevant. In some sense, all definitions of relevant environment require judgment and contain some degree of arbitrariness, yet such judgments are necessary for engaging in worthwhile analysis.

The three levels presented in Figure 2.2—task, competitive/industry, and general environments—roughly correspond to the levels of organization-set, population of organizations, and ecological community. The construct, relevant environment, is introduced to highlight the role of enactment processes in organization, especially as an analyst attempts proactively to understand macroenvironment.

A final comment with respect to Figure 2.2: the levels as posited are applicable not only to single-business firms but also to diversified

Figure 2.2   Levels of Environment

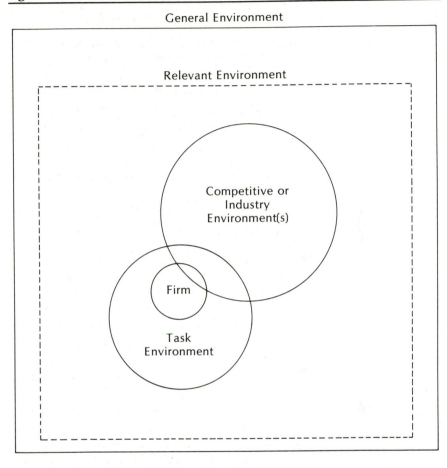

firms with multiple business units. The latter will face a number of competitive and industry environments corresponding to their business units. Further, their task environment becomes complex, as different business units will have distinct elements in task environment in addition to sharing common ones at the corporate level. The concept of relevant environment—aspects of macroenvironment common across all industries to which the analyst pays attention—is relevant for both types of firms—single business and diversified—though working out their implications (Chapter 12) is rendered more complex in the case of diversified firms.

A Model of Macroenvironment

As an analytical construct, the model of macroenvironment decomposes *relevant* environment into four segments: social, economic, political, and technological.

- The *social* segment focuses on (1) demographics, (2) life-styles, and (3) social values of a society. The analyst in this segment is interested in understanding shifts in population characteristics, emergence of new life-styles, or social values.
- The *economic* segment focuses on the general set of economic factors and conditions confronting all industries in a society. This segment has perhaps the most direct impact on all business organizations.
- The *political* segment deals with (1) political processes occurring in a society and (2) regulatory institutions that shape the codes of conduct. This segment is perhaps the most turbulent in the model.
- The *technological* segment is concerned with the technological progress or advancements that are taking place in a society. New products, processes, or materials; general level of scientific activity; and advances in fundamental science (e.g., physics) are the key concerns in this area.

The model is presented in Figure 2.3. As shown, the model also presents various linkages among these segments. The linkages highlight the notion that macroenvironment can be understood only in a *systemic* fashion. Thus, the macroenvironment is presented as a system of interrelated segments; every segment is related to and affects every other segment. The model does not, however, *specify* the types of linkages; these are deemed to be the output of a process of analysis. In other words, the linkages are to be discerned by the analysts during their efforts to scan, monitor, and forecast macroenvironmental trends and patterns.

Each one of the prior segments may display the abstract properties of environment developed in the previous section. Illustrative examples of measures from various segments corresponding to the abstract dimensions are presented in Table 2.2. Two comments are in order here. First, the primary utility of abstract dimensions is to condition the analyst to look for patterns during analysis; they thus provide a lens as well as a language for analysis. Second, during environmental analysis, the analyst will need to move from abstract description to specific detailing of environmental segments if analysis outputs are to be meaningful for strategic action.

Figure 2.3   A Model of Macroenvironment

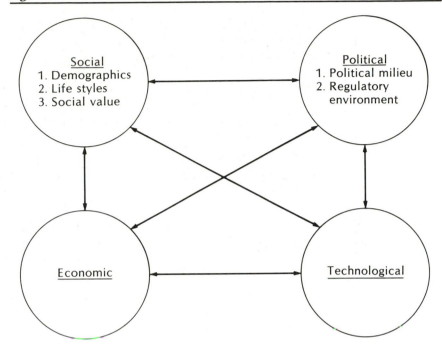

Constructs for Describing Environmental Evolution

The conceptual framework presents three key constructs for describing changes in environmental segments: (1) types of change, (2) forces driving change, and (3) type of future evolution.

Changes in macroenvironmental segments may be *systematic* or *discontinuous*. Changes that are gradual, continuous, and potentially predictable are termed systematic, whereas random, unpredictable, sudden changes are termed discontinuous. Despite theorists (Glover 1966) who disavow discontinuous change and attribute perception of such change to lack of conceptual tools for seeing systematic orderly change, strong pragmatic reasons exist for retaining the notion of discontinuous change: given the cognitive limitations of the analyst, most organizations have at some time or other experienced discontinuity in environmental change. The potential for such discontinuity is present even in the most sophisticated environmental analysis efforts.

For analytic purposes, it is important to go beyond description of change to assess the *forces* driving it. Figure 2.3 showed that various

**Table 2.2 Dimensions of Environment:
Illustrative Examples of Measures from Macroenvironmental Segments**

Segments

Dimension	Social [1]	Economic	Political [2]	Technological
1. Homogeneity-heterogeneity	1. Varieties of households (D) 2. Varieties of life-styles (L) 3. Diversity in social value clusters (S)	Degree of differences in regional/local economies	1. Diversity of interest groups (P) 2. Diversity in viewpoints of agencies (R)	Number of differing technologies competing in the same market
2. Stability-change	1. Rate of population growth (D) 2. Emergence of new life-style (L) 3. Changes in social values (S)	Rate of growth of GNP	1. Increase in the number of PACs (P) 2. Change in regulation (R)	Rate of new product introduction
3. Connectedness	Relationship between life-styles and types of household	Relationship between GNP, interest rates, disposal incomes	1. Relationship among interest groups (P) 2. Procedures for inter-agency coordination (R)	Co-evolution of process and product technologies
		Links among segments		
4. Munificence-scarcity	1. Population density (D) 2. Popularity of life-style (L) 3. Degree of acceptance of a social value (S)	Purchasing power Disposable income	1. Access to interest groups for political action (P) 2. Access to members of regulatory agencies (R)	Availability of technologies in a specific region or nation
5. Concentration-dispersion	Concentration of 1. Population (D) 2. Life-styles (L) in various geographical areas 3. Differences in intensities of social values (S)	Concentration ratios Disparity in income levels Concentration of wealth	1. Differing degrees of political resources available 2. Differences in degree of jurisdiction of agencies (R)	Differences in R&D spending among nations Concentration of technological expertise in various regions
6. Turbulence	Changes in interconnectedness within and among segments			

[1] D refers to demographics, L to life-styles, and S to social values.

[2] P refers to political milieu, R to regulatory environment.

segments are linked together in a systemic manner. The forces driving change in one segment, therefore, often lie in changes in other segments. Thus, shifts in social segment (e.g., migration of population) may affect political segment (e.g., distribution of regional power). Each segment, however, can evolve quasi-autonomously (i.e., the forces driving the change are located in the segment itself). Thus, social values may shift independently of technology. The existence of induced and autonomous evolution necessitates that changes in segments be analyzed *independent of each other* and in conjunction to identify the underlying forces.

Driving forces often interact with one another. These interactions may be *reinforcing, conflictual,* or *disjoint.* When the forces support one another in their effect on changes in a third segment, the effect is reinforcing. When they dampen each other, they are conflictual, and when they do not affect each other, they are disjoint. Consider the following example:

> ■ The actions taken by OPEC in the early seventies resulted in a scarcity of petroleum. These actions put an upward pressure on gasoline prices. At the same time, consumers were becoming increasingly conservation conscious. They began to look for energy-efficient automobiles. This put a dampening effect on prices.

Here, forces in the political segment (OPEC) and those in the social segment (values) are conflictual in their effect on the economic segment (prices).

In addition, the effects of changes in one segment may have primary or secondary consequences for other segments. When the effects are direct, they are called primary consequences. In some cases, changes may not have a direct impact on other segments. Consequences may ensue, however, as a result of direct effects on a third segment. These are termed *secondary consequences.* They are often lagged and take place only after the direct consequences are visible.

Finally, in charting the evolution of change in the future, it is important to characterize whether such evolution is completely predictable from the present trends or whether it is contingent upon actions of the firm or other entities in the environment. This refers to *closed* and *open* versions of the future, respectively. This distinction is often crucial. Unlike in the closed version, open versions should alert organizations to potential action domains that need further analysis, or to arenas where firm level responses may enable it to shape the future evolution of the change.

Linkages to a Firm

As shown in Figure 2.2, the conceptual framework posits two kinds of linkages of macroenvironment to a firm: *indirect* and *direct*. Indirect linkages occur when a macroenvironmental change affects competitive/industry environments, and thus in turn has implications for the organization's task environment (e.g., a firm's strategies). In addition, macroenvironment may have direct implications for the task environment without affecting industry in general (e.g., community action against a firm).

Two comments are in order with respect to posited linkages. First, the linkages present themselves as threats *and* opportunities to firms, thus triggering responses. Second, the direction of linkages is left unspecified. The framework allows consideration of both environments influencing organizations and vice versa.

A comparison of the framework with varying theoretical conceptions of environment is presented in Table 2.3. As will be seen, the framework is focused at the macroenvironment and addresses both informational and resource dimensions of environment. The theme of linkages lies at the core of strategy formulation and implementation (Hofer and Schendel 1978) and is elaborated in the next section.

Linkage to Strategic Management

Macroenvironmental analysis is useful primarily because it serves as a key input into strategic management. The set of key linkages is portrayed in Figure 2.4, which contains a simplified version of strategic management presented by Hofer and Schendel (1978). We briefly indicate three key areas of linkage; this theme is explored in detail in Chapter 12.

First, macroenvironmental analysis provides a crucial set of intelligence inputs into strategy formulation and implementation. In this sense, it should *precede* attempts at strategic analyses.

Second, the analysis has implications both for the content and the process of strategic management.

At the content level, current and future patterns in macroenvironment set the stage for the strategies pursued by a firm: product-market strategies—corporate, business, and functional (Hofer and Schendel 1978)—and political strategies (MacMillan and Jones 1986). In addition, together with these strategies, analysis outputs have implications for the organizational structures adopted by a firm (Galbraith and Kazanjian 1986).

Table 2.3   A Comparison of Models of Environment or Organization (or Both)

Environment	Emery and Trist	Ansoff	International Business Scholars	Population Ecology	Resource Dependence	Industrial Organization	Readaptation	Conceptual Framework of the Book
1. Level of environment	Ecological community	Roughly population: industry	Ecological, global, and national	Population of organizations	Organization-set	Population: industries	Roughly organization-set	Primarily ecological community: implications for other levels
2. Dimensions of environment	Uncertainty and dependence	Primarily uncertainty	Uncertainty and dependence	Uncertainty and dependence	Dependence	Primarily dependence	Uncertainty and dependence	Both, but left to the analyst to discover during analysis
3. Forces driving change	Reside in the ecological field		Not addressed	Variation of forms and in environment/selection	Not addressed	Forces in the macroenvironment and firms	Not addressed	Reside primarily in macroenvironment
4. Type of change	Toward higher levels of complexity	Toward high levels, but could progress or regress	Toward high levels of complexity	Not addressed	Not addressed	Not specified	Not addressed	Different segments evolve at different rates; detection is key task
Organization-Environment Linkage								
Business strategy			Variable among scholars	Yes	Yes	Yes, to some extent	Yes	Yes; to be decided by organization
Political strategy			Variable among scholars	Yes	Yes	Yes, to some extent	No	Yes; to be decided by organization
Structure			Variable among scholars	Yes	Yes	Yes, to some extent	Yes	Yes; to be decided by organization

Figure 2.4 Linkage to Strategic Management

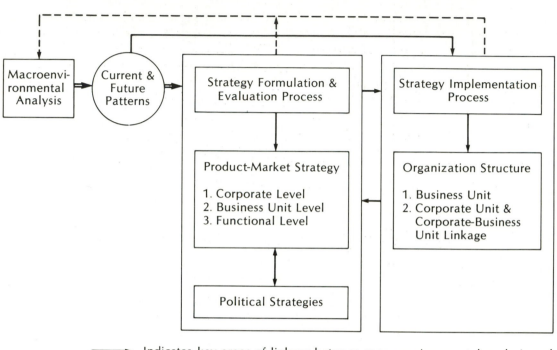

➡ Indicates key areas of linkage between macroenvironmental analysis and strategic management.

—— Linkages delineated in strategic management.

‑ ‑ ‑ ‑ ‑ Induced triggers for macroenvironmental analysis.

The process of strategy formulation and implementation are influenced by the analysis and its outputs because the latter essentially condition the top decision maker's vision of the future.

Third, though environment should be analyzed independent of the organizations, various issues that come up during strategy formulation and implementation sometimes trigger such analysis. Such induced triggers often come about in the form of surprises not detected, or the need for further scanning, monitoring, and/or forecasting of environmental evolution.

SUMMARY

This chapter presented the conception of macroenvironment and decomposed this concept into four major segments: social, political, economic, and technological. Constructs for describing environmental evolution—type of change, forces driving change, and perspective on future evolution—were set forth. Finally, the chapter pointed out the key links to strategy formulation and implementation.

3

The Process of
Environmental Analysis

In this chapter, we present a conceptual overview of *analysis-oriented* activities and processes involved in environmental analysis. We begin by describing four key activities in environmental analysis: scanning, monitoring, forecasting, and assessment. We then elaborate upon the two broad perspectives in environmental analysis, which we have labeled "outside-in" and "inside-out." Finally, we lay out a framework for doing environmental analysis.

Three points need to be kept in mind regarding the discussion in this chapter. First, we have described conceptual issues in environmental analysis to highlight their generic characteristics. Specific characteristics will vary across environmental segments. Second, we focus only on analytic elements in this chapter; issues related to managing the process are dealt with in a later chapter. Finally, we use the term *analyst* to refer to anyone engaged in environmental analysis, and not to the position titles often found in organizations.

SCANNING, MONITORING, FORECASTING, AND ASSESSMENT

Conceptually, the process of environmental analysis can be divided into four analytical stages: (1) scanning the environment to identify warning signals of potential environmental change or to detect environmental changes already taking place, (2) monitoring specific environmental trends and patterns, (3) forecasting the future direction of environmental changes, and (4) assessing current and future environmental change for their organizational implications. Table 3.1 provides an overview of these four activities.

Scanning

Scanning entails general surveillance of all environmental segments and their interactions in order to (1) identify early signals of possible environmental change and (2) detect environmental change already under way.

In its *prospective* mode, scanning focuses on identifying precursors or indicators of potential environmental changes and issues.

Table 3.1   Distinctions Among Scanning, Monitoring, Forecasting, and Assessment

	Scanning	Monitoring	Forecasting	Assessment
Focus	Open-end viewing of environment Identify early signals	Track specific trends and events	Project future patterns and events	Derive implications for organization
Goal	Detect change already under way	Confirm/disconfirm trends	Develop plausible projections of future	Derive implications for organization
Scope	Broad, general environment	Specific trends, patterns, events	Limited to trends, patterns, and issues deemed worthy of forecasting	Critical implications for organization
Time Horizon	Retrospective and current	Real time	Prospective	Prospective and current
Approach	Unconditioned viewing Heterogeneity of stimuli	Conditioned viewing Selective stimuli	Systematic and structured	Systematic, structured, and detailed
Data Characteristics	Unboundable and imprecise Vague and ambiguous	Relatively boundable Gains in precision	Quite specific	Very specific
Data Interpretation	Acts of perception Intuitive reasoning	Weighing evidence Detailing patterns	Judgments about inferences	Judgments about inferences/implications
Data Sources	Broad reading Consulting many types of experts inside and outside of the organization	Focused reading Selective use of individuals Focus groups	Outputs of monitoring Collected via forecasting techniques	Forecasts, Internal strategies Competitive context, etc.
Outputs	Signals of potential change Detection of change under way	Specification of trends Identification of scanning needs	Alternate forecasts Identification of scanning and monitoring needs	Specific organizational implications
Transition	Hunches regarding salience and importance	Judgments regarding relevance to specific organization	Inputs to decisions and decision processes	Action plans
Organizational Outcomes	Awareness of general environment	Consideration and detailing of specific developments Time for developing flexibility	Understanding of plausible futures	Specific actions

Environmental scanning is thus aimed at alerting the organization to potentially significant external impingements *before* they have fully formed or crystallized. Indeed, successful environmental scanning draws attention to possible changes and events well before they have revealed themselves in a discernible pattern.

In the prospective sense, scanning implicitly or explicitly feeds into monitoring early signals or indicators of potential environmental change. In this sense, scanning as an analytical activity becomes useful when environmental change takes time to unfold. This gives an organization time to work out implications for its actions. For example, social value shifts do not occur in days or even in months; technological change often takes many years. Social movements may take years to move from a small pocket of disquiet to a large-scale movement. In these instances, scanning can detect early indicators or precursors of these types of environmental change. For example, scanning might indicate signs of potential shifts toward political conservation or liberalism, the emergence of a more business-oriented judicial and administrative system, or changes in technological possibilities. In these cases, the *immediate* action implications for an organization may not be clear without further tracking and careful assessment of these trends.

In the *current* and *retrospective* sense, scanning identifies "surprises" or strategic issues requiring action on the part of an organization. In this case, the outputs may feed directly into assessment, and may influence current and imminent strategic decisions of the organization.

Scanning frequently detects environmental change that is already at an advanced state. The change has evolved to the point where it is actual or imminent change rather than potential change at some as yet unspecifiable date. A scan of demographic data might pick up population shifts or changes in household formation. A scan of the economic environment might reveal intermittent shortages in local energy or water supplies that have already taken place. Scanning frequently unearths actual or imminent environmental change because it explicitly focuses on areas that the organization may have previously neglected, or it challenges the organization to rethink areas to which it had paid attention.

Scanning is the *most ill-structured* and ambiguous environmental analysis activity. The potentially relevant data are essentially unlimited. The data are inherently scattered, vague, and imprecise, and data sources are many and varied. Moreover, a common feature of scanning is that *early signals* often show up in unexpected places. Thus, *the purview of search must be broad,* but no guidelines exist as to where the search should be focused. In short, the noise level in scanning is likely to be high.

The fundamental challenge for analysts in scanning is to make sense out of vague, ambiguous, and unconnected data. Analysts have to infuse meaning into data; they have to make the connections among discordant data such that signals of future events are created. This involves acts of perception and intuition on the analysts' part. It requires the capacity to suspend beliefs, preconceptions, and judgments that may inhibit connections being made among ambiguous and disconnected data.

Three critical decisions during scanning need highlighting. First, the scope and breadth of the data and data sources inevitably influence analysts' acts of perception. Second, the data do not speak by themselves, analysts have to breathe life into them. Third, critical acts of judgment are required of analysts in their choice of events and precursors to consider for monitoring, forecasting, or assessment (or a combination of these). These decisions depend heavily on analysts' skill and expertise and are not easily formalized.

Monitoring

Monitoring involves tracking the evolution of environmental trends, sequences of events, or streams of activities. It frequently involves following signals or indicators unearthed during environmental scanning. Sometimes it entails tracking trends, events, or activities that the organization accidentally becomes aware of or which are brought to the organization's attention by outsiders.

The purpose of monitoring is to assemble sufficient data to discern whether certain trends and patterns are emerging. Two comments are in order with respect to these patterns. First, patterns are likely to be a complex of discrete trends. For example, an emergent pattern of life-style may include change in entertainment, education, consumption, work habits, and domicile location preferences. In the initial stages of monitoring, the patterns are likely to be hazy, as they are the outputs of scanning; analysts have only a vague notion of what to look for. Second, highly formalized and quantified data bases usually (if) found in archives of organizations represent a characterization based on previously identified patterns and may have limited utility in tracking emergent patterns. Analysts have to breathe life into such data bases; they do this by arming themselves with a general sense of the patterns they are looking for, and extending their data searches to qualitative and quantitative outside sources.

Viewed this way, monitoring almost always follows scanning; the activity ensures that the hunches and intuitive judgments about the weak signals made during scanning are tracked for confirmation, elaboration, modification, and (in)validation. In monitoring, the data search is focused and much more systematic than in scanning. By *focused,* we mean that analysts are guided by a priori hunches (usually made during scanning or brought to the organization's attention by outsiders). *Systematic* refers to the notion that analysts have a general sense of the pattern or patterns they are looking for and collect data regarding the evolution of the patterns. The systematic character of the search renders data regarding trends cumulative. Thus, what were hazy outlines during scanning can now be imbued with details and clarity.

As monitoring progresses, the data frequently move from imprecise and unbounded to reasonably specific and focused. For example, in tracking the emergence of social issues, the first indicators (often picked up through scanning) are feelings of discontent or loosely distributed concerns expressed by a few individuals. These sentiments begin to attract the attention of others, and what is often referred to as a social movement gradually begins to evolve. Such has been the evolution of the consumerist and environmentalist movements at the national level and special or community interest movements at the local level.

A number of data interpretations or judgments are unavoidable in monitoring. As a sequence of events or a potential pattern is tracked, judgments must be made as to what data are relevant, what the valid and reliable data sources are, how the data fit together, how conflicts in the data can be reconciled, and when data are sufficient to declare that a pattern is evident. A tempting suggestion is that these judgments are easier to make in monitoring than in scanning because the pattern is more evident. Yet, it may not be so. Judging when a pattern is evident is often difficult; it may be simply a fad or a figment of the analysts' fancy. Analysts may be imputing groundless linkages among disparate, unconnected data points. This problem is further confounded when different individuals within the organization make different and conflicting judgments—a not uncommon occurrence.

The outputs of monitoring are threefold: (1) a specific description of environmental trends and patterns to be forecast, (2) the identification of trends for further monitoring, and (3) the identification of areas requiring further scanning. Thus, the outputs of monitoring go beyond the simple provision of inputs to forecasting. Monitoring may identify trends or apparent trends that were not included in the scope of the original monitoring program. Also, as noted previously, a not unusual occurrence is for monitoring activities to indicate areas where further scanning may be desirable.

Forecasting

Scanning and monitoring provide a picture of what has already taken place and what is happening. Strategic decision making, however, requires a future orientation: it needs a picture of what is likely to take place. Thus, forecasting is an essential element in environmental analysis.

Forecasting is concerned with developing plausible projections of the direction, scope, speed, and intensity of environmental change. It tries to lay out the evolutionary path of anticipated change. How long will it take the new technology to reach the marketplace? Will the present social concern with some issue result in new legislation or administrative agency action? Are current life-style trends likely to continue? These kinds of questions provide the grist for forecasting efforts.

Forecasting has two conceptually separable though integrally related activity elements. The first concerns projections based on trends that are evident and which can be expected, with some margin of error, to continue unabated in a given period of time in the future. For example, many demographic trends may be projected with reasonable accuracy over five to ten years. The second element relates to alternative futures that may come about not only on the basis of current trends but also on the basis of judgments regarding events that may take place or that may be made to happen by an organization or outside entities. These represent possible futures. The distinction corresponds to the one drawn in the previous chapter regarding closed and open futures. In the former sense, forecasting (like projections) involves a closed perspective on the future, whereas in the latter sense (as alternative futures), it corresponds to the version of an open future.

A number of key analytical tasks and outputs are involved in forecasting. The first concerns untangling the *key forces* that drive the evolution of a trend. This is a necessary prerequisite to charting out the trend's evolutionary path. The second concerns understanding *the nature of the evolutionary path,* (i.e., whether the change is a fad or of some duration, or cyclical or systematic in character). The third concerns more or less clearly *delineating the evolutionary path* or paths leading to projections and alternative futures. The critical outputs of forecasting are specific understandings of the future implications of current and anticipated environmental changes and decision-relevant assumptions, projections, and information.

Forecasting is typically well focused in comparison to scanning and monitoring. Emphasis is placed upon environmental changes of importance to the organization. Forecasting inherently requires that the organization identify fairly precisely what it wishes to forecast. To forecast social value change, the analyst needs to identify specific value changes to be forecast—for example, political, religious, or economic values. To forecast technological change, the specific technologies to be forecasted have to be clearly identified.

Since the focus, scope, and goals of forecasting are more specific than in scanning and monitoring, forecasting is usually a much more deductive and *rigorous* activity. A wide variety of forecasting techniques are available, ranging from simple extrapolation techniques to methodologies involving multiple participants making forecasts in a number of iterations such as Delphi, to scenario development which involves individuals laying out different paths of likely future developments. These techniques are explored in greater detail in Chapter 13. Note that forecasting as an activity may take some time from initial commitment to doing a forecast to actually acquiring a forecast's outputs. For example, a delphi-based forecast, depending upon the number of iterations involved, may take six to nine months or more. The development of multiple scenarios may also consume many months.

Forecasting also involves numerous data interpretations and judgments. How strong is the supporting and refuting evidence that the trend will continue, intensify, or broaden in scope? What underlying forces are driving the trend, and how strong are they?

Assessment

Scanning, monitoring, and forecasting are not ends in themselves. Unless their outputs are assessed to determine implications for the organization's current and potential strategies, scanning, monitoring, and forecasting merely provide "nice-to-know" information. Assessment involves identifying and evaluating how and why current and projected environment changes affect or will affect strategic management of the organization.

In assessment, the frame of reference moves from understanding the environment—the focus of scanning, monitoring, and forecasting—to identifying what that understanding of the environment means for the organization. Assessment thus endeavors to answer the following questions. What are the key issues presented by the environment? What are the implications of the issues for our organization? An analytical framework to identify key environmental issues is presented in Chapter 11, and various levels at which implications can be addressed are detailed in Chapter 12.

Interrelationships among Scanning, Monitoring, Forecasting, and Assessment

The prior discussion has emphasized the distinctions among scanning, monitoring, forecasting, and assessment. Though they are conceptually separable activities within environmental analysis, scanning, monitoring, forecasting, and assessment are *inextricably intertwined.* As shown in Figure 3.1, each activity can and should directly influence the others.

For example, upon unearthing an emerging trend through scanning, one might quickly jump to potential implications for the organization (assessment) by implicitly forecasting the future path of the trend. If warranted by the potential impact, one may then continue scanning and monitoring. Also, forecasting often proves difficult, if not impossible, because of insufficient knowledge and data about the topic or trends being forecast, thus forcing a return to scanning and monitoring efforts. Deriving implications (assessment) often alerts the organization to the need to conduct further scanning, monitoring, and forecasting. As we shall see in Chapter 11, deciding what to forecast requires consideration of the impact (assessment) on the

Figure 3.1 Linkages Among Scanning, Monitoring, Forecasting, and Assessment

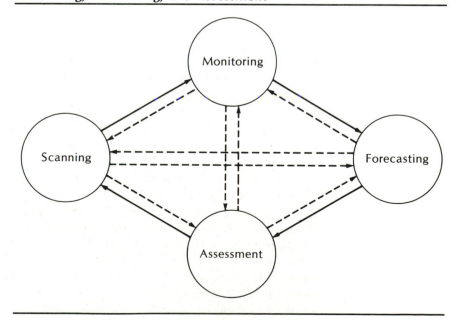

organization of what is being forecast; it makes no sense to forecast the direction of trends and patterns that are not relevant to the organization. In short, environmental analysis is not as simple and as linear as moving from scanning to monitoring to forecasting to assessment.

An Illustration: Discovery of "Yuppies"

A consumer goods firm was interested in environmental analysis for some time. In the late 1970's, one of the analysts had a "premonition" about an emergent trend in life-styles. His occasional encounters with young professionals in Los Angeles, his reading of the print media—especially such popular magazines as *Esquire* and *Harper's*—his conversations with specialized agencies tracking life-style changes, and results of public polling convinced him that something new but potentially significant was emerging in the life-styles area. He had a hunch that this group of individuals was sufficiently similar to but distinct from the rest of the population. If sufficiently large, this group might constitute a market segment worth pursuing. He had some idea of who they were, though he did not know how to describe them except in vague terms such as "like Mr. Joseph Tower."

The analyst, hot on a trail, persuaded his superior to commit some resources to a study of the apparent phenomenon. The analysts began to track writings by and about people he believed fit the prototype he had in mind. He conducted open-ended interviews with some of them to understand if and how their life-styles were different from those of others. As he reflected on these interviews, an initial description presented itself. They were young (25–35 years), male and female, mostly situated in cities, well educated, upwardly mobile, professionals. The analyst followed up the description with a survey, which pointed up similar consumption patterns (Calvin Kleins, Yves St. Laurents), leisure patterns (active, tying leisure activities to professional concerns), living habits (postponing marriage and childbearing), domicile preferences, and a set of social values. The characterization here is brief, yet individuals of this genre later came to be known as "yuppies."

The analyst, however, needed precise answers relevant for his organization beyond a clear delineation of their characteristics. He needed to know if the group was large and if this was a persistent phenomenon or a fad. Determining these answers was relatively easy, as he had access to a wide array of specific data sources. He noted that the key forces driving this life-style were demographics, stable social values, and purchasing power. Based on these key factors, the analyst projected that in ten years there would be a stable population of 10–15 million yuppies.

The analyst brought all of this information to the attention of selected product managers in order to assess specific marketing and product development implications. Product designs and marketing strategies oriented to this segment were initiated within two months.

Table 3.2 summarizes the preceding example within the analytic framework presented in this chapter. Three observations deserve mention. First, we chose this example as it provides a straightforward scanning-monitoring-forecasting-assessment cycle. The example should not be interpreted normatively—that is, that this example represents the ideal cycle. Second, details of data sources and conclusions will vary from instance to instance and will depend on the environmental segments under study. Third, given the focus on lifestyle, the analyst scanned only one of the environmental segments; in many cases, the process will be much more complex, because a number of segments will need to be considered.

Table 3.2 Illustration: Relationships to the Analytic Framework

	Scanning	Monitoring	Forecasting	Assessment
Data Sources	Encounters with specific individuals General reading of print media Specialist organizations tracking lifestyle Public polls	Careful reading of print media Interviews with prototypes Surveys	Internal and external formal data bases Specific models (regional dispersion, growth estimate)	Internal marketing product managers
Data Interpretation and Analysis	Something new in life-styles Potentially significant	Choice of details to focus on	Forces driving: demographics, purchasing power, social values	Implication for segmenting existing markets
Outputs	Identification of a new phenomenon Prototypes: "Mr. Joseph Tower"	Description of yuppie: consumption patterns, leisure patterns, working/living habits, education, age, socioeconomic details	10–15 million estimated growth rate	Product modification
Transition	Analyst conviction reinforced by superior's approval	Believing that the group is large enough to be relevant		

TWO APPROACHES TO ENVIRONMENTAL ANALYSIS

One can conceptualize and execute two distinct though related approaches to environmental analysis. One approach, which we call the "outside-in" or macro-approach, adopts a broad view of the environment, focuses upon longer-term trends, develops alternative views or scenarios of the future environment, and then derives implications for the industry surrounding the firm and for the firm itself. An alternate approach, which we call the "inside-out" or micro-approach, adopts a narrow view of the environment, develops a picture of what is currently happening through ongoing monitoring as a basis for forecasting the immediate future environment, and then derives implications for the industry and the firms within it. These two approaches to environmental analysis are profiled in Table 3.3.

The Outside-in Approach

The outside-in or macro-approach to environmental analysis as an ideal type can be succinctly described. Unfettered by current concerns, the organization engages in scanning, monitoring, and forecasting in order to identify and examine plausible alternative future environments that may confront it. The driving force underlying this approach is the desire to ensure that the organization understands the longer-term dynamics of change within each environmental segment *and* interactions across these segments *before* it attempts to derive or deduce organization-specific implications.

Two dominant questions drive the outside-in approach: (1) What are the major alternative plausible courses of events or scenarios

Table 3.3 The Outside-in and Inside-out Perspectives

	Outside-in	Inside-out
Focus and Scope	Unconstrained view of environment	View of environment constrained by conception of organization
Goal	Broad environmental analyses before considering the organization	Environmental analysis relevant to current organization
Time Horizon	Typically 1–5 years, sometimes 5–10 years	Typically 1–3 years
Frequency	Periodic/ad hoc	Continuous/periodic
Strengths	Avoids organizational blinders Identifies broader array of trends Identifies trends earlier	Efficient, well-focused analysis Implications for organizational action

that are likely to evolve in the environment over the foreseeable future (usually 5–10 years)? (2) What are the implications of each of these views of the future for the competitive context of the organization and for the organization itself? A number of things should be noted about these questions. First, their point of departure is the environment. What is likely to happen in the environment is the dominant concern. Stated differently, the organization itself becomes the focus of attention only *after* alternative plausible pictures of the environment have been developed. Second, and relatedly, the conception of the environment is largely open-ended; it is not constrained by considerations of the firm itself or the industry surrounding it. Whatever data, events, or trends that are unearthed through scanning and monitoring are considered on their merits within the context of the projected evolution of the environment.

The utility of the outside-in approach resides in its potential to surface trends and change early, and thus provide the organization with time to plan appropriate responses. The thrust and purposes of the outside-in approach necessarily mean that scanning is a pivotal component. The outside-in approach entails a broad-brush, largely unconditioned scan of what is happening in the environment. An effective outside-in approach therefore not only should alert the organization to a broader array of environmental trends and patterns than the more narrowly focused inside-out approach but also should identify trends and patterns earlier than the more narrowly focused inside-out approach.

Another major benefit of the outside-in approach is that it helps avoid the blinders that are heavily associated with an emphasis upon the organization. For example, if managers are preoccupied with the organization's current technologies, they may well miss developments in related and sometimes apparently unrelated technologies in the not too distant future.

Since the outside-in approach involves scanning, monitoring, and forecasting the broad environment, the nature of the data, data interpretations and judgments, and outputs previously discussed under scanning, monitoring, and forecasting are also germane. The scope and focus of the data analysis become more specific and structured as the analysis moves from scanning to forecasting. The data interpretations and judgments are increasingly based on more solid and detailed evidence as one moves from scanning to forecasting.

Organizations are not likely to apply an outside-in approach on an ongoing basis to the entire environment. Few organizations have the resources and time to do so. Many organizations, however, adopt a continuous outside-in approach to specific environmental segments—for example, scanning, monitoring, and forecasting demographic shifts, economic trends, or technological developments.

The Inside-out Approach

The inside-out approach, on the other hand, takes the organization as its point of departure—the organization's products, markets, technologies, and strategies. Scanning, monitoring, and forecasting are driven by a current conception of the organization: Given our present and anticipated products, markets, technologies, and strategies, what elements of the environment should the organization scan, monitor, and forecast?

In an inside-out approach, scanning in its pure form as previously described is not likely to be practiced. The organization does not do a broad, unconditioned search of the environment. It does not seek new signals or variables to monitor and forecast beyond the domains of its current scanning and monitoring activities. An example of the inside-out approach might be a fast-food organization that confines its environmental analysis of life-styles to understanding peoples' consumption and leisure habits. It does not make any effort to scan for changes in life-styles beyond the domain of consumption and leisure pursuits—for example, family structure or work patterns.

The utility of the inside-out approach is that it provides efficient, well-focused information and environmental analysis. If the conditions are appropriate for it, the organization can continue to narrowly scan, monitor, and forecast in specific environmental segments. Efficiency stems from the absence of the need, as in the outside-in approach, to cast a wide net in its scanning and monitoring activities. Efficiency will also be enhanced, since monitoring is much more likely to be in familiar territory.

The limitations of the inside-out approach reflect the strengths of the outside-in approach. Its narrow focus may result in many trends or events being missed or, at least, not being captured until much later. The firm that adopts a narrow focus in scanning, monitoring, and forecasting technological change is likely to miss the evolution of relevant technologies until they directly affect the firm's performance. For example, a firm manufacturing products for use in hospital operating rooms that restricts its environmental analysis to technologies relevant to its own products will not capture the technological changes in different domains (e.g., drugs) that may directly affect its sales: an increase in noninvasive treatments of disease through the use of drugs means that surgery is required less often.

Linking the Two Perspectives

The two perspectives are integrally related. They are essentially opposite sides of the same coin and can easily be integrated. The outside-in perspective ultimately leads to inside-out analysis: What are the short-run and medium-run implications of our broad environmental scan for the organization (e.g., strategy issues, and so on)? The inside-out perspective can help sharpen points of departure for the outside-in approach. An example of the latter occurred when a bank, adopting the narrow focus of the inside-out approach, began to notice the importance of information technology in almost all phases of its operations. It then launched a major scan of bank-related technological developments to indicate strategic and operational implications.

Indeed, an organization cannot do environmental analyses that focus upon the broad environment and derive specific implications for the organization without adopting both perspectives. Many organizations do both with varying degrees of integration. We emphasize that organizations will find it productive to adopt both approaches to environmental analysis and to know which approach they are employing.

A FRAMEWORK FOR ENVIRONMENTAL ANALYSIS

No one generally accepted or "right" way exists for doing environmental analysis. Organizationally, firms structure themselves differently to do environmental analysis. Wide differences are also present in the analytical frameworks that organizations employ in doing environmental analysis. The purpose of this section is to provide a general analytical framework for environmental analysis. The section provides an overview to guide the discussion of environmental segments in the following chapters and is a composite of pieces of analysis conducted by many firms. It is also a normative framework in that it suggests a series of steps that any organization should go through if it is to fully understand its environment. The steps are summarized in Figure 3.2, and the following text briefly discusses each step.

Defining the Environment

The first step in the analytical framework is to clearly delineate what is meant by "the environment." This step is important not only because it influences much of the rest of the analysis but also because different firms adopt different definitions of environment. As discussed in Chapter 2, our operating definition of the environment is everything outside the industry—those elements in the broader society that can influence (and be influenced by) an industry and the

Figure 3.2 A General Normative Framework For Environmental Analysis

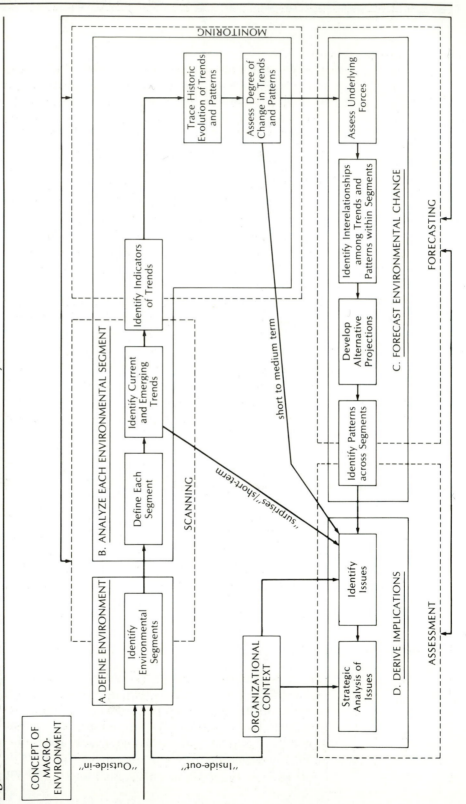

firms within it. For the purposes of this book, and as noted in Chapter 2, we define the environment as consisting of seven segments: demographics, life-styles, social values, technology, economy, and the political and regulatory milieus. At this stage, it is important to identify which segments are to be analyzed and to consider whether the approach is inside-out or outside-in.

Two criteria may be presented with respect to definition of environment and selection of environmental segments. First, the *time frame* of analysis should guide such selection. In the short run, the analysis is dominated by task and industry environment concerns. Macroenvironmental analysis often presents surprises (or discontinuities), or ongoing monitoring generates information that is crucial at these levels. In the medium run, macroenvironmental analysis presents critical inputs for assessing industry/competitive environments. In the long term, broad macroenvironmental analysis from an outside-in perspective is necessary. These concepts are presented in Table 3.4. Second, the *size of the firm* will have implications for the resources that can be devoted to environmental analysis. Macroenvironmental analysis that is broad may be affordable only by large- or medium-large firms; smaller firms will probably have to focus primarily on the task environment or at best, selected (macroenvironmental) segments from an inside-out perspective.

Analyzing Each Environmental Segment

Analyzing the environment as a whole is impossible, since it is too complex and interconnected. The environment must therefore be decomposed into segments. As we shall see in later steps, the analyses of individual segments must be integrated precisely because of the interconnections among environmental segments. Within each environmental segment, the following general set of questions should guide the analysis.

How Is the Segment Defined? As with the environment as a whole, each environmental segment needs to be defined. The definition of each segment determines the focus and breadth of the analysis. Although the definition of any segment is necessarily somewhat arbitrary, consideration of what each segment entails serves to sharpen the organization's understanding of the scope and composition of each segment as well as how the segments may be related. In

Chapters 4 through 10, we provide definitions of the seven environmental segments considered in the book.

What Are the Current and Emerging Trends and Patterns? Once the segment is defined, an effective point of departure is to identify the dominant current changes and emerging patterns within the segment. The ultimate purpose of scanning and monitoring is to do precisely this: to identify changes under way or precursors of impending and likely change (or both).

Conceptually and pragmatically, strong reasons exist for paying particular attention to identifying emerging trends. Conceptually, scanning and monitoring are designed to furnish the early signals of potential trends. Pragmatically, the intent is to capture the emergence of trends before they have impact on the organization. If trends are identified early enough, firms can anticipate and respond to them.

What Are the Indicators of These Trends and Patterns? Knowing that a trend exists is not enough. To monitor, forecast, and assess the direction and magnitude of a trend, we need to be able to operationalize the pattern—that is, establish indicators by which the pattern can be tracked and predicted. We need to know what data or evidence allows us to assert that a trend is apparent and what direction it may take.

For example, indicators of a trend toward conservation or liberalism in the political sphere might be evidenced by election results,

Table 3.4   Relative Importance and Characteristics of Macroenvironmental Analysis for Various Time Frames

Time Frame	Focus		
	Task	*Industry*	*Macro*
Short-term	High	Moderate	LOW SURPRISES MONITORING INSIDE–OUT
Medium-term	Moderate	High	MODERATE INDUSTRY(IES) ATTRACTIVENESS
Long-term	Low	Moderate	HIGH OUTSIDE–IN

public opinion polls, proposed legislation and legislative votes, court decisions, content analyses of newspaper editorials, feature articles, and political speeches. These data provide the evidence that a pattern exists.

What Is the Historic Evolution of These Trends and Patterns?

Knowing the current status of a pattern or potential trend is not enough. Indeed, knowing only the current status may be misleading unless we also have some understanding of the evolution of the pattern over time. This step is analogous to the distinction between point estimates and trend lines in statistics.

An understanding of the *current* scope, intensity, speed, and direction of a trend is *partially* furnished by a depiction of its historic path. With most trends, tracing their evolution in broad terms is typically possible. Demographic and many economic and regulatory patterns are relatively easy to trace. Life-style and some technological developments may be more difficult. Social values and political trends may be the most difficult to trace. Again, indicators are required to develop trend lines.

What Is the Degree of Change Within These Patterns?

Identifying the *degree* of change currently evident within a trend is of paramount importance. Is the trend gaining momentum, slowing down, or remaining relatively stationary? The reference point for the degree of current change is the historic evolution of the pattern.

At a general level, broadly identifying the degree of change of a trend is sometimes possible by noting which phase of its life cycle it's in. Trends often have distinct life cycles; they emerge, develop, mature (peak), and decline. They may not necessarily disappear. Although specifying a trend's life cycle is not always easy (even in retrospect), trying to do so is useful as a means of understanding its evolution to date.

Forecasting Environmental Changes

To assess the potential implications of changes for an organization, the analyst has to develop an understanding of the future evolution of the changes or more precisely, the trends and patterns constituting the changes. To do this, the analyst must perform three tasks: (1) identify and examine the forces underlying or driving the changes, (2) discover interrelationships among the changes, and (3) develop alternative forecasts (or more precisely, projections) of the evolution of change.

Assessing the Underlying Forces. Changes do not just appear, and trends do not just happen. To identify changes is not to explain them; something is driving them. Values and life-styles don't change merely of their own accord. Regulatory change reflects many forces. Technological change is dramatically influenced by social, economic, and political forces. Therefore, before one can develop a forecast, identifying the forces underlying or driving the changes is imperative.

Assessing the forces driving changes emphasizes the interconnections among environmental segments. As shown in Chapters 4 through 10, the trends evident in one segment are often the product of forces in other segments of the environment. The challenge is to identify the most pertinent forces, assess the direction and magnitude of the influence they exert, and determine the likelihood of future change. These tasks clearly move the analyst from description (i.e., identifying indicators) to analyses (i.e., explaining what has been detected or described) and forecasting (i.e., projecting what is likely to happen).

An important point is that rarely will all forces push a trend in the same direction. In environmental analysis, countervailing forces almost always seem to exist. Hence, assessing whether the forces driving trends are reinforcing, conflicting, or unrelated is important.

Identifying Key Interrelationships Among Trends Within Segments. A systematic view of the environment and organization-environment linkages suggests that changes are not isolated phenomena; they are interconnected in multiple ways. Some may reinforce or support each other, some may be in conflict, and some may not be directly related. Consideration of the interrelationships among trends raises the complexity of environmental analysis to a much higher level than the analysis of specific changes.

Unfortunately, no simple methodology exists for searching for and developing linkages among trends. This step requires that the analyst be inventive and creative. The linkages among trends are frequently not obvious. Indeed, the capacity to see the nonobvious is what distinguishes the truly capable analyst.

The following methodology is a composite of the approaches adopted by a number of organizations to identify interrelationships among trends *within* specific environmental segments. First, look for interrelationships within *subsegments.* For example, in the case of life-styles, what trends are interrelated within the subsegments of family structure, work, education, consumption, and leisure? In the case of family structure, for example, how are trends with regard to cohabitation (i.e., unmarried individuals of the opposite sex living together), singles (i.e., individuals living alone), single-parent families, divorce rates, geographic mobility, and so on related? Do they evidence a (continuing) breakdown in family life? Do they reflect new definitions of "family?" Do different life-styles exist among different types of families?

Second, look for relationships across subsegments. Continuing with the example of life-styles, what are the interrelationships among trends in the areas of family structure, work, education, consumption, and leisure? For example, how do work, education, consumption, and leisure patterns differ across different types of households?

Developing Alternative Projections.   If one accepts as a guiding principle (as most individuals involved in environmental analysis do) that the future cannot be *predicted,* then developing alternative projections around likely and sometimes possible future directions of changes becomes imperative. Multiple projections are necessary to avoid the limitations inherent in making only a single best guess or forecast. In making only one forecast of a trend, organizations too often gloss over the difficulties involved in projecting the future (e.g., conflicts among forces driving trends). In short, accepting a single projection as fact becomes too easy.

A range of projections allows different pictures of the future to be created. Each projection must be developed in sufficient detail to allow its validity to be assessed: What is the evidence that the trends are valid? Are the alleged forces propelling the trends? Do the asserted interrelationships among forces make sense? Have conflicts among the trends been taken into account? What assumptions have been made about the future (e.g., will the underlying forces continue)? Questions such as these allow each scenario to be evaluated.

Identifying Interrelationships Among Environmental Segments.   Any division of the environment into segments is somewhat arbitrary; it is done for analytical convenience. From a systems perspective, the segments are necessarily interconnected. As we have noted in many places, the segments discussed in the book are necessarily intertwined in many ways. Thus, during the process of environmental analysis, trends, patterns, and events must be searched out for interrelationships across segments in order to develop an understanding of the environment as a whole.

As in our discussion of interrelationships among patterns within segments, no simple methodology exists for searching for and developing linkages among segments. However, some key questions and ideas useful for this process are presented in detail in Chapter 11.

Assessing Implications for Strategy Formulation and Implementation

As previously noted, the purpose of environmental analysis is to derive implications for the organization. This consists of two steps, both of which are elaborated in later chapters.

Identifying Environmental Issues. All trends, patterns, and events are not of equal importance to any organization. Some may have direct impact, others may only have indirect impact, and some may have little, if any, impact. Also, few organizations have the resources to monitor and track all trends—even those identified by organizational members as potentially important. Determining those trends (within and across segments) that have or are likely to have the most impact (either negative or positive) on the organization is therefore necessary. These trends may then be designated as issues; that is, they are declared to be worthy of analysis as to likely future direction (forecasting) and impact (assessment) on the organization.

Strategic Analysis of Issues. Although Chapter 12 addresses the derivation of implications in detail, we emphasize here the breadth and variety of implications that can be drawn from environmental analysis. The ultimate implication is impact of the environment upon the firm's current and potential strategies, but it is often difficult to discern this impact without first assessing impact of the environment upon the organization's general expectations or assumptions and the industry or industries that the firm is in (i.e., impact upon suppliers, customers, substitute products, new entrants, competitive dynamics). Once these implications have been noted, delineating their impact upon the organization's current strategy and potential strategy options is then possible.

Some Comments on Figure 3.2

Four points need to be kept in mind with respect to Figure 3.2. First, multiple time-bound cycles in environmental analysis noted earlier are presented in the figure. Discovery of "surprises" or discrete issues during early scanning activities may require immediate action on the part of the organization; this is a short-term cycle. In a similar vein, monitoring activities may engender short- and medium-term actions, while a complete cycle is typically useful for long-term actions. In environmental analysis, it is important to distinguish among these issues and consider action implications separately. Second, depending on resources, time, and inclination, an organization may choose to analyze an emerging pattern in a segment or in multiple segments.

These decisions determine the *breadth* of environmental analysis. Typically, broader analyses are necessary for longer-term cycles. Third, to identify issues and assess implications from outputs of scanning, monitoring, and forecasting, the analyst has to have a good understanding of the context of the organization. Inputs from environmental forecasts and projections are by themselves not enough. This is why we earlier defined issues as the intersection of environment and organization. Environmental forecasts are not action relevant unless they have an organizational context. Finally, note in Figure 3.2 that scanning, monitoring, forecasting, and assessment are *recursive* steps, as shown by reverse (dotted) lines, and that these activities overlap each other. The processes assume different characteristics depending on the environmental segment (content) addressed, a consideration that is elaborated in the seven ensuing chapters.

SUMMARY

This chapter described the four key activities involved in analysis of macroenvironment: scanning, monitoring, forecasting, and assessment. Two approaches to analysis—inside-out and outside-in were discussed, and finally a normative framework for analysis was presented.

4

Demographics

Demographics represents the most easily quantifiable or measurable segment of the social environment. *Demographics* means the size, age structure, geographic distribution, ethnic mix, and income distribution of the population. These elements of the demographic environment lie at the heart of many long-term changes in society.

Demographics is perhaps the most easily understood of all the environmental segments. The demographic elements just noted require little explanation. Thus, this chapter does not focus on key concepts for describing demographic change but instead highlights some of the changes in each of these elements and delineates the activities involved in their analysis.

DEMOGRAPHIC CHANGE

The demographic arena is a dynamic sector. Since World War II, considerable and continuing change has been its dominant characteristic. The following text highlights some of the more recent demographic changes.

Population Size. The size of the U.S. population is increasing, but at a slow rate.

■ The total size of the U.S. population rose from 180.7 million in 1960 to 205.1 million in 1970—a 13.5 percent increase. In the next decade, the population increased 11 percent to 227.7 million in 1980. The estimated U.S. population in 1982 was 232.1 million. The rate of growth in the total population has slowed considerably.

Age Structure. Dramatic demographic shifts are occurring in the population's age structure. Over the past four decades, major changes have occurred in the relative sizes of different age groups. These waves, or instability, will continue for a long time to come. In short, the United States has moved into a new demographic era in which every decade's age composition differs significantly from that of the previous decades.

■ The age structure of the population changed significantly between the 1970 and 1980 censuses. The population group aged 14 years and younger decreased by almost 7 million (11.5 percent) to 51.3 million in 1980. However, the population groups in the college and prime household-forming ages (18 to 39) and the elderly population (65 and over) have grown rapidly since 1970. Although the total population grew 13.5 percent from 1970 to 1982, the 18–39 age group grew 40.6 percent (from 60.8 to 85.5 million, or from 29.8 to 36.9 percent of the total population), and the 65 and over age group grew 34.3 percent (from 20 to 26.8 million, or from 9.8 to 11.6 percent of the total population). The number of persons in each 10-year age group above the mid-50s increased at rates above the average of 11.4 percent for the total population. Of the 26.8 million persons aged 65 and over in 1982, 2.5 million were 85 and over. The latter group has been growing at a more rapid rate than the total elderly population. Between 1970 and 1982, the number of 5- to 13-year-olds dropped 17 percent, and the number of 14- to 17-year-olds dropped 5.6 percent. Those figures reflect the decline in the number of births since the mid-1960s. However, because of the almost 20 percent increase in the number of births since 1975, the number of children under 5 has reversed its downward trend.

■ The aging of the population is reflected in the rise in the median age (the age at which half the people are younger and half older) from 27.9 in 1970 to 30.6 in July 1, 1982. The 1982 figure exceeded the previous high reached in 1952 (30.3), after which the combination of relatively high numbers of births and relatively small numbers of persons passing the median age lowered the median age to 27.9 in the 1967–71 period. Then, as the number of births remained relatively low and large numbers of persons passed the median age, the median age began to increase and will continue to do so.

In large measure, the recent and projected volatility in the age structure is a consequence of the boom and bust in fertility rates since World War II. In postwar America, the public mood changed from a concern with scarcity to expansion and growth, and its most personal expression was a soaring birthrate. This demographic phenomenon was so dramatic, it was given a name: the baby boom.

■ The so-called baby boom era spans the period 1946 through 1964. In these nineteen years, 76.4 million babies were born in the United States. For eleven consecutive years, 1954–1964, more than 4 million babies were born each year. Nearly 70 million of the boom babies between the ages of twenty-one and thirty-nine are alive today, and they account for over one-third of the entire population (and the aforementioned massive increase currently being witnessed in this age cohort). The baby boom created a child-centered society, which is becoming an adult-centered society as the boom generation ages.

The baby boom, however, was followed by a baby bust. The boom years peaked with 4.3 million births in 1957. The late 1960s and early 1970s saw a substantial falloff in births, plummeting to approximately 3 million per year in the 1970–72 period.

Geographic Distribution. The age structure is not the only demographic element that is changing. Geographic distribution and growth rates are also exhibiting significant shifts.

■ During the 1970s, the states with the fastest rates of population growth were all in the West or in the South. Between 1970 and 1982, only 10 percent of the 28 million increase in the U.S. population was in the northeast and northcentral regions, and their share of the nation's population declined from 52 to 47 percent.

■ Geographic shifts are also occurring between metropolitan and non-metropolitan areas. Reversing a longtime trend, the population in non-metropolitan areas grew more rapidly during the 1970s than the population in metropolitan areas. In 1980, however, 73 percent of the U.S. population still resided in metropolitan areas. Only the smaller metropolitan areas as a group had a faster rate of growth in the 1970s than in the 1960s, and only the metropolitan areas in the South increased faster than nonmetropolitan areas. Nonmetropolitan counties with the closest commuting ties to metropolitan areas had higher growth rates than the more remote rural counties.

■ Even though the suburbs of metropolitan areas grew faster than non-metropolitan areas, the central cities of metropolitan areas as a group lost population in the 1970s.

■ The number and percentage of individuals whose occupation is farming have declined since World War II. The number has dropped from 23 million in 1950 (15.3 percent of the population) to 9.7 million in 1970 (4.8 percent) to 5.6 million in 1982 (2.4 percent). Not surprising, then, is that increases in those living in the nonmetropolitan population took place almost entirely in nonfarm areas. The largest share of the farm population, 45 percent, lived in the northcentral region in 1982. The South, which had the largest share until 1965, ranked second in 1982 with 35 percent. The West and Northwest contained just 13 and 7.5 percent, respectively, of all farm residents.

Ethnic Mix.   The ethnic mix of the U.S. population is also manifesting change. Some ethnic groups are growing more rapidly than others.

■ During the decade of the 1970s, the black population grew by 17 percent (compared with 11.4 percent for the total population) from 22.6 million in 1970 to 26.5 million in 1980. Over the same period, persons of Spanish origin registered a 60.44 percent increase from 9.1 million to 14.6 million. The increase of the Spanish-origin population is well outside the range of natural increase and reflects improved census coverage, increased group awareness, and improved publicity, which led to the inclusion of an unknown number of illegal aliens.

■ The ethnic mix also reflects geographic shifts. Central cities lost more white population. Although suburban growth slowed considerably during the 1970s, the suburbs gained black population at a faster rate than they gained white population. The total number of blacks living in suburbs grew by about 760,000 in the 1960s and 2.3 million between 1970 and 1982. During the 1970s, the proportion of the total black population living in central cities declined for the first time in many decades. Only 55 percent of the nation's black population lived in central cities in 1982, compared with 59 percent in 1970. Also, some evidence indicates that the Spanish-origin population registered higher rates of increase in central cities, suburbs, and nonmetropolitan areas since 1970 than whites or blacks.

Income Levels.   Income levels and their distribution across the population help inform us about purchasing power, discretionary income, and wealth distribution. An important point is that these elements are affected by rate of economic growth and the composition of families.

■ Slower economic growth and profound changes in the composition of families contributed to the overall decline in purchasing power of families during the 1970s. Before adjusting for changes in consumer prices, median family income (family income is the sum of the income of all family members aged fifteen or older) more than doubled from $10,290 in 1971 to $22,390 in 1981. During this period, however, consumer prices rose by nearly 12.5 percent, resulting in a decline of about 3 percent in median family income after adjusting for changes in prices.

Detection of shifts in demographic characteristics and their implications is the key objective of analysis of this environmental segment. The discussion that follows focuses on the four key activities— scanning, monitoring, forecasting, and assessing—described generally in the previous chapter.

SCANNING AND MONITORING

Scanning and monitoring data to identify current, emerging, and potential trends and patterns is comparatively more straightforward in the demographic arena than in the case of any other environmental segment. The demographic arena is more focused, the indicators of trends are reasonably specifiable, the data are readily available, and many organizations specialize in providing analyses of demographic data. This is not to suggest that reading the data is simple and easy. It is not, as those who misforecast the proclivity of the baby boomers to reproduce will readily attest.

Scanning involves becoming immersed in demographic data. It entails collecting, organizing, and reviewing demographic data from a wide variety of sources. Organizations engage in a variety of activities to scan the demographic area. They attend seminars and presentations by specialist organizations; they subscribe to specialist publications (e.g., *American Demographics*); they obtain special or periodic publications or statistics from the Census Bureau, federal, state, and local government agencies, university programs, and consulting firms. Some organizations occasionally invite demographic experts to make in-house presentations. Scanning unavoidably entails much reading and reflection. Reflection can be brought only by the scanner, but it is critical to satisfying the purposes of scanning.

The purpose of scanning activities is to detect demographic changes or trends already taking place and the precursors of trends. The scanner, then, must go beyond merely collecting and collating demographic data. The data must be organized and interpreted. The data must be translated into answers to three questions: (1) What change is already taking place? That is, what trend lines are already apparent? (2) What are the incipient or emerging trends? That is, what combinations of data points (past trends, events, precursors) suggest and support the beginnings or early stages of a possible trend? (3) What are the possible precursors of change? That is, what are the events, facts, transitions, and so on that may be the harbingers of change?

Many of the indicators that can be used in scanning (and to monitor demographic trends) are noted in Table 4.1. These indicators or variables can be used to identify demographic trends, emerging trends, and precursors pertaining to population size, age structure, geographic distribution, ethnic mix, and income distribution, as well as linkages among these demographic elements. Table 4.1 is not intended to provide an exhaustive listing of indicators but merely to identify the type and variety of variables that can be used in scanning and monitoring. The Census Bureau and many other entities provide

Table 4.1 Demographic Subsegments: Sample Indicators

Population Size	Age Structure	Geographic Distribution	Ethnic Mix	Income Distribution
Number of persons by Geographic areas, e.g., country, region, state, county, city, town	Number of persons by age group, e.g., 0–5, 5–10, 10–15	Movement of persons across geographic areas by • age group • ethnic mix	Size and growth rate of ethnic groups by • age group • geographic region	Income levels by • age group • geographic region • ethnic group
	Rate of growth/ decline by age group	Growth/decline in movement		Average individual income
Birth rate	Median age			Average household income
Mortality rate				

not just historical data along these and many other dimensions but also projections of their future direction. They frequently provide alternate projections based upon different sets of assumptions.

For scanning and monitoring demographic changes, almost exclusive reliance can be placed on secondary sources. Many such data sources exist. The ultimate source is the Bureau of the Census, which is responsible for conducting the national census every ten years, a large number of specific studies on an annual basis, and periodic special studies. Each state and many cities have a specific agency or center that provides detailed demographic analyses of their own regions. Other federal government agencies such as the Department of Labor and National Technical and Information Services also make available specific types of demographic analysis. A large number of consulting and data resource firms have well-established specialties in demographic analysis. Some universities have population study centers, and the Inter-University Consortium for Political and Social Research also conducts demographic studies. The National Center for Health Statistics, in its coverage of vital statistics, provides data on trends in areas such as fertility and life expectancy. Many trade and industry associations conduct studies utilizing demographic data. For example, the U.S. League of Savings Associations studies changes in home-buyer demographics, and the American Council of Life Insurance's Social Research Services conducts many studies for its membership. Many of these organizations conduct custom studies for individual clients.

FORECASTING

Despite the plethora of available data, the multiplicity of data sources, and the variety of demographic analyses that different organizations provide, understanding demographic change and developing demographic projections is not easy. Indeed, the history of demographic analysis is strewn with forecasts that did not come to pass. For example, many of the confident predictions made about the baby boomers during the 1960s proved erroneous.

Underlying Forces

The example just noted indicates how easy and dangerous it can be to buy into demographic (or any other kind of environmental) forecasts. One needs to know not just how the forecast is made (i.e., what data and analytical tools and techniques are used) but also why the forecast or projections are made (i.e., what rationales, logic, evidence, and assumptions underlie these depictions of the future) and for what purpose the forecast is made. The latter concern addresses a fundamental issue in understanding and using any environmental forecast: What are the forces (sometimes termed *drivers*) that are driving the projected (demographic) trends? These driving forces need to be identified and analyzed before one can make a forecast or assess whether one is going to accept or reject a forecast made by someone else. Otherwise, one makes or accepts a forecast on blind faith, without understanding why the projected patterns or events are likely to occur.

The forces driving demographic change reside both within the demographic arena itself and in other environmental segments. *Interactions among demographic elements* themselves may be a force that drives demographic change.

■ For example, changes in the ethnic mix may be reflected in the age structure, geographic distribution, and income levels. The rapid influx of persons of Spanish origin into many cities has increased the proportion of children under sixteen years of age, and the increase in the black population living in suburbia has lowered the age structure of many suburbs. The migration of the elderly to the Sun Belt states has increased the median age and affected the ethnic mix of these states.

Demographic forces such as fertility rates and life expectancy rates also directly affect demographic change through their impact on age structure and distribution. We emphasize that interactions or linkages among the subsegments or elements within the demographic arena at least partially explain some of the demographic change.

As with each other environmental segment, demographic change is also driven by forces outside the demographic arena. Indeed, a safe suggestion is that unless these forces are identified and their impact on specific demographic changes assessed, gaining an understanding of why change is occurring or what change is likely to occur is impossible.

Long-term demographic change is particularly driven by social value, life-style, technology, and economic forces.

- *Social* values such as preferences for smaller families lead to a reduction in the birthrate. Social value change with regard to ethnic relations, civil rights, access to education, and so on has facilitated movement of minorities from cities to suburbs.
- *Life-style changes* are closely related to demographic change. The rate and type of household formation affect birthrates and geographic mobility. The increasing participation of women in the work force has led to later births of first children for many women. Increasing education levels has helped to create greater equalization of income.
- *Economic environment* also influences demographic change. Economic conditions most obviously impact income levels. Economic and climatic conditions and physical resources such as land availability and air quality affect geographic mobility. They variously influence people to move to the West and South. Physical resources such as the extent and quality of the stock of housing may impact birthrates (family size) and death rates (through the amount of housing devoted to care for the elderly).
- *Technology* significantly affects demographic change. Developments in medical care technology have reduced infant mortality and extended life expectancy through disease control and enhancement of surgical capabilities. Birth control technology has allowed people to better manage family size and spacing. Technological developments relevant to demographic change go far beyond health care, birth control, and the aging process. Technologies involved in improving transportation and communication capabilities facilitate movement from cities to suburbia and nonmetropolitan areas.
- *Political* and *regulatory* forces also help shape demographic change. Who wins and loses in the political battle being waged over abortion will affect birthrates. Geographic and ethnic shifts

are often impeded or supported by political skirmishes and judicial decisions at the local or regional levels.

It is not these forces individually but the degree and direction of *interrelationships* among them that are critical for forecasting demographic change. As we discussed in Chapter 2, forces from within and from outside the demographic arena may reinforce each other, conflict or drive in opposite directions, or be little related, if at all. It is easy to see how these forces might reinforce each other. For example:

■ With regard to the trend toward longer life expectancy, medical technology advancements, greater social value placed upon the aged, greater attention devoted to the problems of the aged by the political and regulatory processes, in conjunction with sufficient economic resources (either through themselves or through voluntary or governmental sources), have all contributed to better medical and social care for elderly citizens.

Understanding current change and determining future change is rendered problematic, however, because the driving forces may be conflictual; they may push change in opposite directions. The push and pull among conflictual forces accounts for much of surprise in environmental change; some forces may gain strength while others weaken. Conflictual forces are evident with regard to many trends (and changes in trends) in the demographic arena. For example:

■ The recent increase in the birthrate has been attributed to an upsurge in the number of women of childbearing age (a demographic force reflecting the aging of the baby boomers), some changes in life-styles (single women wishing to form households), social value change (a growing acceptance of single mothers, day-care facilities, and a return to the values inherent in parenting), and a general improvement in economic conditions. Yet, counterforces are also evident that may slow down this trend or cause it to change in direction. Life-style shifts such as the increase in singles among the twenties and thirties age group, the increase in cohabitation and in two-career families, social value shifts reflected in these life-style changes, and the diffusion of birth control technology all work against an upswing in the birthrate.

Driving forces from within any environmental segment do not necessarily reinforce each other. Note the conflict among life-style elements in their impact on birthrate changes. Indeed, as we shall see often in this book, they may directly conflict.

Developing Forecasts and Projections

As with any segment of environmental analysis, some conception of future demographic developments is necessary as an input to strategy development and evaluation. We emphasize that future developments cover short-run as well as longer-run depictions of possible trends, patterns, and events. As emphasized in Chapter 3, developing plausible conceptions of the future or alternative futures takes what is happening now (i.e., the current state of affairs) as its point of departure. Thus, a critical component of alternative futures development is assessing what is likely to happen in the immediate future. A preoccupation with the long run often leads to neglect of the benefits of considering the short run.

Irrespective of short-run or long-run considerations, specifying precisely what elements of demographics are to be forecast or projected is imperative. To assert that an organization is interested in population forecasting does not tell us with any degree of precision what the organization wishes to forecast. Conceptions of alternative demographic futures are frequently built around individual dimensions (or combinations of dimensions), such as number of people in each life cycle stage (typically five- or ten-year spans), population size and growth within particular regions, mobility of people from region to region or from city to suburb, changes in ethnic mix, changes in income levels, and changes in fertility rates. More comprehensive forecasts are built around interactions among these dimensions, such as changes in income by life cycle stage and by geographic region.

As with any macroenvironmental forecast, the specification of what is to be forecast should be geared to the purposes of the forecast. The demographic dimensions (age, sex, race, mobility, income, and so on) and level of detail is a function of how the forecast is to be used. For example, much greater detail is required in market size and segmentation analysis than in assessing the broad implications of demographic change for different segments of an industry.

A peculiarity of the demographic arena is that many organizations are in the business of providing demographic forecasts. The Bureau of the Census, other governmental agencies, many consulting firms, and industry, trade, and professional associations all develop demographic forecasts. These vary considerably in complexity and detail. The offerings of the organizations can be divided into three categories: *published reports, custom-tailored studies,* and *interactive systems.* The Bureau of the Census and other organizations put out many publications that include demographic forecasts and projections. Some of these publications are extremely detailed and long-ranging. Many consulting firms develop forecasts, tailored to client specifications. Some firms allow access to their forecasting models, thereby permitting clients to manipulate the models by changing the characteristics of variables, the relationships among variables, and their underlying assumptions. Many organizations utilize one or more of these offerings of demographic forecasts and adopt them to meet their own specific needs.

The presence of so many organizations specializing in demographic analysis is made possible by another peculiarity of the demographic arena: the availability of abundant quantitative data. Thus, demographic forecasting tends to involve some kind of computation procedure. These procedures or forecasting techniques range in complexity from *simple extrapolations* of demographic trend lines (e.g., population totals, birthrates, income levels) to *transition matrices* to *elaborate models* linking the details of many demographic variables. The pursuit of model elegance, however, can never be substituted for validly capturing the forces driving demographic change. No forecasting technique is intrinsically superior in its ability to make plausible demographic projections. Thus, anybody confronted with the challenge of using and adapting the demographic forecasts of others or creating demographic forecasts de novo, irrespective of the forecasting technique employed, must raise the following two questions:

What Logic Gives Rise to the Forecast or Projections? Projections or forecasts of demographic variables (e.g., size of population, birthrate, fertility rate, ethnic mix, geographic mobility) and their interrelationships are necessarily predicated upon underlying rationales or cause-effect relationships. These cause-effect relationships are the previously discussed driving forces and their interrelationships. We emphasize that the explanations that buttress a forecast should be made *explicit* as part of the forecasting process. Only by doing so can we understand why the projections are as they are. By the same token, if one is using or adapting others' demographic forecasts, ascertaining the driving forces underlying their forecasts is equally imperative. If one finds their logic faulty, disagreement will likely follow pertaining to their forecasts or projections.

What Assumptions Underlie the Forecast or Projections? In developing depictions of future direction and change along demographic variables or dimensions, many assumptions must inevitably be made. Not surprisingly, different sets of assumptions will lead to different forecasts or projections. As is the case with many of the Bureau of the Census forecasts, different sets of assumptions in the context of the same driving forces give rise to distinct projections. For example, different assumptions about birthrates and death rates generate different total population levels. Different assumptions about fertility rates, economic growth, and governmental fiscal policies give rise to different patterns of income distribution.

The linkage between driving forces and assumptions is analogous to the use of simulation models: while leaving the model's relationships among individual variables constant, by changing the model's assumptions, different results are obtained. Indeed, many demographic forecasts are the product of *simulation* models. Again, we emphasize the need to make explicit what assumptions underlie individual demographic forecasts or projections.

In summary, for many business strategy purposes, demographic forecasts can be readily obtained from many external sources. Because of the quantitative nature of demographic data, these forecasts use a wide variety of computation or forecasting tools and techniques. Many organizations further adapt these forecasts to satisfy their own individual needs. Irrespective of the source of demographic forecasts, any individual forecast can be interpreted only if the driving forces and assumptions underlying it have been explicated.

ASSESSMENT: DERIVING IMPLICATIONS

Demographic change directly or indirectly impacts every industry and every organization. One matter, however, is noting this broad general implication, and quite another is deriving specific implications for an individual organization. Demographic data, no more than any other type of environmental data, do not speak for themselves. As observed by one senior executive in a discussion with the authors: "The challenge is to derive insight from the numbers and tell me how they will impact my business. Demographic changes by themselves are meaningless." That statement could be the catch-cry for all environmental analysis.

Five general themes that are largely distinctive of the demographic segment run through consideration of implications of changes in this segment. First, changes in this segment represent *closed* versions of the future; a single firm or industry can do little to influence future demographic shifts or evolution of emergent changes. Second, most changes in this segment are gradual and *continuous;* this facilitates early detection of trends and formulation of strategic thrusts. Third, demographic shifts together with technological and resource shifts lie at the bottom of many *long-term macroenvironmental shifts.* Hence, their implications for other segments (Chapter 11) present *second-order* opportunities and threats, which firms may exploit in strategy formulation for the long-term advantage. Fourth, in many cases, demographic shifts need to be considered *jointly* with life-style shifts (presented in the next chapter) to formulate strategic thrusts. Finally, direct implications of demographic shifts are primarily felt in the *short* and *medium term* at the level of *business-unit* strategies. Even when the firm has multiple business units, implications of demographic shifts need to be considered separately for each of the units.

Implications of demographic shifts at the business-unit level need to consider industry, business strategy, and functional levels. Linkages between demographic shifts and impact on different types of industries can be quickly noted.

■ The projected decline in the number of children under sixteen for the next few years will affect a wide variety of firms serving the children's market: baby foods, children's clothes, toys, fast food, and so on. The impact of the increase in the twenty-five to forty-five year-old group and especially the upsurge in the thirty-five to forty-five year-old group will be felt in many different types of industries: housing, furniture, automobiles, food, financial services, and so on.

The continuing increase in the elderly population can be expected to open up *new market needs* or niches and impact many long-established industries. For example, many financial service institutions (i.e., banks, insurance firms) are now creating special offerings for the elderly market segment. Many leisure goods firms are now targeting the elderly market.

■ Bowling establishments, golf courses, entertainment centers, and housing and holiday resorts offer special packages to attract more seniors, particularly in off-peak times. Disney World has been especially successful in attracting senior citizens with special vacation packages. Some transportation firms (airlines and bus lines) have developed marketing programs aimed specifically at senior citizens. Even in basic product areas, such as food, some firms have begun to address the peculiar needs of the elderly market segment. Various firms now produce salt-free products aimed (in part) at the elderly market, since one out of every four persons aged sixty-five or over requires a salt-free diet.

The previous discussion emphasizes the capacity of demographic change to impact many industries. Typically, demographics is at the core of such industry-level variables as *product life cycle, market potential,* and *growth;* strength of *market segments* (often jointly with life-styles in consumer markets); and regional (geographic) *distribution* of markets. Demographic shifts often have profound impact on these variables. For business strategists, early detection of demographic shifts and their implications enables exploration of growth opportunities and shift of resources away from declining regions, segments, or industries.

The following is a sequence of questions that any organization should ask to derive the implications of the prevailing demographic context and anticipated change.

What Are the Industrywide Implications? How is demographic change affecting (and how will it affect) the industry in current and potential sales? Many consulting firms specializing in demographic analysis make broad projections along these lines.

> ■ One firm projected the following changes in household consumption patterns during the 1980s as a consequence of demographic change induced by the baby boomers: expenditures for necessities (food at home, shelter, household energy, transportation energy, clothing, and medical care) would increase by 26 percent, while expenditures on discretionary goods would increase 32 percent; expenditures on home furnishings and operations (sofas, appliances, china, telephone, water, and so on) would increase by 49 percent; expenditures on medical care would increase by 45 percent; and expenditures on recreational durables (e.g., cross-country skis, televisions, tickets to sports events) would increase by 14.2 percent.

What are the implications for specific industry segments? Demographic change variously affects different industry segments. Which segments are positively or negatively affected? How and why are they affected?

> ■ In the food service industry, non-sit-down fast-food establishments have been negatively affected by demographic change, while sit-down, lower-priced restaurants have been positively affected. As the baby boomers get older and have more discretionary income and as the number of children below age sixteen declines, demand for take-out fast food declines.

What Are the Implications for Business-Unit Strategy? The industrywide implications in turn set the context for business-unit strategy formulation. This is evident in many of the examples cited previously. Three pivotal questions need to be asked at this stage:

1. What demographic assumptions underlie industry change and business-unit strategy? How are they likely to change?
2. What opportunities are presented by demographic shifts and their industry implications?

3. What threats (e.g., closing of markets, regional redistribution of markets) are generated by demographic shifts?

In addition, demographic shifts often have implications for functional-level strategies such as human resource and marketing strategies. For example:

■ The aging of the U.S. population has resulted in many more employees aged fifty-five and over. As the baby boom generation gets older, competition is much keener in the lower managerial ranks in many companies. As a consequence, many firms have had to institute new programs and policies to deal with these demographic changes.

SUMMARY

The demographic segment deals with such factors as the size, age structure, ethnic mix, income levels, and geographic distribution of the population. Data for demographics are abundant; for many business strategy purposes, demographic forecasts can be readily obtained from many external sources. Because of the quantitative nature of the demographic data, these forecasts use a wide variety of computation or forecasting tools and techniques. Irrespective of the source of demographic forecasts, any individual forecast should be interpreted only after explicating the driving forces and assumptions underlying it. Further, these interpretations should be followed by specific consideration of the impact of the demographic change on the industry or industries in which the firm is competing.

5

Life-Styles

The demographic data discussed in the previous chapter provide broad parameters as to the size, age distribution, location, ethnic mix, and income levels of the U.S. population. These data, however, do not describe how people live; that is, they tell us little about people's life-styles. People's life-styles are their patterns of living in the world as expressed in household formation, work, education, consumption, and leisure activities. We therefore categorize life-styles into five components: the type of family structure or household one chooses to establish, the type of work one performs, the type of education one chooses, the goods and services one consumes, and the leisure activities one engages in. These activities are highly *interrelated*. Note that life-styles are often closely related to the demographic dimensions discussed in the previous chapter. Also, life-styles are the outward manifestation of people's attitudes and values, which is the focus of the chapter.

LIFE–STYLE CHANGE

Life-style changes are so pervasive that they have become an enduring characteristic of industrial societies. Toffler (1980), for example, notes that postindustrial societies are characterized by emergence of new life-styles at such a rapid rate that it is now necessary to speak of "consumption" of life-styles. For analytical purposes, life-style changes can be described along the five dimensions mentioned earlier. Typically, however, changes occur in clusters of variables; this underscores the notion that the factors constituting life-style are highly interrelated.

Consider, for example, the changes occurring in the United States along the life-style dimensions.

Household Formation. The last twenty-five years have witnessed dramatic shifts in the composition, rate of change, type, and size of households in the United States.

■ There were an estimated 83.5 million households in the United States in 1982. About 61 million were family households and 22.5 million were nonfamily households (a family household requires the presence of a householder—a person who owns or rents the living quarters—and at least one other person related to the householder by birth, marriage, or adoption).

Significant change is occurring in the type and rate of household formation.

■ Between 1970 and 1982, the number of family households increased 19 percent, while the number of nonfamily households increased by 88 percent. Although most households are still family households, their share of the total declined from 81 percent in 1970 to 73 percent in 1982. With regard to the three distinct types of family households specified by the Census Bureau, between 1970 and 1982, married couple families increased 11 percent, other families with male householders (no wives present) increased 62 percent, and other families with female householders (no husbands present) increased 71 percent.

■ Many, but not all, of what are called "other families" are one-parent households (i.e., have own children under eighteen present). Approximately 34 percent of other family households maintained by males and 62 percent of those maintained by females were one-parent situations. The increase in one-parent households has been one of the major changes in household composition over the past decade. While the number of two-parent households has declined by 4 percent since 1970, the number of one-parent households increased 99 percent among those maintained by the father alone and 105 percent among those maintained by the mother alone. The rates of increase in one-parent families maintained by either the father or mother were not significantly different.

■ About 13.1 million of the 22.5 million nonfamily households were maintained by women, and 91 percent of these women lived alone. By comparison, about 79 percent of the 9.5 million males maintaining nonfamily households lived alone. Although most nonfamily households were maintained by women in both 1970 and 1982, the percentage increase over the twelve-year period for those maintained by men was about twice as high as that for women. Consequently, the portion of all nonfamily households maintained by men increased significantly from 34 percent in 1970 to 42 percent in 1982.

Although the number of nonfamily households has increased dramatically, the percentage of the total household population involved is relatively low.

■ In 1982, the 22.5 million nonfamily households represented 27 percent of all households, but they contained only 12 percent of all persons living in households. In 1970, the 11.9 million nonfamily households represented 19 percent of all households and contained 7 percent of the household population.

Change is also occurring in the number of persons per household.

■ The average number of persons per household has been declining steadily since 1965 and reached a new low in 1982 of 2.72 persons, compared with 3.14 in 1970. This decline is largely due to the low level of fertility during the 1970s (discussed in the previous chapter) and the changes in the household composition noted previously. Households maintained by married-couple families contain the most members with 3.33 persons in 1982. Although relatively small families (consisting of a husband and wife and one or two children) increased modestly between 1970 and 1982, a substantial decline occurred in the number of larger families where both parents and at least three children are present. Nonfamily households in 1982 were small, containing an average of only 1.19 persons. Overall, households with only one or two members increased from 46 to 55 percent of total households between 1970 and 1982, while households with five or more members dropped from 21 to 12 percent of the total.

Work.   Work-related trends also tell us much about people's lifestyles: whether they work, what kind of work they do, what expectations they possess about work, where they work, how long they work, and whether the work is paid or voluntary. As we shall see, these questions are integrally linked to the prior discussion of household structure and composition.

■ The most striking work-related life-style trend is the increasing participation of women in the work force. In 1940, 27 percent of women aged fourteen and older were in the work force. By 1982, more women were in the labor force than worked at home or engaged in other non-labor-force activities. Women are moving into many types of jobs that were previously almost exclusively held by men. The proportion of women in almost all professional and technical jobs is increasing. The last decade has seen an influx of women into managerial positions: between 1972 and 1980, the number of women employed as managers doubled.

One consequence is that the two-income or two-earner family household is now more common than traditional one-earner family households.

■ In 1968, two-earner families about equaled traditional earner families both in number and proportion. Two-earner families are now much more prevalent than traditional single-earner families. Two-earner family households are considerably more prevalent among the younger age groups.

■ Other work-related trends include: more elderly continuing full-time or part-time work upon reaching age sixty-five; more people taking early retirement from their "career" jobs, some of whom return to the labor force on a full-time or part-time basis; and a decline in the willingness of individuals to move geographically, often at the expense of job promotions.

Education.   Education type and attainment levels tell us much about how people wish to spend their lives: the type of work they seek, the type of consumption and leisure patterns they may engage in, and the attitudes and values they may exhibit.

■ The United States is becoming better educated as measured by participation in and graduation from educational institutions. In March 1982, 71 percent of persons aged twenty-five and over had completed at least a high school education as compared with 53 percent in 1970. The proportion of persons completing high school has been increasing more rapidly for blacks than for whites—from 53 percent in the twenty-five to thirty-four years age group in 1970 to 79 percent in 1982.

■ The proportion of persons with one year or more of college and those who are college graduates continues to rise. This is true for whites, blacks, and those of Spanish origin. Between 1970 and 1982, for persons between twenty-five and thirty-four, the percentage of whites with college degrees rose from 16.6 to 24.9; for blacks it rose from 6.1 to 12.6; and for those of Spanish origin, it rose from 5.4 to 9.7. The proportion of women among this age group who are college graduates is rising faster than it is for men: from 20 to 27 percent for men and from 12 to 21 percent for women.

Consumption.   Consumption patterns are an integral element of life-styles. The homes, furnishings, durable goods, autos, clothes, food, beverages, travel, personal services, and so on that people consume tell us much about how they live (and the style in which they wish to be seen living). They also reveal much about people's attitudes and values. Consumption patterns can and do change over time—sometimes precipitously.

■ Significant changes have occurred in types of homes purchased (e.g., the emergence of condominiums), autos (e.g., from larger to smaller autos, from domestic to foreign), furnishings (e.g., the rise and decline of many styles), durable goods (e.g., the status attached to particular items such as microwave ovens), clothes (e.g., shifts in fashions and styles) beverages (e.g., movement from regular to diet drinks), and personal services (e.g., the increase in the use of others to perform functions such as laundry, housecleaning, and lawn and garden maintenance).

Change in consumption patterns can occur rapidly.

■ A number of metropolitan areas in the last few years have experienced a major decline in the demand for condominiums. Much consumption behavior tends to follow fashion and fads. Some furniture stylings, food types, clothes, and beverage drinks tend to be "in" or "out" with different demographic and household segments. Scandinavian furniture and Perrier water became vogue products for a period of time. Clothes styles obviously follow faddish trends.

Leisure.   Leisure activities represent a significant element of the way people live their lives. They tell us much about how people spend a large proportion of their time. Leisure activities vary by individual. At the aggregate level, they manifest change over time.

■ In recent years, health enhancement and physical fitness activities such as jogging, bicycling, calisthenics, swimming, tennis, and racquetball have experienced a major upsurge in participation. The popularity of jogging and tennis now seems to be waning. Broader segments of society now attend cultural events: symphony, theater, ballet, opera, and shows in general. Movie attendance varies from year to year; videotape recorders have clearly affected this leisure activity for many families. Home-centered leisure activities are also subject to change. Cable TV is drawing viewers away from the national television networks, garden and lawn work is less popular among baby boomers than older adults, and younger generations eat fewer meals at home than do older adults.

Life-style changes unfold over time: new life-styles emerge, diffuse at varying rates, and are replaced by still newer ones. Analysis of this segment entails detecting new life-styles, tracing their diffusion, and deriving their implications.

SCANNING

Scanning the life-styles arena is cumbersome and complex. The subsegments within life-styles are broad in scope; they interrelate to constitute many distinct life-styles. Change can occur much more quickly than in the case of demographics, and the sources of relevant data are many and diverse.

Two key considerations underlie scanning in this segment. First, new life-styles cannot be predicted in a manner specific enough to render drawing implications possible. Hence, a key task in scanning is discovery of emergent life-styles. Detection is facilitated by *qualitative* indicators, though a wide number of quantitative indicators can enable detailing the specifics of new life-styles. Second, and relatedly, organizations need to (and many consumer goods firms do) pay attention to *primary* sources of data in addition to secondary sources, unlike the demographic sector.

Much of the approach to life-styles scanning was captured in the discussion of yuppies in Chapter 3. Scanning the life-styles arena entails keeping up-to-date with a wide variety of information sources, both secondary and primary. As shown in Table 5.1, secondary sources differ somewhat depending upon the subsegments of interest: household formation, work, education, consumption, and leisure. The analyst must sift through these many data types—in the process, effecting many sets of perception. We emphasize again that the data do not speak for themselves. For example, a scan of the leisure subsegment would yield a lot of quantitative and qualitative data. The analyst's task, however, is to read the data—that is, to discover what trends seem to be emerging and what harbingers or precursors of change may be evident.

Primary data sources also need to be used in scanning and monitoring life-styles. A number of firms use focus groups as a means of identifying and tracking life-style trends. Some firms regularly assemble panels of experts to discuss life-style trends and changes. Many firms conduct interviews with experts on a regular basis.

MONITORING

Monitoring trends requires careful tracking of specific indicators. Table 5.2 suggests the types of indicators that might be tracked. As noted in the discussion of scanning, the types of indicators tracked will vary depending upon the trends that are of concern.

For illustration purposes, the following is a brief outline of the monitoring process employed by a consumer goods firm that was interested in tracking a number of trends that collectively constituted what was often dubbed the "physical fitness craze."

■ Of particular interest to the firm were trends pertaining to participation in tennis, bowling, and jogging. The firm tracked sales of relevant equipment, shoes, and clothing; sales of specific companies selling these products because they frequently served distinct market segments; the building of new facilities and the usage of existing facilities; the proportion of individuals within different age groups participating in these leisure activities; and the competitive behaviors of firms competing in these market segments, such as pricing and promotions. By tracking indicators such as these, the firm was able to keep tabs on what was happening in these leisure areas. The data for monitoring these indicators were readily available through company annual reports and quarterly statements, industry and trade association literature and analyses, security analysts' reports, specialist magazines, periodic sampling of distributors, retailers, and end-use facilities, and frequent contact with industry participants and observers (e.g., editorial staffs of specialist magazines).

Scanning and monitoring life-styles is often facilitated by the existence of multiple organizations dedicated, at least in part, to studying life-styles. A large number of consulting firms, market research houses, and advertising agencies conduct regular and ad hoc life-styles studies. Some of these organizations make these studies available for a fee; others provide them free. Many congressional committees also conduct hearings, solicit testimony, and issue reports on

Table 5.1 Life-Style Subsegments: Data Sources

Household Formation	Work	Education	Consumption	Leisure
Census Bureau	Dept. of Labor	Dept. of Education	Dept. of Commerce	Federal/state/local agencies
State and local demographic agencies	Dept. of Commerce	State and local education agencies	Other federal agencies	Industry/trade associations and press
	State and local agencies	Individual educational associations	Industry/trade associations and publications	Consumer reports
Consulting firms specializing in demographic and life-style research	Economic reports and statistics	Educational institutions	Economic reports and statistics	Consulting firms
Some specialist magazines	Specialist magazines and newspapers	Specialist journals and magazines	Consumer reports	Professional societies —Medical —Sporting
			Corporate annual reports	Leader groups Follower groups
			General business press	
			Security/financial analysts	
			Leader groups Follower groups	

many facets of life-styles. As is the case in demographics, many industry, trade, and professional organizations conduct life-styles studies covering such elements as household formation, single families, home ownership, work patterns, educational trends, and leisure activities. Specialist magazines exist on most aspects of life-styles; these publications and their editorial staffs are typically a fountain of information on specific facets of life-styles.

FORECASTING LIFE–STYLE CHANGE

Forecasting life-style changes is much more problematic than demographic change for two reasons. First, over the long run, life-style changes are rarely gradual. Second, description of changes in the

Table 5.2 Life-Style Subsegments: Dimensions

Household Formation	Work	Education	Consumption	Leisure
Types of family, nonfamily, and "other family" households —Headed by male or female —Number in family —Number of children —One or two parents —Average number of persons per household —Growth rate for each household type —Absolute number and percentage of total for each type	Size and growth of work force Participation in work force by demographic variables —Age —Sex —Income —Race Types of work performed —Job type —Full-time —Part-time Work conditions —Hours —Pay Work expectations —Rewards —Quality —Mobility Paid vs. voluntary —Community service	Number and growth rate by educational level —High school —College, etc. Educational participation type/level by demographic variables —Age —Sex —Income —Race Educational attainment level by demographic variables	Volume and growth of consumption expenditures by category —Homes —Durable goods —Clothes, etc. Changes within each category —Type of house —Size of auto —Size of durable goods —Price range of clothes, etc. Expenditures by demographic variables	Volume and growth rate of participation in leisure activity by category —Physical exercise —Indoor games —At-home activities —Entertainment —Etc. Changes within each category —Type of sport —Type of physical exercise, etc. Participation by demographic variables

early stages is likely to be qualitative, which incorporates a large judgmental component. Although general contours of life-styles in the long term may often be predictable, such forecasts frequently either lack the specificity requisite for strategy formulation or have such low probability of occurrence as not to be useful. Therefore, forecasting life-style changes primarily involves forecasting diffusion of changes identified during scanning and monitoring, and is typically useful for the medium term. Providing a framework for assessing life-style changes in this latter sense of the term is possible.

Forces Driving Life-Style Change

The forces driving the life-style change reside both within the life-style segment and in other segments of the macroenvironment. Forces within the life-styles arena—that is, interactions across the subsegments of household formation, work, education, consumption, and leisure—impact life-style change.

- The increasing number of childless families and the postponement of children are often driven by the work, consumption, education, and leisure preferences of both spouses. A not surprising finding is that as more women attain higher levels of education, a rising proportion of women are joining the work force, thus enlarging the pool of two-income families. The increase in the number of young adults who have never married is a function of higher educational levels, and work, consumption, and leisure preferences. Conversely, household formation also affects the other subsegments. The increase in two-income families affects work, consumption, and leisure patterns. Two-income families tend to purchase more convenience items and services that reduce the time the family must devote to such tasks as food preparation, laundry, and child care.

The primary driving forces underlying life-style change, however, emanate from outside of the life-styles arena. Demographics, social values, technology, economic change, and political and regulatory forces all influence life-styles. Each of these sets of forces may affect each subsegment in different ways.

Demographics influences each subsegment. Consider the following example:

- The number of households headed by persons under the age of thirty increased by more than 5 million during the 1970s, but during the 1980s, the increase will be less than 3 million. In contrast, households headed by the thirty to forty-four age group will grow almost twice as much as it did in the seventies, as the baby boom generation moves into these years. Changes in the size, age structure, geographic distribution, ethnic mix, and income levels affect demand for different types of education and jobs, and shape consumption and leisure patterns.

Social values directly influence each life-styles subsegment.

■ Value shifts such as greater acceptance of divorce, separation, living alone, and cohabitation facilitate greater diversity in family and nonfamily households. Value shifts also cause changes in work, education, consumption, and leisure patterns. Many values had to change before the influx of women in the work force could have occurred. The placement of greater value upon personal health and physical fitness has greatly affected the consumption of many goods and services and innumerable leisure activities.

Technology affects life-styles in many ways—often in ways that are not immediately obvious.

■ Technological developments resulting in home conveniences such as food preparation machines, microwave ovens, frozen foods, and so on have made it much easier for singles to live alone. Technological advances are strikingly changing the nature of work that people do and the work options available to them. These changes have facilitated many of the work-related changes discussed at the beginning of this chapter. Technological change also affects leisure pursuits. For example, through the introduction of videotape recorders, many people now watch movies at home rather than in movie theaters.

Economic change may induce life-style changes. For example:

■ A common assertion is that a downturn in the economy leads to a reduction in household formation: people are less inclined to get divorced, young adults are more inclined to live at home, and single senior citizens may be more inclined to live with their families. Conversely, sustained economic growth opens up job opportunities, thus facilitating growth in two-earner families and greater participation in the work force by women and the elderly.

Political and regulatory forces, though not as pervasive as demographic, social value, and economic forces, may contribute to life-style change through their impact on other segments. The women's movement, as a social and political force, has clearly aided many life-style changes noted in this chapter.

Interactions among the Driving Forces

None of these sets of forces alone drive life-style change. They may reinforce each other, they may conflict, or they may bear little relationship to each other. Assessing how these forces interact is therefore important. A reasonable suggestion is that almost every life-style change noted in this chapter is the product of the interaction of multiple forces within and outside the life-style arena.

Consider, for example, the increasing trend toward two-earner families.

■ Work-related factors such as the rapid growth in female participation in the work force, household formation factors such as the reduction in family size and postponement of children, the rising educational level of women, and consumption factors such as greater desire for immediate gratification have all contributed to an increasing number of two-earner families. These life-style forces were being propelled by social value change pertaining to the role of women in society and the increasing acceptance that responsible child care can be provided by someone other than a parent. As the early baby-boom generation reached the labor force, these values shifts became noticeably more pronounced, reflected in the fact that two-earner families are considerably younger than traditional earner families. Yet, note also that changes in the economy—the trend toward service industries such as financial services, real estate, health care, and government—generated many types of white-collar job opportunities for both spouses but especially for women. Relatedly, technological innovations simplifying household chores as well as creating many new kinds of jobs or altering old occupations allow women more freedom to choose work rather than staying at home.

Yet, the forces driving two-earner families are not a one-way street. Some forces are at play that are slowing down the rate of increase in two-earner families.

■ The life-style trend of professional and nonprofessional women withdrawing from the labor force to have children and raising them through their early years reduces the number of two-earner families. So, too, does a decline in economic activity. Moreover, technology is a two-edged sword: it may eliminate some jobs just as it creates some. Technology may thus eliminate either spouse, temporarily or permanently, from the labor force. The reemergence of traditional values, such as the proclamations of some church and political leaders about the rights and merits of women serving as homemakers, may keep some married women out of the work force.

In short, assessing current life-styles and developing projections of life-styles change require an understanding of which forces are driving life-styles, which direction specific life-style trends are moving, and whether these forces reinforce or counterbalance each other. We now turn to assessing and projecting life-style change.

Assessing and Projecting Life-Style Change.   Scanning, monitoring, and often forecasting efforts reveal established trends, changes in trends, and precursors of trends. As discussed in the previous section, a complex set of forces drives these current and potential life-style changes. A framework for analyzing these life-style changes and the forces affecting them is needed in order to postulate answers such questions as: Will the life-style change persist, or is it a fad? Will it broadly diffuse? How rapidly will it disseminate? What future events might affect it? The following questions constitute a framework that some organizations have found useful in assessing and projecting life-style change.

How Does the Life-Style Change Fit with Current Life-Styles? A life-style change that is compatible with the current life-styles of significant groups of individuals is much more likely to blossom into a sustained development than if it is not compatible. Work, consumption, education, and leisure changes often fit with prevailing life-styles.

> For example, the increasing number and variety of adult education programs reflect greater participation and competition in the work force, and greater commitments of leisure time to self-development.

An extremely important point is that major life-style changes in their early stages often seem incompatible with dominant elements of prevailing life-styles. For example, the emergence of working mothers, those over age sixty-five continuing to work, and the initial acceptance of diet foods and beverages were life-style changes that *seemed* to and did run counter to many aspects of prevailing life-styles. Yet, they blossomed into significant and sustained life-style changes. The point here is twofold: (1) elements of life-styles did support these changes, and (2) strong forces outside of life-styles were driving these changes. Dependence upon either alone is insufficient to understand life-style change.

How Is the Life-Style Change Affected by Demographics? As noted in the discussion of demographic change, people's behaviors—that is, how they live—are highly related to demographic variables such as age structure, geographic distribution, ethnic mix, and income levels. One therefore needs to pinpoint as carefully as possible which demographic factors or forces are most related to the life-style change.

How Compatible Is the Life-Style Change With Current Values? Life-style changes that endure are supported by prevailing values.

> The singles boom and the rise in cohabitation are highly compatible with the values of the twenty- to thirty-five-year-old age group. Consumption trends that last fit with people's values. Some people's desire for time-saving, convenient, and economical home ownership has led

them to move from suburbia back to the cities. Diet foods and beverages have proved to be a widespread consumption shift because they dovetailed with values supporting health care and physical fitness maintenance.

How Applicable Is the Life-Style Change to Different People in Various Ways?

Unless a life-style change is applicable to many groups of people and can be adopted in various ways, it is not likely to lead to a large-scale development. The major life-style changes noted in the beginning of this chapter, such as single-parent families, the singles boom, cohabitation, women in the work place, consumption of diet foods, and the physical fitness boom, all satisfy this criterion.

What Groups Have Adopted or Are Likely to Adopt the Life-Style Change?

Although a life-style change may be compatible with and supported by existing life-styles, demographics, and values and may be applicable to different groups in various ways, it must still diffuse in some sequence through different groups in society. Thus, one can watch for early adopters or leader groups and then follower groups. Follower groups, however, may be more important in many respects than early adopters, because if unexpected groups adopt the behavior or change, one can attach greater significance to it as an indicator of its dissemination.

For example, when the number of working women started to increase in the late 1950s and 1960s, most of those entering the work force were older women who typically worked for low wages. When mothers of young children began to work, it represented a significant intensification of this life-style change.

What Institutional and Other Forces Might Affect the Life-Style Change?

As noted previously, political, regulatory, technological, and economic factors may propel or retard life-style change. It is important to identify trends and events in these arenas that might facilitate or impede diffusion of the life-style change across different groups. This simultaneous trends approach seeks to identify packages of trends that may be promoting or slowing down the life-style change. For example, the women's movement, civil rights, workers' rights, and senior-citizens-related legislation have furthered the participation of women and senior citizens in the work force.

What Future Change Could Most Affect the Life-Style Change?

The previous questions primarily focus upon understanding the life-style change in the context of the current environment.

Logically, they inherently bring up questions about future changes in the environment. Identifying possible key future changes in the environment that could affect the life-style change is usually possible. Merely identifying these factors may serve to focus monitoring efforts and to counsel caution in accepting projections in life-style changes.

ASSESSMENT: DERIVING IMPLICATIONS

In deriving implications of life-style changes, the analyst needs to keep in mind five themes that undergird analysis in this segment. First, the long-term prediction of life-style changes (except in general terms) is hazardous; hence, the action-relevant implications of life-style changes is for *medium-* and *short-run* strategy formulation. Second, for long-term purposes, life-styles may be viewed more as derivative of forces in other segments, and hence such derivative effects need to be analyzed. Third, and relatedly, life-style changes open up avenues for new products or market niches; hence, deriving implications is necessarily a *creative* act. Fourth, life-style changes need to be considered *jointly* with demographic factors for strategy-relevant implications. Finally, the primary impacts of life-style changes are likely to be felt at the level of business-unit strategy.

As in the case of demographics, implications of life-style changes (for business units) may be considered at industry, business strategy, and functional strategy levels.

Life-style change suggests that simple conception of markets around broad demographic variables is no longer sufficient in many industries. *Heterogeneity* in life-styles implies that one can no longer simply focus upon the baby-boom market, the women's market, the senior citizens' market, the young adults' market, and so on. These broad categories conceal more than they reveal in terms of market segments. For example:

■ Different segments of the baby-boom cohorts have formed different types of households: large and small family households, and many different types of nonfamily households. Moreover, these different types of households manifest distinct work, education, consumption, and leisure preferences. They manifest consumption patterns that range all the way from "down-market" to "up-market"; they demand products that run the gamut from regular to the unusual and exotic.

■ To take another example, Bartos (1982) argues convincingly that the women's market is now extraordinarily diverse. She contends that to distinguish between working and nonworking women is to miss a multitude of distinct market niches. Bartos found in her study that working women exist in all stages of the life cycle; they hold different kinds of jobs, even within life cycle stages; they work for different reasons; they manifest different attitudes toward their families; and they seek different things out of life. Bartos also notes that even the notion of "homemaker"—that is, a woman who chooses not to work but to stay at home to raise her family—may be misleading. She distinguishes between stay-at-home housewives and plan-to-work housewives, with the latter group continuing to shrink as more women follow through on their plans.

It is not just heterogeneity but the number of individuals that pursue distinct life-styles that makes this such an attractive means to *segment* and *target* markets. The growing size of many household types, the volume of women pursuing work for different reasons, and the numbers engaged in different leisure activities all represent attractive markets for many businesses.

Part of the importance of life-styles is that the way in which people live, and want to live, goes beyond demographic factors in helping to explain what groups of individuals purchase which types of products. Indeed, recent research suggests that demographics alone is not sufficient to explain purchasing behavior. In short, life-style characteristics help predict customer segments that attribute positive values to products or services and thus aid in developing strategies around distribution, advertising, and image creation to reach these market segments.

Life-style change, for example, often strongly underlies the emergence of new industry segments.

■ Life-style changes that have to do with health and physical fitness enhancement have helped create or substantially enlarge many industry segments around health foods, diet foods, and beverages, leisure equipment and clothes, and so on.

Life-style change can also impact well-established industries. Consider the following:

■ Women now make more purchasing decisions. The Ford Motor Company, for example, claims that almost 40 percent of its autos are now purchased by women, compared with marginally more than 10 percent five years ago. The home construction industry has felt many of the winds of life-style change: home type and design have been strongly influenced by changes in family structure, consumption, and leisure patterns.

At the level of industry, life-style changes therefore affect *strategic groups* by opening up avenues for new market segments or obsoleting others, and *key success factors* by generating demand for new or different product features or styling and necessitating different delivery systems. In turn, they may impact the *mobility barriers* of various strategic groups. These effects are particularly important for consumer goods firms, though they also have indirect consequences for other business entities.

Although the prior discussion has noted some general linkages between life-styles and market or industry segments, each firm is confronted with the task of deriving implications of life-style change for its own unique strategic context. The following sequence of questions facilitates this linkage.

How Can Life-Style Change Impact Current Products? Unless this type of specific question is asked, knowledge of life-styles is likely to remain in the "nice-to-know" realm. Consideration of this question forces the organization to relate life-style change to its current product offerings. It must ask such questions as: How will life-style change affect demand for our current products? Which products will be favored? Which will be disfavored? How will life-style change cause these impacts? The last question compels an examination of the specific ways in which life-styles are currently impacting the firm's offerings: How does the product fit different life-styles? How will anticipated changes in these life-styles affect product acceptance—will they result in more or less value being perceived in the product? What life-style changes would most positively or negatively affect sales of current products?

How Can Life-Style Change Give Rise to Product Opportunities? A primary attribute of strategic thinking is the identification and creation of product-market opportunities. Many firms will find it beneficial to go beyond impacts on current products by assessing whether life-styles change contains the seeds of opportunities for new products or modifications of existing products. Such questions as these should be asked: What products or product attributes fit different current life-styles and anticipated changes? How might current products be adapted to satisfy these needs?

How Can Life-Style Change Impact Customer Segments? This question is implicit in the previous two, but asking it separately is important because addressing customer issues in the absence of concern with specific products yields useful insights. Specific questions to address include: What are the life-styles of current and potential customers? Do current and anticipated life-style changes imply that current and potential customers will view (existing) products differently? Is the number of people exhibiting these life-style characteristics growing, declining, or remaining stationary?

How Can Life-Style Change Impact How the Firm Competes? Beyond the range of products offered, life-style change can also have implications for how a firm competes against its competitors. The fundamental question is, what are the implications of current and anticipated life-styles for how the firm should compete on such dimensions as price, quality, service, product features, image, and functionality? Life-style changes may suggest creating different images of the product. Some cosmetics that were previously promoted as beauty aids are now promoted as offering better skin care and facial health. Because of many life-style changes, product warranties and after-sales service are increasingly important in many product-market segments. In short, different life-styles cause individuals to differentially value product attributes such as price, features, and performance.

SUMMARY

Life-styles, defined as how people live, represent the most visible manifestation of the social environment. Despite their visibility, a dominant peculiarity of life-styles is that they are difficult to categorize, and segment into component parts. Life-style patterns are not easy to construct or detect. Although broad categorizations such as suburban, two-career, and single-parent family life-styles convey general understandings of some life-style types, for many strategy analysis purposes, they are not specific enough. They may tell little about product opportunities, differences across customer segments, or purchasing behavior. Thus, any firm in conducting life-style analyses must identify key life-style trends (which may go far beyond simple categorizations of life-styles, such as surburban or single-adult life-styles), determine which trends or sets of trends constitute issues, and specifically assess how these life-style issues affect current and likely strategies.

6

Social Values

Values are the fundamental cornerstone of a society. Society's values are reflected in all its institutions, modes of behavior, mores, and norms. Value change is almost always a major driving force underlying social, political, technological, and economic changes. Yet, as noted by so many authors (e.g., Baier and Rescher 1969), our understanding of values and value change is limited.

Perhaps the most widely quoted definition of values is provided by Kluckhohn (1962, 395): "A value is a conception, explicit or implicit, distinctive of an individual or characteristic of a group, of the desirable which influences the selection from available means and ends of action." Thus, the choices we make (e.g., life-styles, voting, or business decisions), reflecting our ends or goals as well as the means we adopt to implement or achieve our choices, manifest our values.

VALUE CHANGE

Much value change has clearly taken place in the United States since World War II. During this time period, decisions by individuals and institutions regarding ends and means in the political, social, legal, technological, and economic arenas reflect profound value change. The following is a sampling of decision contexts in which value changes are manifest.

- *Political:* increased commitment of resources to the military budget; change in the acceptance of political authority (e.g., the power of the presidency); movement from equality of opportunity to equality of results; greater participation by many groups such as church and community groups in the political process; the continual emergence of new issues in the agenda of the legislative process; changes in electoral results

- *Regulatory:* the increase in social regulations such as consumer and environmental protection; the lifting of regulations (deregulation) in many industries; change in the commitment of some agencies to administer regulations (e.g., the EPA relaxing enforcement of some of its rules); changes in Supreme Court rulings over time

- *Technological:* the conflict between automation and robots on one hand and job security on the other; the pursuit of technical efficiency versus considerations of social equity; expanding technological progress in the military arena versus the social arena; the costs and benefits of new technology such as life support systems

- *Social:* changing attitudes toward work; demands for greater participation in organizations; rising consumer expectations; increasing activism among women and minority groups; greater acceptance of sex and violence on television; public campaigns against smoking; an upsurge of concern with personal health and physical fitness

- *Economic:* less acceptance of economic growth as an unqualified benefit to society; much more concern with the distribution of the benefits produced by the economic system; less willingness on the part of society to accord individuals or organizations the unfettered freedoms often associated with laissez-faire notions of competition

Although we may broadly speak of social, political, economic, legal, and technological values and their change over time, two points merit special emphasis.

First, social, political, legal, economic, and technological values are highly interrelated. Indeed, they are often difficult to disentangle. Thus, speaking of value clusters is appropriate—for example, the values undergirding competitive capitalism or socialism, or the values buttressing arguments in support of or in opposition to a major role for government in the management of the economy.

Second, we need to distinguish between core values and peripheral, or secondary, values. Our core values are the most dominant, enduring, and central of our individual or institutional values. Peripheral values change much more quickly. For example, values associated with the work ethic, a limited role for government, and technological progress are core values for many Americans (Lodge 1975).

Types of Value Change

Rescher (1969) provides an elaborate yet simple conceptual framework for the analysis of value change. He identifies multiple means by which values may be upgraded or downgraded, that is, increase in prevalence and importance: (1) value acquisition/abandonment, (2) value redistribution, (3) value rescaling, (4) value redeployment, and (5) value restandardization.

Value Acquisition/Abandonment.   Values may be acquired anew or totally abandoned. At the extremes of value acquisition and abandonment, changes at the level of society are possible but rare. Note, however, that such extreme value change can be incorporated into society's laws through judicial system mandates. For example:

- Historic Supreme Court decisions, such as the affirmation of the availability of abortion or the right to integrated schooling, institutionalized specific values even though all members of society did not subscribe to them.

Value Redistribution.   A value may be upgraded (or downgraded) through redistribution when it comes to be more (or less) widely held throughout society. It involves a change in the extent or in the pattern of a value's distribution in the society; that is, more individuals acquire or abandon the value. For example:

- Value redistribution has undergirded the environmentalist, women's, and consumerist movements. A small group of activists espouse a set of values that progressively diffuse through society until they are held by a substantial segment of the population.

Value Rescaling.   Value change also occurs when values move up or down our hierarchy of values as individuals or as a society. Rescaling reflects increased commitment to some values and decreased commitment to others. Rescaling is among the more drastic varieties of value change. For example:

- Values pertaining to religion have been rescaled downward by many individuals in the United States, whereas many have recently argued that nation-oriented values (e.g., patriotic virtues, national pride, concern for the national welfare) have encountered an upward rescaling. The reordering of values inherent in rescaling is also applicable to governmental policies. For example, the political, technological, and economic values associated with national defense have been sharply rescaled upward within the federal government under the Reagan administration, while the political and social values associated with social programs have been rescaled downward.

Value Redeployment. Values generally hold within a domain of application but may be extended or narrowed in area of coverage. Such redeployment is a common form of value change. For example:

■ The value of legal and political equality has been extended to include the rights of black Americans and other minorities. The values embodied in civil rights have been extended beyond simply voting rights and religious rights to include employment, education, and housing access and opportunities. Employees' rights have also greatly increased in scope in the past few decades.

Value Restandardization. Values as "concepts of the desirable" presume some means of assessing the extent to which values or preferences are realized. Thus, another mode of value change is change in the standard of implementation of a value, that is, the extent to which it is attained within its domain of application. Existing standards for application can be altered or new ones introduced. For example:

■ The standard of living reflects both varieties of value change. The minimum standard is continually being increased, while new dimensions are also frequently added.

Four points deserve mention regarding types of value change. First, different types of change may occur in specific values, rendering detection of such changes difficult. Second, some types of change are more frequent than others. Thus, value redeployment and restandardization are typically more frequent than rescaling or abandonment. Third, core values as noted earlier are less likely to be affected, whereas peripheral values may exhibit extreme forms of change (e.g., abandonment or acquisition). Finally, these concepts are primarily useful for conditioning the analyst during scanning. In other words, they provide a language for considering value changes; the specific changes need to be clothed in greater detail.

SCANNING

Scanning is more difficult, complex, and precarious in the values arena than in any other environmental segment. Values are not readily manifest; individuals are often unable to articulate their values. Moreover, frequently the values that individuals espouse and the values that are operant are not congruent (Argyris 1982). This renders value change difficult to detect and measure. Further, there are few measurement scales as exist in the other environmental segments. In short, value analysis is relatively underdeveloped compared with analysis of the other environmental segments.

Conceptually, the value arena can be scanned in two related ways: first, through attempts to directly identify, code, and thus measure values and value change; second, through inferring value changes from people's behaviors and opinions—these are captured during scanning the other environmental segments. The first is often accomplished by a small but growing number of value analysis specialists; the second, by environmental analysts during general scanning activity.

Value Analysis Specialists

Although few organizations regard themselves as value analysis specialists, a number of organizations collect data from which value change inferences can be drawn. The following types of organizations assess value change to some extent: public opinion research organizations, news media polls, market research agencies, some think tanks, some consulting firms (e.g., Stanford Research Institute), some government agencies, and some congressional committees. These entities collect values-related data such as changes in political preferences, attitudes toward government, nuclear power, or new technologies, family-related values, the importance of religion in people's lives, life-style preferences, commitment to preserving the environment, and so on. These organizations typically produce reports of their findings.

Scanning the Other Environmental Segments

Because values influence our words and deeds, and because of the paucity of values-specific data, detecting value change or precursors of value change becomes a process of drawing value-related inferences from trends and events occurring in the other environmental segments. The presumption here is that demographic, life-style, economic, technological, political, and regulatory change reflect, to some degree, underlying value change. By noting these changes, one can move toward inferring the value change that underpins them and that may be required to sustain them. The latter is especially important because it is not enough to simply detect value change after trends have peaked or events have taken place. Rather, one must be able to use value change as a means of assessing and forecasting trends and events in the other environmental segments.

The indicators for scanning and monitoring in each of the other environmental segments can provide the basis for scanning the values arena. For example:

■ Demographic and life-style changes may reveal many value changes: preferences for geographic location, style of living (e.g., cohabitation versus marriage, small versus large families), career versus family (e.g., job promotions versus family stability), and leisure activity (health-related foods, and so on). The adoption of or opposition to technological advances may also reveal value change: the availability of birth control technology and nuclear technology has caused many individuals to rescale and restandardize their values. In the political arena, the positions of interest groups, legislative proposals, and election results may indicate value change.

In common with the other environmental segments, broad-based reading of multiple sources is required. This may be especially important in the context of values because the sources of value change are so many and varied. In the extreme, all the data sources noted in this book may provide indicators of values and value change.

Precursors of Value Change

Because of the important role that values play in precipitating and driving environmental change, identifying value change as early as possible is particularly important. The identification of the precursors of value change thus assumes great significance. The intent here should be to identify events and trends that may give rise to value change or, more likely, add momentum to value change that is already taking place.

■ Judicial decisions, regulatory decisions, the introduction or adoption of new technology, the emergence of new social or political interest groups, confrontations in the political arena, new leisure habits, and demographic mobility changes could all be signals of new developments in value change.

MONITORING

Because value change is difficult to observe directly, (i.e., values manifest themselves in our actions and words), monitoring value change involves tracking indicators from the other environmental segments. Thus, the types of indicators as discussed in the other environmental segment chapters provide the raw material for monitoring value change.

Monitoring, in the context of values, illustrates some of the generic aspects of what is involved in this activity. First, the analyst has to identify the relevant indicators that signal value change. Whether these are the outputs of scanning, past monitoring activity in the organization, or are accidentally discovered by the organization, they provide the focus for the monitoring effort. In the case of values, the indicators are almost unlimited; as noted, all the indicators discussed in the other segment chapters are potentially relevant as means of tracking value change.

Second, the analyst has to go beyond simply searching for and tracking indicators. The analyst has to draw inferences and discern trends. Monitoring value change necessarily involves drawing inferences from what will be hazy data in the initial stages of monitoring. For example:

■ The early stages of a social or political movement typically provide fuzzy data. The scope and direction of these movements will be far from clear, yet the analyst will have to try to distill the value changes that may underlie their evolution.

Third, as the analyst is tracking specific trends, he or she is also aggregating trends into patterns. The analyst is creating a broader mosaic than any individual trend. These patterns in the context of values may be value clusters: political values, religious values, family values, work-related values, physical-environment-related values, and so on. Again, the analyst must infuse this meaning into what initially may seem to be unrelated trends and events.

Fourth, while monitoring specific trends and patterns over time, the data become clearer. As we discuss in the other environmental segment chapters, the nature of technological changes, the thrust of a social movement, the scope of life-style changes, and demographic shifts all become more evident with the passage of time. Their implications, however, will not be easier to determine, though the change itself will be easier to delineate. This enables one to speculate as to the strength and direction of underlying value changes as patterns in the other segments are identified.

Fifth, the recursive nature of monitoring and scanning is also evident. Monitoring value change will often lead the analyst to raise questions about the value change that may require further scanning. For example:

■ In monitoring political values change, the analyst may begin to sense connections with changes in other value contexts, such as family values or work values. This may then require scanning in these domains and later possibly developing value change patterns linking political, family, and work values.

As seen in the previous discussion, scanning and monitoring values necessarily entails a speculative component. This is particularly manifest when long-term value changes are the object of inquiry.

FORECASTING VALUE CHANGE

In comparison with the economic, demographic, and technological arenas, comparatively little attention has been devoted to assessing and forecasting value change. As noted by Baier and Rescher (1969, 108), "the predictive instrumentalities for the study of value change are sadly lacking at present." Value change, however, is a major driving force underlying social, political, economic, and technological change. Thus, concern with value change is unavoidable in any attempt to understand the current environment and perhaps more importantly, project alternative futures. The focus of this section, therefore, is twofold: to provide an understanding of the forces that give rise to value change and to lay out an analysis framework to provide guidance to any effort to project future value change.

Forces Driving Value Change

As discussed in Chapter 2, change may occur within any environmental segment somewhat autonomously. In the context of values, this means that a change in some values may cause a change in other values. If individuals, institutions, or societies are visualized as adhering to a hierarchy or system of values, changes in some values cause change in other values in the hierarchy or system. This kind of value change is captured in the notion of value upgrading or downgrading via rescaling. For example:

- For many individuals, the upgrading of values pertaining to the environment led to the downgrading of values pertaining to the economy (economic growth and efficiency assume lesser importance).

Viewing a values hierarchy as a system of interrelated values pertaining to different domains (e.g., political, legal, economic, technological, and social values) enables one to assess how a change in values in one domain may have direct or derivative effects on values in the other domains. For example:

- An upgrading of religious values may directly cause a downgrading in technology-related values: technology becomes viewed as less important to our well-being in this life and the hereafter. Changes in political and social values directly affect economic values. Social values change in the realm of the work ethic, consumption, and leisure (work is no longer viewed by many as unavoidable and a duty; leisure is increasingly regard-ed as a valid activity in its own right) impacts economic values such as the desirability of economic growth, efficiency, and productivity.

Change in values, however, is never completely autonomous. In-deed, significant value change is usually in response to change in the other segments of the environment. The following briefly highlights some of the environmental forces that may cause value change.

Demographics.   Shifts in age distribution, geographic mobility, and ethnic mix may cause value shifts. For example:

■ The aging of the population may cause value redistribution (values pertaining to security become more widely held). Changes in ethnic mix may lead to value redeployment (equal opportunity is extended to include access to education, housing, and employment).

Life-styles.   Changes in household formation (i.e., family structure) may exert strong pressure on all modes of value upgrading and downgrading. For example:

■ Some values may be severely decreased in distribution (preference for two-parent families, desire for women to stay at home to raise the family, desire that children should be cared for only by their parents). Some values may be redeployed (concept of family no longer requires two parents). Education also contributes to value change. A better-educated population may lead to value restandardization (quality of life is no long-er defined as simply possession of material goods).

Economic.   Changes in the economic arena can cause value change. For example:

■ Rising affluence gives rise to opportunities for value upscaling (e.g., self-fulfillment needs move up individuals' hierarchy of values) and val-ues restandardization (e.g., the standard of living changes—unlike the mid-1950s, it now includes possession of material goods not then broadly possessed, such as a television set). Scarcity of economic resources, such as the shortfall in water supplies, arable land, or building land in some regions, has led to an upgrading of values pertaining to these natural resources.

Technology.   Technological change is perhaps the major driving force in value change. It creates opportunities for choice that give rise to value change. In the extreme, technological change may give rise to value acquisition through its capacity to create new options.

■ Hazard (1969) contends that the automobile, for example, has upgraded values concerned with pleasure, power, privacy, convenience, and human dignity and has downgraded values pertaining to love and affection, devotion to family, law and order, freedom from interference, reverence for life, and courtesy.

Politics.   Forces in the political arena, such as political interest groups and social movements, constitute major conduits in value change.

■ Such groups try to foster acceptance of their values among other groups (value redistribution) and to extend the domain of application of the relevant values (restandardization). The rise of the antinuclear, environmental, and women's interest groups are good examples.

Regulatory.   The regulatory arena can provide a major impetus to value change in many ways. For example:

■ Judicial decisions may serve as a major springboard for value change, either in its early stages through path-breaking decisions (e.g., the Supreme Court decision desegregating public schools) or through decisions legitimizing within the eyes of the law value change that is already significantly under way (e.g., the Supreme Court decision recognizing a woman's right to abortion).

Interactions Among the Driving Forces

The complex interactions among the forces driving value change, and the impact, in turn, of value change upon these forces, exemplify environmental turbulence and connectedness. No single force alone drives any value change. We illustrate by way of an extensive example:

■ The values associated with the physical environment have changed dramatically for large segments of the U.S. population over the last three decades. During the 1950s and the early 1960s, we can infer from business and social behaviors that the dominant values pertaining to the physical environment were that it could and should be exploited in the interests of furthering economic growth and enhanced quality of life: the environment was there to be exploited for the betterment of the country's inhabitants.

■ However, one of the consequences of continued economic growth and development was a build-up of environmental degradation: land, air, and water were becoming ever more polluted. Technological developments that were fueling the engines of economic advancement were also contributing to increased pollution; as industrial output increased, so too did spill-off of pollutants into the air, water systems, and onto land.

■ From the late 1950s, harm to the environment was becoming increasingly apparent: water, food, and fish became contaminated in many areas; a variety of health problems were linked to chemicals used in agriculture and industry.

■ Yet, in the late 1950s, environmental pollution was not an issue on the public agenda. Indeed, one can scan the newspapers of that time period and find little attention devoted to degradation of the environment. In the early 1960s, however, events were beginning to fall in place that put concern with the physical environment on center stage of the political arena. Some local groups in different parts of the country began to pressure public representatives and governmental agencies to redress specific environmental problems. These local problems drew national attention with the publication of Rachel Carson's book *Silent Spring* in 1962. Spurred by this work, local interest groups began to emerge around the issue of environmental protection. Social critics began to address the issue, public and private institutions began to research the issue, and public representatives began to push for a cleaner and safer environment.

■ The change in values that took place in the 1960s was given institutional form in the early 1970s with the establishment of the Environmental Protection Agency.

Thus, we see that technological, economic, social, and political forces were intermingled in changing society's values around the issue of environmental protection.

Assessing and Projecting Value Change

Attempts to forecast value change have often taken the form of qualitative techniques such as social value profiles or value diffusion matrices (Wilson 1977). Such techniques rely heavily on the judgment and awareness of those involved in forecasting. At the heart of such techniques lie a number of key questions, which should be confronted by the analyst.

What Is the Focal Value Trend or Pattern?   Delineating what is to be analyzed and forecast is especially important in the case of values, since they are so elusive and intangible. It is also important because often it is a cluster of value trends or a pattern of values that is of interest—for example, trends toward conservatism or liberalism, a rise or decline of religious values or family values, or the emergence or decline of values supporting or opposing technological developments.

What Are the Indicators of the Value Change? A specification of the focal values is a prerequisite to the specification of indicators. The choice of indicators may influence the direction, degree, and intensity of the alleged value change. Typically, some judgment is required as to what the relevant indicators are. For example:

> ■ The argument has recently been made that traditional family values have been in decline in the United States for some time. Others have argued that we are now witnessing the early stages of the reemergence of traditional family values. At issue here is, what is meant by family values? Elements constituting "traditional family values" might include a family of married parents with two to four children, which takes care of the grandparents in the home, manifests strong bonds between each generation, attends religious services regularly, and is active in community and social affairs. A number of indicators will be required to monitor and assess change in a cluster or pattern of values.

What Is the Nature of the Value Change? What type of value change may be occurring? Is it value acquisition/abandonment, redistribution, rescaling, redeployment, or restandardization? It could also be some combination of these.

How Compatible Is the Value Change With Other Values? In general, the greater the compatibility of any value change with broad societal values or, more specifically, with the values of a particular group (e.g., young adults, senior citizens, the farming community), the more likely the value change will be adopted. For example, the value shifts or trends giving rise to the alleged pattern toward greater conservatism are highly compatible with the core values of many segments of the U.S. population. Similarly, the values underlying the emergence of yuppies, as discussed in Chapter 3, are compatible with many values shared by many other Americans.

Who Is Manifesting the Value Change? Collection of data via indicators and an assessment of the nature of the value change presumes an identification of those who are exhibiting the value change. This question is critical because it provides an assessment of the potential significance of the value change: What is the sociopolitical importance of those already subscribing to the value change (e.g., are they opinion leaders)? What is their magnitude in numbers?

What Other Groups Might Adopt or Oppose the Value Change? This question is especially important in the early stages of value change. For example, what political and social groups are likely to support or oppose the value positions espoused by some churches on such issues as nuclear technology, capital punishment, or the use of federal funds to support the poor?

Also, given some precursors of a value change, a consideration of this question yields a preliminary assessment of its diffusion potential and speed.

What Resources Are Available to the Protagonists and Antagonists of the Value Change? Value shifts frequently occur slowly and almost imperceptibly in their early stages. Some value shifts, however, receive momentum from groups who are willing to devote resources to their propagation. This is typically the case with regard to value changes embodied in the emergence and evolution of interest groups and social movements (e.g., the consumerist, environmental, and women's movements). Government-initiated or -supported value shifts (e.g., that cigarette smoking is not good for your health) may also be the beneficiary of extensive resources. Resources may also be mobilized against perceived value shifts—for example, the efforts of the moral majority to counteract the values underlying political liberalism. By the word *resources* we mean the capacity to effect support or opposition to a value change, such as numbers of people, access to the media, and so on.

What Costs and Benefits Flow From the Value Change, and Who Receives Them? One reason that a value change may not diffuse too broadly throughout society is that it may be too costly for (other) groups to acquire and uphold the value. The word *cost* here may be defined along multiple dimensions: money, status, or prestige, time commitment, degree of effort, and so on. Costs may be broadly interpreted as the stresses and strains caused by the pursuit of a value. For example, some of the elements of the alleged comeback of traditional family values may be constrained by the costs associated with sustaining a traditional family: the effort and commitment required to sustain a marriage, the monetary cost of raising three or more children, and the opportunity forgone to realize a higher material standard of living.

The corollary is that the greater the perceived benefits of a value change, the quicker it will diffuse and be supported. The benefits attributable to birth control have led to its general acceptance, despite some associated costs, except for some groups who deem birth control incompatible with their core values. Thus, different groups may assess differently the costs and benefits associated with any value change.

What Forces Are Driving the Value Change? Implicit in the previous discussion is concern with the forces facilitating and inhibiting the value change and the sustainability of these forces. As previously noted, our conceptual understanding of the causal forces exerting value shifts is limited. Yet, at a minimum, an effort must be made to sketch out the forces that are plausibly at work.

ASSESSMENT: DERIVING IMPLICATIONS

Value changes have important implications for the strategic context of the firm. In discussing these implications, three themes merit emphasis. First, value changes occurring currently often have long-term implications not clearly discernible to a firm. Second, these long-term changes ensue from the influence of values on other environmental segments. Third, value changes bring about potential changes in the political and regulatory arenas and sometimes discrete issues for a firm.

Value change can exert direct impact on the strategic context of business firms in many ways. For example, value change can impact the acceptance accorded to firms' current and potential products in the marketplace; it is often evidenced in strong public support for or opposition to the products of whole industries or industry segments.

■ The military, space, nuclear, chemical, pharmaceutical, and other industries have been directly spurred or slowed by value changes. Public reaction to environmental pollution has caused many chemical firms to drop products and modify others. Many firms working on biomedical technologies have been subjected to public criticism from groups opposed to this type of research.

Value change contributes to industry structural change through its impact on customers' tastes and product attribute preferences. These changes frequently result in product substitutions. To take some consumer goods examples:

■ Diet forms have become a substitute in many food and beverage categories. Low-nicotine cigarettes are substituted for regular cigarettes.

The implications noted earlier can have differential consequences for segments of a specific industry. For example:

■ In the food and beverage industry, health and life-style–related value change has contributed to a major growth in the wine segment of the beverage market at the same time that beer consumption has somewhat declined. Chicken consumption has increased, while red meat consumption has declined.

Value change impacts many industries and the strategies of firms within them through its effect upon consumption patterns. For example:

■ The increase in two-earner families has greatly enhanced the need for convenience foods and more convenient (quicker) food preparation methods.

Value change causes much more indirect implications for the strategic management of firms than other sources of environmental change; that is, the impact of value change is exerted through change in the other environmental segments. These indirect implications are especially waged through the political and regulatory arenas. Many of the political and regulatory changes that are noted in Chapters 9 and 10 have their source in the types of value changes discussed in the beginning of this chapter. For example:

■ Many industries or individual firms have found themselves confronted by demands from local, regional, or national interest groups to take their products off the market, to change how they compete, or to change their corporate policies (e.g., withdraw their investments in South Africa, hire more minorities).

As more individuals subscribe to the values underlying these demands and are willing to vent their beliefs in public, the intensity of these demands increases and action of some kind becomes necessary of the part of the focal firms. Thus, one major indirect implication of value change is the need for firms to develop a political strategy, that is, a strategy to deal with those groups in society that do or may place direct or indirect demands upon them.

Although value change has primary and secondary consequences for every other environmental segment, its major primary consequences are felt in the life-style and political arenas. Life-styles in the form of family structure and work, leisure, and consumption patterns are a direct manifestation of values. Values directly influence the life-styles we follow and the content and intensity of the battles waged in the political arena. As we indicate in Chapter 9, the issues that arise in the political arena and how they are resolved are a direct manifestation of values held by competing groups such as political parties, social movements, and interest groups.

SUMMARY

Value change must be inferred from the behavior and words of individuals. Thus, value change is the least evident form of macroenvironmental change. Yet, it is also a major driving force in much of the change witnessed in the other environmental segments.

7

The Economic Environment

The economic segment of the macroenvironment has perhaps the most general impact on business organizations. Thinking of any type of business enterprise that is not affected by the vagaries of economic activity is difficult. Indeed, most large business organizations continually assess the likely impact of prevailing and potential economic conditions on their business operations.

Defining the Economic Environment

The economic environment refers to the nature and direction of the economy in which business operates. In a broad sense, the economy includes the stock of physical and natural resources and the aggregation of all the markets where goods and services are exchanged for payment. More specifically, economic activity is reflected in levels and patterns of industrial output, consumption, income, savings, and investments, capital and labor availability, and price movements. Such indices in common (business) language as gross national product, inflation, interest and unemployment rates, foreign exchange fluctuations, concentration of wealth, and consumer prices refer to various aspects of the economic environment.

In this chapter, the assumption is that readers are familiar with the basic principles of micro- and macroeconomics. The discussion is therefore oriented to the generation and use of the outputs of economic analysis.

ECONOMIC CHANGE

Change is an enduring characteristic of the economic environment. Economic change can be discontinuous or evolutionary. The decades

105

of the 1970s and 1980s have been characterized by such frequent economic change that economic uncertainty is now regarded as a fact of life. Though a number of models have been advanced over the years to explain economic change, the predictive abilities of these models is far from perfect—a point to which we will return.

For the purposes of analysis for strategic management, addressing two dimensions of economic change is useful: (1) type of change and (2) levels of change.

Types of Economic Change

Economic change can be broadly categorized into structural change and cyclical change.

Structural Change.   The first category of economic change refers to change within and across sectors of the economy: movements in economic activity from some types of industries to others and movements in the relationships among key economic variables. Structural changes are largely permanent and irreversible. Consider the following:

■ The frequently noted movement from a manufacturing-based economy to an information economy or from an industrial economy to a service economy captures the notion of structural change. The percentage of GNP attributable to manufacturing industry continues to decline; the service sector continues to increase. For example, of the 7 million jobs created in the United States in 1984, 5 million were in the service sector and only 2 million were in the manufacturing sector.

Structural change has also taken place within sectors of the economy.

■ Within the manufacturing sector, major shifts have occurred: the output of the so-called smokestack industries such as steel and aluminum has not just declined as a percentage of total manufacturing output but has also declined in absolute terms in recent years. On the other hand, high-technology-oriented industries such as electronics, computers, and medical equipment continue to gain in importance. Structural change within the manufacturing sector is also reflected in the emergence of new industries or segments within existing industries, such as biotechnology, robotics, and fiber optics.

Although our focus in this book is on the macroenvironment, an appropriate point here is that an important element of structural change in the economy is the considerable restructuring that has occurred within many industries in the last decade.

The second facet of structural change is change in the relationships among key economic variables. For example, energy costs have risen much faster than many other raw material costs since the early 1970s. The relative levels of exports and imports as a percentage of GNP have also changed considerably: imports have risen to the point where the United States now has a trade deficit in excess of $100 million. The relationship between inflation and unemployment has also changed considerably in the past two decades.

Structural change indicates a qualitative shift in the economic environment. Such change requires us to review our understanding of how the economy works. This in turn suggests that assumptions pertaining to the economy that underlie a strategy need to be reconsidered.

Cyclical Change. The second category of economic change refers to upswings and downswings in the general level of economic activity. Cyclical change is evidenced in the volatility manifested in key economic variables. Compared with the 1960s and early 1970s, the later 1970s and 1980s have witnessed increasing volatility in such key indicators of economic activity as GNP, interest rates, inflation, the consumer price index, industrial investment, and housing starts. The scale and rate of change in these variables in the past decade have been much greater than had been the case in the previous two decades. Cyclical change in the economic arena underlies the notion of business cycles.

Theoretically, one can consider the implications of cyclical change without major shifts in assumptions. In many cases, however, these changes are intertwined with structural change. This renders isolating cyclical changes (in the presence of structural change) problematic. For practical purposes, the twin concepts of structural and cyclical change provide the lenses through which an analyst can begin to understand the economic environment.

Levels of Economic Change

Economic change can occur at multiple levels. Broadly, four levels can be considered: global, national, regional, and local. Structural change at the global level is reflected in increasing interdependence among the national economies. The economic environment can no longer be analyzed in terms of a closed national economy. Global cyclical economic change entails changes in balance of trade positions, foreign currency exchange positions, and in the relative strengths of countries in different industrial sectors. At the national level, issues related to interest rates, budget deficits, and inflation assume importance. At the regional and local levels, issues reflect the structure and dynamics of the geographic location under consideration: regions dominated by older industries (e.g., steel, automobiles, chemicals) have experienced economic change different from that of regions with newer high-technology industries.

The notion of levels of economic change highlights two interrelated issues. First, change at higher levels often carries implications for lower levels, though some of these implications may be delayed or lagged. For example, global economic change has implications for the national economy, though the implications may not be immediately manifest. Second, economic changes will increasingly need to be analyzed at multiple levels in order to derive action-relevant implications.

In the economic arena, analysis is facilitated by a multitude of data sources. As we shall see, however, deriving implications is not always easy. We now turn to these analysis-related issues.

SCANNING

Scanning and monitoring is perhaps easier in the economic arena than in any of the other environmental segments discussed in this book. A plethora of data on economic activity is readily available, most of it on a monthly or quarterly basis. In addition, numerous governmental and private firms specialize in scanning, monitoring, and forecasting economic activity.

Table 7.1 shows a listing of numerous indicators that can be employed to scan the economic arena. It illustrates the wide variety of measures that have been developed to track and analyze economic activity. Most of the indicators shown in Table 7.1 are reported on a monthly basis by the Bureau of Economic Analysis, an agency within the Department of Commerce.

The data for the economic segment are primarily quantitative and, as noted, available in abundance from secondary sources. Nonetheless, making sense of the data is complicated: the forces driving the trends have to be derived, requiring a qualitative understanding of the shifts in the economy. Fortunately, this is facilitated by a number of governmental, university, and private enterprises that specialize in this activity.

MONITORING

The indicators noted in Table 7.1 also provide the basis for monitoring economic activity. Many economic trends and patterns can be

Table 7.1 Sample Economic Indicators

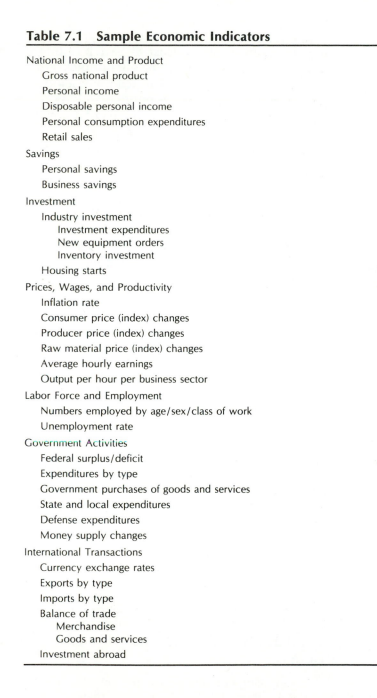

National Income and Product
    Gross national product
    Personal income
    Disposable personal income
    Personal consumption expenditures
    Retail sales
Savings
    Personal savings
    Business savings
Investment
    Industry investment
        Investment expenditures
        New equipment orders
        Inventory investment
    Housing starts
Prices, Wages, and Productivity
    Inflation rate
    Consumer price (index) changes
    Producer price (index) changes
    Raw material price (index) changes
    Average hourly earnings
    Output per hour per business sector
Labor Force and Employment
    Numbers employed by age/sex/class of work
    Unemployment rate
Government Activities
    Federal surplus/deficit
    Expenditures by type
    Government purchases of goods and services
    State and local expenditures
    Defense expenditures
    Money supply changes
International Transactions
    Currency exchange rates
    Exports by type
    Imports by type
    Balance of trade
        Merchandise
        Goods and services
    Investment abroad

monitored almost as quickly as they happen. As noted in the discussion of scanning, much of the requisite data is available on a monthly or quarterly basis.

Scanning and monitoring economic activity is important for many reasons, not the least of which is that changes in economic trends and patterns can come about quickly. Economic analysts talk about indicators that tend to lead, coincide with, or lag the broad movements in aggregate economic activity, such as GNP, inflation, and employment. The Department of Commerce's Bureau of Economic Analysis has developed a number of economic time series to relate leading, coincident, and lagging indicators to economic change and cycles. The output of this analysis is available monthly and is used by many organizations as one means of monitoring economic activity.

So much data and so many sources are available that a major problem in scanning and monitoring the economic arena is an abundance rather than an absence of data. Many governmental agencies provide economic data: the Departments of Commerce, Labor, Energy, and Treasury. State and local governmental agencies provide regional economic data. Industry and trade associations often provide data on economic indicators believed to be important for their specific industries or markets. A seemingly endless number of organizations—consulting firms, research organizations, financial institutions (investment houses, stock brokerage firms, banks, and so on)—and university-based institutes and research centers specialize in economic analysis. Much of the output of these different sources of economic data can be found on a regular basis in the popular business press and the more specialized industry and trade press.

A major focus of the primary providers of economic data noted earlier is the identification and analysis of economic trends (as well as the creation of economic forecasts). Thus, many of these organizations largely serve as monitors of economic activity, providing interpretations of the raw data collected.

FORECASTING

Economic forecasting has had a long history, and a number of different techniques have been in existence for some time. They may range from input-output models (Leontief 1951) to simulation models (e.g., world dynamics models, Meadows et al. 1972) to econometric forecasting.

■ Input-output models trace the flow of goods through various sectors of the economy; tables for these are regularly available from the Department of Commerce. Simulation models were developed to seek long-run trends at various levels of the economy and are usually conducted on a periodic or an ad hoc basis. Their primary utility in recent years has been to alert decision makers to the complex interdependence of economic variables and to the need for systemic approaches to solving problems.

Econometric forecasting is probably the most utilized economic analysis technique. It attempts to forecast movements in economic indicators on a short to medium basis.

■ Econometric forecasts can vary considerably in scope and detail. Some may address only one variable (e.g., GNP, interest rates, money supply, unemployment). Others may cover detailed projections of economic activity for particular industries or geographic regions. One may even obtain forecasts that include projections of most of the variables shown in Table 7.1. Some organizations ask the providers of economic forecasting services to custom-tailor forecasts to meet their unique requirements.

Because of the widespread use of economic forecasting and the extensive treatment devoted to it in many business school curricula, we treat the topic of forecasting in the economic arena somewhat differently from the way it is treated in the other environmental segments. First, we highlight some of the forces driving economic change. Then, the recent track record of economic forecasting is examined. Finally, a number of issues pertaining to environmental analysis are identified.

The Driving Forces

The economic arena clearly illustrates change taking place as a result of forces within the economic segment of the environment and forces emanating from the other environmental segments. Economic change is most often discussed in terms of the impact of forces within the economic arena. Changes in the variables noted in Table 7.1 receive wide discussion with regard to their impact on each other. For example:

■ A change in the level of the money supply may affect many of the variables noted in Table 7.1, such as the size of the budget deficit, unemployment, and inflation. Inflation affects interest rates, employment, and exports and imports. Interest rates affect housing starts, investment levels, and industry output.

Econometric forecasting models try to capture the relationship among these types of variables. Equally clear, however, is that the economic system does not change completely autonomously. Forces in the other environmental segments also influence economic change. Consider the following examples:

Demographics. The size of the population, changes in the age structure, and geographic distribution profoundly impact economic developments.

■ As the baby boomers grow older and as the population aged sixty and older increases, the pattern of demand for goods and services is dramatically changed and the composition of the labor market shifts. Geographic flows of population from the snow-belt to the sun-belt states contribute greatly to differing levels of economic activity in these regions.

Life-styles. The manner in which people choose to live their lives strongly impacts economic activity.

■ Changes in household formation, such as the increase in single-parent families, the decline in average household size, and the growth in non-family households (mainly individuals living alone), affect many aspects of economic activity, such as the need for specific goods and services (e.g., household conveniences and furnishings, types of housing, and day-care services). Consumption and leisure patterns may directly and indirectly impact many economic indicators: retail sales levels, inventory levels, investment commitments, the consumer price index, and so on.

Social Values. Largely indirectly but nonetheless significantly, value change influences the scope and level of economic activity.

■ Changes in values pertaining to the physical environment have affected production and consumption in many industries. Value change, as manifested in political and regulatory change, has greatly affected how economic resources are and should be distributed (e.g., taxation policies, governmental subsidies).

Technology. Technological change is often referred to as the engine of economic growth. Technological development in the form of new products (e.g., personal computers) propels much of the economic activity in many industries.

Political. Changes in governmental policies can impact almost every indicator shown in Table 7.1.

■ Fiscal policy changes affect interest rates, inflation, and investment behavior. Governmental subsidies support the economic structure and viability of many industries such as tobacco, farming, and steel.

Regulatory. Much debate has long raged as to the positive and negative impacts of specific regulations on economic activity. Regulations most visibly affect the structure of industries.

These examples illustrate the pervasive influence of other environmental segments on economic changes. These changes may vary from short- to medium-term (as in the case of political and regulatory changes) to long-term (as in the case of demographics and values). Most econometric forecasting approaches have treated these forces as exogenous to their models or have adapted the models on a continuing basis to accommodate these changes. This has resulted in some key problems in dealing with these forecasts.

Economic Forecasting: Some Recent Problems

Many of the difficulties involved in forecasting change in the macroenvironment stem from the plethora of driving forces and the interrelationships among them. Modeling these interrelationships is especially difficult. These difficulties have recently been evidenced in the efforts of economic forecasters. Several of the problems encountered in economic forecasting are worth noting.

Misforecasts. In recent years, many economic forecasts have badly missed the mark. For example:

■ *Business Week* magazine, in a review of the performance of over forty economic forecasts on the economy in 1982, found that although a majority of these forecasts were based on some form of econometric model, only two of the forty-four forecasts were correct in estimating that GNP would decline during 1982.

Forecast Inaccuracy. Many economic forecasts have made predictions in the right direction but have missed the magnitude of change involved. For example:

■ GNP grew at an 8 percent rate in the first half of 1984, while most forecasts predicted a growth rate of 4 percent to 6 percent.

Long-Range Forecast Problems. Forecasts of economic activity for time periods exceeding more than one year have proved particularly treacherous. For example:

■ A number of econometric models have consistently and incorrectly forecast that U.S. energy consumption would return to the pattern that existed before the 1979–1980 price increases.

Variance in Forecasts.   With regard to almost any indicator noted in Table 7.1, finding major differences in forecasts is quite possible. Significant variance seems to be the norm in forecasted levels of the federal budget deficit, interest rate changes, GNP, and the money supply.

Lessons Derived From Economic Forecasting

Much can be learned from the efforts of economists to build econometric models as a means to assess and project economic activity. All of these lessons have applicability to macroenvironmental forecasting beyond the domain of the economic arena.

Reality Is Difficult to Replicate.   Despite the scale and intricacy of many econometric models, they fail to capture the complexity of the world they purport to forecast. Given the complex reality of the macroenvironment as suggested throughout this book, expecting any analytical model to do justice to that complexity is simply naive. Thus, some degree of error with regard to the outputs of these models (the forecasts) is to be expected.

Structure Does Not Always Dictate Behavior.   The experience of economic forecasting should strongly remind us of the distinction drawn by systems theorists between the structure of a system and its behavior. Even if the structure of a system of relationships is accurately captured by a model (e.g., a system of relationships depicted in an economic model), it does not follow that we will be able to accurately predict the behavior of that system. As noted by Mayes (1983, 17), "to some extent the problem is that purely statistically in a time-series relationship, dominated by trends, a number of alterative specifications of economic behavior will provide sufficiently accurate representations of reality that their goodness of fit and simulation and forecasting properties will satisfy the requirements of those who wish to use them."

The problem is that inadequacies in the model show up only when major departures from prevailing trends take place.

Explanation Is Not Prediction.   We need to distinguish between explanation (or description) and prediction. Describing and explaining the current state of the economy is one matter; predicting movement of key economic variables is quite another. Being able to describe and explain the current trends and patterns in the economy is a prerequisite to forecasting economic change; however, it is not sufficient. Stated differently, because of the interconnectedness and turbulence in the forces driving the macroenvironment, simple extrapolation is rarely sufficient as a means of forecasting; it merely tells us what to expect if present trends continue.

Relationships Among Variables Change.   A major reason why structure does not dictate behavior and that explanation is not a guarantor of prediction is that the relationships among economic variables or indicators change over time.

> ■ A good example is the relationship between GNP and energy consumption. The ratio between GNP and energy use was relatively constant until the rapid price increases of the 1970s. But since then, the ratio of energy use to GNP has been declining steadily. Perhaps the best example is the dramatic change that has taken place in the relationship between inflation and employment in the last twenty years.

Key Driving Forces Reside Outside the Economic Arena.   A dominant factor underlying the previous observations is that change in the economic system is often caused by forces outside of the economic arena. For example:

> ■ Much of the turbulence experienced by the economic system during the mid-1970s can be traced to the energy crisis of 1973–74. Major political events can also introduce extensive instability into the economic system. Political upheavals in foreign countries and wars can wreak havoc with economic stability.

Driving Forces Are of Unequal Importance.   In explaining current economic change and in forecasting future economic change, we need to determine which factors are largely random, which are cyclical, and which are trend setting (i.e., leading to long-term structural change). Long-range projections of economic activity should not be biased by current cyclical and random fluctuations.

Change Can Occur Quickly.   The recent experience with economic forecasting confirms an old maxim: Change can occur quickly. Although the record of economic forecasting is good, many forecasts have badly missed the mark in the short run. Thus, simply because a forecast addresses the short run (i.e., less than six months) does not guarantee its accuracy.

Accuracy Is Often Overstated.   Economic forecasts illustrate another important point pertaining to environmental forecasting. Correctly assessing the direction of trends and garnering some idea of the magnitude of change is often more important than a high degree of accuracy in the forecast. As we shall see in later chapters, a high degree of accuracy in not necessary for a forecast to be a useful input into strategy analysis.

The Importance of Assumptions. The differences in forecasts are often attributable to differing assumptions adopted by forecasters as inputs to their forecasts. For example, if forecasters employ different assumptions about likely interest rates, their projections about many other economic variables influenced by interest rates are likely to be different. Thus, knowing the assumptions underlying a forecast is just as important as knowing the forecast's output; the latter makes sense only when we know the former.

Judgment Is Unavoidable. In using econometric models as aids in economic forecasting, a number of judgments are required: What variables should be included in the model? What relationships should be posited among the variables? What assumptions should be made? These types of judgments critically shape the model's outputs (i.e., forecasts).

This recent experience with economic forecasting should not be construed as an argument against forecasting the economic environment or against using forecasts as an input into strategy analysis. Based upon the experience of many firms in using economic forecasting as an input to their strategy analysis, a number of considerations that have wide applicability to macroenvironmental analysis merit emphasis.

First, economic analysis provides one important basis for sensitivity analysis. It facilitates the development of scenarios—the systematic asking of "what-if" questions. What will the impact be on our industry if the economy grows or declines? What will happen to our markets if interest rates decline or increase? Many providers of economic analysis provide such scenarios in the form of pessimistic, middle, and optimistic forecasts or scenarios.

Second, a key output of economic analysis is some set of assumptions about future economic conditions. For example, the acceptance of some projected rate of GNP for the forthcoming year means that that growth rate becomes an assumption for strategic planning purposes. Varying assumptions is an important means of creating scenarios.

Third, economic analysis often stimulates the search for more information on the external environment. Rather than accepting the outputs of an economic forecast as the final word on what may happen in the economy, decision makers use the outputs to ask what other data are required to fully understand what is happening or likely to happen in the economy. For example, what factors outside of the economic arena are driving the projected increase in interest rates? Raising this type of question compels consideration of the interconnectedness among the segments of the environment.

Fourth, the prior discussion points up another characteristic of successful environmental analysis: because of the speed with which change can occur, a need exists to update forecasts as often as possible. Many providers of economic analysis update their forecasts on a monthly basis.

The previous discussion may be crystallized into a number of key questions that need to be posed before drawing strategy-relevant implications of economic forecasts:

1. What are the key assumptions behind a forecast? What alternative sets of assumptions are employed by different forecasters?
2. What is the variability in these forecasts? Why do they differ?
3. What do these forecasts tell us of the type of change: cyclical, structural, systematic, or random? At what levels are changes taking place?
4. How should the forecasts be interpreted in light of the developments in other segments of the environment—on a short-, medium-, and long-term basis?
5. How should alternative assumptions be incorporated into sensitivity analysis?
6. How often should these forecasts, the assumptions, and the driving forces behind them be updated?

ASSESSMENT: DERIVING IMPLICATIONS

That economic conditions directly impact the fortunes of industries and firms is axiomatic. All strategic plans are anchored in assumptions about the economy. Such factors are ubiquitous in strategy formulation (Hofer and Schendel 1978). In this regard, four themes merit restatement. First, economic forces affect different industries in different ways. Second, economic factors affect strategy formulation at all levels: corporate, business, and functional. Third, they form one set of crucial inputs into sensitivity analysis. Finally, they should be updated continuously, and such updating should be reflected in budgeting practices as well as in the evaluation of strategies.

Economic changes affect different industries in different ways:

■ The markets for the products of firms in heavy industries (e.g., steel, aluminum), consumer durables (e.g., refrigerators, television sets, furniture), construction, and real estate rise or fall in line with upturns or downturns in the economy. Different conditions, however, may prevail in different segments of the economy. Demand in some industries may be buoyant, while in others it may be stagnant or declining.

■ Another important point is that different industries may be sensitive to different indicators noted in Table 7.1. For example, the machine tool industry as a major supplier of business equipment to many industries is particularly impacted by aggregate business investment plans. Consumer goods firms pay close attention to the consumer price index and the level of retail sales.

Economic changes (for an industry) need to be interpreted in the context of the industry; broad generalizations are of relative little value for deriving action-relevant strategies.

Economic changes affect corporate-, business-, and functional-level strategies:

■ At the corporate level, portfolio analysis, especially when it concerns market growth and level of available resources, is to some extent sensitive to economic upswings and downturns. In a similar vein, patterns of acquisition and divestiture have shown a relationship to economic cycles.

The implications of economic assumptions for sensitivity analysis are prevalent in the strategy literature. Equally important is stressing that misforecasts and misjudgments in economic assumptions (or their accuracy), as in the case of any other environmental assumptions, should be considered as one of the factors explaining business performance and deviation from targets during the implementation and monitoring phases of strategic management.

SUMMARY

This chapter has highlighted the recent experience with economic forecasting. Caveats regarding accuracy and precision in these forecasts are noted, and some questions that should be raised while interpreting the forecasts are presented. This chapter has emphasized the role of judgment in considering the seemingly precise outputs of these forecasts as well as the pervasive influence of economic assumptions in strategy formulation.

8

Technology

Technological change is the most visible and pervasive form of change in society, as it brings in its wake new products, processes, and materials. It directly impacts every aspect of society around us—for example, transportation modes, energy forms, communication, entertainment, health care, food, agriculture, and industry. It alters the rules of the game in international trade and competition.

Despite its obvious consequences, technology is not easy to define. The dictionary explains technology as "the branch of knowledge that deals with industrial arts, applied science and engineering" and, more broadly, "as the sum of the ways in which a social group provides itself with the material objects of its civilization." Its essence is thus the knowledge of how to do things. For our purposes, we broadly define the technological arena as embracing the institutions and activities involved in the creation of new knowledge (what is often referred to as "science") and the translation of that knowledge into new products, processes, and materials.

TECHNOLOGICAL CHANGE

A vast literature exists on technological change, technological forecasting, and the impact of technology on society. Although an extensive summary of this literature is outside the scope of this book, it is important to sketch some key notions about technological change in order to highlight issues involved in analysis of this segment. These key notions may be summarized along three dimensions: (1) general characteristics of the process of technological change, (2) forms of technological change, and (3) technology life cycles.

119

The Process of Technological Change

The process of technological change is complex and often appears chaotic. However, some general characteristics of the process may be noted.

Technological Development Takes Place at Many Levels. A number of stages are apparent in the birth, growth, development, and diffusion of technologies:

1. Fundamental or basic research seeks the principles and relationships underlying knowledge. This stage represents the scientific discovery of a new physical phenomenon or a new theoretical concept,
2. Applied research further crystallizes the true nature of the knowledge and demonstrates its potential utility through the use of bench scale approaches,
3. Development reduces this knowledge to practice in workable prototype form,
4. Engineering refines the knowledge for commercial exploitation or other practical end uses,
5. Operations such as manufacturing finally put the technology to use, and it becomes adopted and used by others (Quinn, J.B. and Mueller, J.A. Transferring Research Results to Operations. *Harvard Business Review* (January–February 1963) pp. 49–66).

The demarcation lines between these levels is often hazy; nevertheless, a different level of technical skill and business orientation is needed for each. Hence, these levels are normally performed by different groups of individuals in a society and often within firms.

The first two stages embrace what is often referred to as "invention." The third and fourth stages constitute what is typically labeled "innovation." The fifth stage is "diffusion," the time required for the technology to become accepted in general use. Although the distinctions among these stages are somewhat imprecise, the preceding scheme points up the fact that technological developments from invention to diffusion take place over a considerable period of time. Thus, innovation lag—the period of time between the recognition of a scientific solution to a technological need and the emergence of the first viable product utilizing the solution—may range from six to twenty years. Generally, invention typifies revolutionary change: it represents new knowledge and is a breakthrough or major discontinuity compared with the previous state of knowledge. Innovation and diffusion, on the other hand, more generally manifest evolutionary change, a series of small changes that clearly build upon past knowledge and conditions.

Technological Change is an Evolutionary Process. Changes are continually unfolding in this segment. The factors that contribute to the development of specific technologies are so numerous that search for a limited number of determinants has proven less than successful (Sahal 1981). Further, the process of technological change displays two related properties: multifinality and nonlinearity. The process is multifinal in that change may take place in multiple directions simultaneously. Consider the following examples:

■ Developments in semiconductor technology have led to further developments in computers, electronics, and military hardware.

■ Bar codes are no longer found just on food packaging but also in warehouses, assembly lines, and shipping docks—in short, wherever people want to keep track of products or parts. The Department of Defense now requires codes on goods that it buys from more than 50,000 suppliers.

Technological change is nonlinear in that developments often take place irregularly with a lot of dead ends, and results often become visible only after some specific prior developments have taken place. For example:

The successful commercialization of 100 percent solid-state television sets occurred only after a number of firms failed in their efforts to make the transition to solid-state technology. This sequence of failures took place over a five-year period.

Indeed, further developments in a specific technological application must sometimes wait developments in other technologies.

Technology Change Agents Are Many. The agents or creators of technological change are almost innumerable and vary significantly across the stages of technological change noted earlier. Government institutions such as NASA, the Batelle Research Institute, independent research entities such as Bell Laboratories, and universities and some large corporations engage in much of the work that is dubbed scientific discovery (which leads to inventions in the form of new products, processes, or materials). Independent entrepreneurs, business firms, and some governmental agencies play leading roles in innovation and diffusion.

The evolutionary process of technological change indicates that most technological developments can be broken down into a series of small steps. In the case of technological change, however, the distinction between continuous and discontinuous change depends on the location of the observer. Innovation within an established industry is often limited to incremental improvements of both products and processes. Discontinuous change in the form of major product change is often introduced from outside the established industry. Its source is often new, small, start-up firms, or the invasion of markets by leading firms in other industries or by government-sponsored research.

From the perspective of the latter entities, the so-called radical changes will be seen as an accumulation of incremental innovations. Each of the incremental steps is a creative act and depends on the results of active experimentation or availability of local information of a specific nature. The accumulation or synthesis of these facts, not available to outsiders, is what often bestows the discontinuous quality on the change.

Forms of Technological Change

The overriding characteristic of technological change, relative to the other segments, is its manifestation in tangible outputs: products, processes, and materials. It brings about new products, product refinements, and product substitution. Many times technological change leads to new or improved process technologies, or new or improved materials that enhance product quality, performance, and reliability.

The forms of technological change often vary depending on the stage of the product life cycle. These forms of change, as postulated by Moore and Tushman (1982), are summarized in Table 8.1. As the table shows, product design changes are usually much more frequent in the development and growth stages of the product life cycle, while process design changes are more frequent during later stages.

The complexity of technological change is often attributable to changes occurring simultaneously in various forms of technological development. We emphasized, however, that the threat of discontinuous innovations that produce different levels of products or processes to perform a particular function is greatest during late maturity and decline stages of the product life cycle (Cooper and Schendel 1976).

Technology Life Cycles

Specific technologies often exhibit life cycles, which have differing implications for different industries. To highlight this concept, considering two related ideas is necessary.

Table 8.1   Forms of Technological Change Over the Product Life Cycle Stages

	PRODUCT LIFE CYCLE STAGE		
	INTRODUCTION	*GROWTH*	*MATURE*
TYPE OF INNOVATION	MAJOR PRODUCT INNOVATION →	INCREMENTAL PRODUCT/MAJOR PROCESS INNOVATION →	INCREMENTAL PRODUCT/PROCESS INNOVATION
LOCATION OF INNOVATION	ENTREPRENEUR →	MARKETING/R & D →	MARKETING/PRODUCTION → PRODUCTION
BASES OF COMPETITION	PRODUCT PERFORMANCE →	PRODUCT DIFFERENTIATION PRICE →	PRICE IMAGE MINOR DIFFERENCES
PRODUCTION PROCESS	JOB SHOP → BATCH →	ISLANDS OF AUTOMATION →	ASSEMBLY LINE → CONTINUOUS FLOW
DOMINANT FUNCTION	ENTREPRENEUR →	MARKETING/R & D →	MARKETING/PRODUCTION → PRODUCTION/SALES (PROMOTION)
MANAGEMENT ROLE	ENTREPRENEUR →	SOPHISTICATED MARKET MANAGER → ADMINISTRATOR/INTEGRATOR →	STEWARD
MODES OF INTEGRATION	INFORMAL COMMUNICATION →	INFORMAL COMMUNICATION TASK FORCES TEAMS → INFORMAL COMMUNICATION TEAMS PROJECT MANAGER →	FORMAL COMMUNICATION SENIOR MANAGEMENT COMMITTEES
ORGANIZATIONAL STRUCTURE	FREE FORM →	FUNCTIONAL ORGANIC → PROJECT/MATRIX →	FUNCTIONAL/BUREAUCRATIC

Source: Moore, W.L. and Tushman, M.L. Managing Innovation Over the Product Life Cycle, in *Readings in the Management of Innovation*, Tushman and Moore, eds. Boston: Pitman Press, 1982, p. 143.

First, products or processes are often composed of a number of specific technologies. For example, personal computers consist of several distinct technologies: central processing units, printers, monitors, modems, and communication links. These specific technologies can be further decomposed. Note, however, that specific technologies possess differential competitive impact as illustrated in A.D. Little's (1981) technology classification: base, key, pacing, and peripheral.

Base technologies are shared by competitors in the industry and thus offer little basis for competitive advantage. These technologies, however, sometimes create technological entry barriers. *Key technologies* offer the opportunity for competitive differentiation. Especially in technology-intensive industries, firms channel R&D expenditures into developing or refining key technologies, and differing technologies often compete for supremacy in this area. *Pacing technologies* have the potential to replace base or key technologies. Typically, however, they arise outside the established industry. *Peripheral technologies* have no competitive or strategic significance. They are often low value-added features with little impact on product and process features.

Second, to focus on technology life cycles, considering the notion of performance parameters or characteristics is important. Performance characteristics refer to those characteristics of a specific technology that are deemed important in the function of a product or process. Typically, each specific technology is associated with a limited number of performance characteristics. Technology life cycles refer to the changes in performance characteristics over time. Performance characteristics often exhibit an S-shaped curve.

Consider the illustration in Figure 8.1. Maximum speed is the key performance characteristic. Differing technologies (e.g., automobiles versus trains) have differing characteristics, but typically, the form of the curve is S-shaped.

Base technologies typically have peaked out in their dominant performance characteristics. Key technologies exhibit rapid improvements. As for pacing technologies, the performance characteristics are likely to be associated with a high degree of uncertainty and must await further improvement to be considered a serious competitor to existing technology.

As we shall see later, the notion of technology life cycles is useful for monitoring and forecasting purposes.

SCANNING

Scanning in the technological arena is an activity that is rendered difficult because of conceptual and data-related problems. Conceptually, as seen from the foregoing discussion, technological developments take place simultaneously and at different lead times, and often the potential of specific developments is not clear even to those engaged in them.

In addition, some characteristics of the relevant data sources render scanning difficult. First, much of the evolution of technological change is not in the public arena; this is especially true for developments in the early stages: fundamental science, research, and the initial stages of development. Second, and relatedly, much of the relevant data is confined to specialists: scientists, researchers, consultants, academics, and relevant governmental personnel. Thus, data pertaining to fundamental scientific research primarily reside

Figure 8.1   Example of S Curve

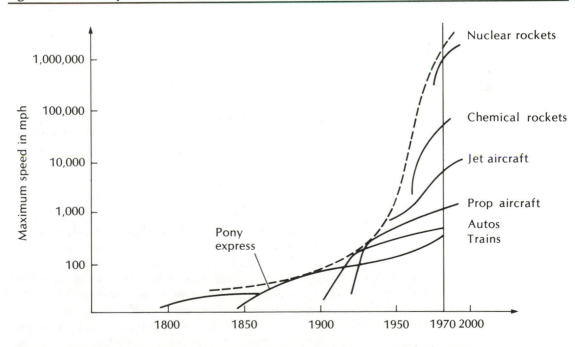

Source: Wheelwright & Makridakis. *Forecasting Methods for Management* 3d ed., 1980.

in scientific communities, whereas technology-specific data reside within many specific application-oriented organizations such as corporations, consulting firms, and some research organizations.

Tapping these data sources poses some problems. Effort is required to locate these sources of data. Many of these specialists use much technical jargon, which makes communication more difficult than in the other environmental segments. Even in the case of technological change in the innovation and diffusion stages, a lot of highly local knowledge exists that may not be easily transmitted but remains in the minds of individuals. Finally, many technology experts are not forthcoming with information, as technological developments are frequently shrouded in secrecy and deemed confidential. This is true even for some government sources, especially when technological developments are tied to issues of national security and defense.

These data problems indicate that scanning (and monitoring) efforts in the technological arena should have an investigative element. Data sources must be identified, and primary sources must be spoken to. Considerable resources and time may need to be devoted to this effort. Scanning cannot be largely confined to secondary sources as may be the case in the demographic and economic arenas. In the technological arena, primary sources are critical because the appearance of technological developments as news often takes place at the innovation and diffusion stages, at which time a firm would have lost considerable lead time for strategic action.

For many organizations, scanning in the technological arena should be focused at multiple levels: general technological trends and specific technologies. General technological trends may be scanned on a global or national level. At the global level, macrolevel data (nation by nation) pertaining to R&D expenditures are broken down by industrial sectors, level of scientific development, level of scientific and educational efforts, and government expenditures for R&D are typically available in advanced economies. Such data provide indicators of potential pockets of technological developments. Data at this level are often useful for indicating patterns of changes in the long run—patterns that are becoming increasingly important as we move toward a more globally interdependent economy.

Extensive technological data along these lines exist at the national or federal level. Many federal agencies provide considerable data pertaining to their domain (e.g., the Department of Energy, the Environmental Protection Agency, the National Institutes of Health). Some federal agencies primarily address technology issues (e.g., the Office of Technology Assessment). Note also that many nongovernmental institutions play major roles in shaping technological developments. For example, the American Cancer Society plays a key role in cancer research.

Scanning specific technologies in their embryonic stages and over their lifetimes is the primary scanning focus for many firms. However, underscoring the necessity to scan for technologies far outside the firm's field of operations or base technology is important for two reasons. First, as noted earlier, disruptive or discontinuous technological changes often have their source outside what is generally conceived as the industry. For example:

■ Analyses of technological change in the textile industry require that the chemical, plastics, paper, and equipment industries be included. Analyses of technological change in the electronics industry require a scan of technological developments related to component, circuit, and software producers. In the electronics industry, changes in fields as far away as biological sciences may have implications.

Table 8.2 lists examples of sources of data for scanning both general technological trends and specific technologies. We emphasize again that to spot emerging technologies, reliance must primarily be placed on primary external sources of data. Secondary sources are primarily useful for scanning technological change at later stages.

MONITORING

Monitoring technological change assumes added importance due to the cumulative and often unforeseen effects of changes at each phase of the technological change process. Unfortunately, monitoring technological change also confronts some problems largely peculiar to the technological arena. First, indicators such as performance characteristics are often specific to individual technologies. Second, the relevant indicators vary over the phases of technology evolution or life cycle. Third, uniform, complete, credible, and timely data (compared with the other environmental segments) are often absent. Fourth, standard formats for data collection do not exist. Thus, as noted in the case of scanning, data sources and indicators need to be identified, and formats for data collection need to be established for monitoring to proceed.

FORECASTING

Technological forecasting has received a lot of attention in the last twenty years. A large literature emerged on the topic in the late 1960s and early 1970s. The following are some key issues, distilled from this literature, (Schon 1967) that to some extent distinguish forecasting as conceived and practiced in the technological arena from forecasting in the other environmental arenas.

First, technological forecasting often conjures up images of predicting specific technological changes (e.g., inventions and commer-

Table 8.2 Sources of Data for Technology Scanning

General Technology Trends	Specific Technologies
Scientists/technologists in different disciplines/fields	Scientists
Scientific/technology leaders, e.g., American Association for Advancement of Science	Engineers
	Relevant science/technology experts
Public policy analysts	Relevant government agency personnel
University researchers	Current and ex-employees of suppliers, competitors, and distributors
Consultants specializing in science/technology issues	Industry and trade association personnel
	Consultants
Employees in science/technology-related government agencies, e.g., Patents Office, Office of Technology Assessment, National Science Foundation	University faculty and research
	Staff of relevant science/technology publications
Staff of science/technology journals/magazines	Staff of organizations specializing in monitoring specific industries
Executive departments, e.g., Commerce, Energy	General government documents, e.g., executive departments, regulatory agencies, congressional hearings
Regulatory agencies, e.g., EPA, FDA, Patents Office	Government-sponsored studies, e.g., Office of Technology Assessment, National Science Foundation
Agencies that fund/review science/technology developments, e.g., National Science Foundation, National Academy of Engineering, Congressional Budget Office	Patent statistics
Congressional hearings	Consultants' reports
Research institutes	Specialist industry research organizations' publications
University research programs	Industry/trade association publications/statistics
Consulting firms	Specialized science/technology publications
Science/technology journals, e.g., *Science, Scientific American, Proceedings of National Academy of Sciences*	Materials provided at science/technology seminars, trade shows, conventions
General business/science/technology publications and indices, e.g., *Predicast, Business Periodicals Index, Statistical Reference Index*	Company records, e.g., annual reports, government filings
	Documented analyses by supplier and user groups

cialization of technologies). Technological forecasting as typically conceived and implemented, however, takes on a heavy assessment element. The intent of forecasting is to identify and assess the impact of technological change—not just when and how the change is likely to occur. For example, corporations, labor unions, and government agencies undertake such forecasts. These forecasts are important because technological change is so closely linked to social, economic, and political change. Even an apparently nontechnological economic forecast rests on the assumption that no significant technological change will counter the forecast.

Second, the tasks and approaches to technological forecasting vary across the stages of technological change (i.e., invention, innovation, and diffusion). Forecasts of inventions fall generally into the category of informed opinion. This requires a thorough grasp of some science or technology field. These forecasts may take the form of one person's opinion or a Delphi where the opinions of a number of experts are pooled or averaged.

> ■ An example of a systematic effort of this type of forecasting is the U.S. Air Force's Project Forecast, where opinions are gathered from experts about developments of new physical phenomena and implications for future systems such as aircraft are derived.

Many, if not most, business-related technology forecasts focus on the rate and direction of diffusion. This makes a great deal of pragmatic sense: the time period of diffusion is often long so that there is still time to take action. Approaches to forecasting diffusion differ. One approach utilizes historical diffusion curves and then goes on to identify characteristic curve shapes (S-shaped curves, for example) or to formulate conditions governing rate of diffusion. A second approach focuses on diffusion of technology on an industry-by-industry basis.

Third, technological forecasting in the business arena often involves the creation and diffusion of new products, processes, and materials. The creation of these technological changes is not the result of natural processes but of creative decisional acts on the part of individuals and organizations. Thus, the technological environment is very much open regarding its future evolution.

Fourth, the technological arena is noticeably bereft of adequate theories that spell out the necessary and sufficient conditions of technological change, rendering prediction hazardous. The timing and nature of fundamental breakthroughs and inventions often cannot be anticipated, and diffusion is very much dependent on social, political, and economic influences.

Fifth, technological forecasts sometimes seem to function as self-fulfilling or self-defeating prophecies, especially when they are made by a prominent public institution (e.g., some agency of the federal government). Alleged predictions often preform public opinions and shape deeply held assumptions.

Sixth, and related to the previous issues, given the difficulties in forecasting, scanning and monitoring assume importance. Tracking technological changes on an ongoing basis becomes necessary given the "noise" level in technological forecasts and predictions. Forecasts of the future should be regarded as mechanisms for creating insights rather than as definitive postulations of what will transpire.

Forces Driving Technological Change

The foregoing discussion should make it clear that technological change may sometimes occur autonomously, that is, largely independent of the forces in the other environmental segments. Many examples of technological change leading to further technological developments could be cited. Advances in semiconductor and microprocessor technology have led to technological developments affecting a wide variety of products such as computers, electronic equipment, automobiles, refrigerators, and energy control systems. Advances in space-related technology frequently find their way into technological improvements in industrial, commercial, and consumer products.

Forces in the other environmental segments, however, do impact technological change. Political, regulatory, and economic forces often play a significant role in shaping the scope and direction of fundamental research as well as the thrust of more applied technological developments.

Political.   Through its authorization of funds and its oversight role of governmental departments and agencies, Congress provides direct and indirect supports and incentives for all phases of technological change, both within federally controlled and supported institutions and the private sector. These supports and incentives (e.g., direct funding of R&D, tax policies, technology transfer programs) have contributed significantly to the development and diffusion of many technologies. To take one example:

> ■ Prior to the discovery of the transistor in 1948, European firms were the equal of American firms in advanced component technology. In the early fifties, the military services became convinced of the strategic importance of transistors and semiconductor devices. As a result, the Department of Defense financed semiconductor R&D on a large scale. Between 1955 and 1961, direct government funding for semiconductor R&D and production refinement totaled $66 million. Beginning with the tran-

sistor, almost all the important inventions and innovations in component technology have been made in the United States—most of them the consequences of direct or indirect governmental support (Schnee, Jerome. Government Programs and the Growth of High Technology. *Research Policy*, January, 1978).

Regulatory.   Regulations directly or indirectly facilitate or impede every phase of technological development.

■ Regulations may sometimes impact what research can be worked on and what organizations can work on it, the acquisition and use of patents, and even the diffusion of research outputs and technological changes. Regulatory agencies such as the Federal Drug Administration and the Department of Commerce's Bureau of Standards must give their approval before many of the outputs of technological change can be sold in the marketplace.

Regulatory agencies can also redirect the thrust of technological developments. For example, the Environmental Protection Agency has strongly influenced technological development away from pollution creation and toward pollution control.

Economic.   Economic conditions exert a primary impact on the level and pace of technological change. The argument has often been made that innovation and diffusion (and to a lesser extent, basic and applied research) are driven more by the prevailing market or economic conditions than by the availability of scientific and technological knowledge (Kelly and Kranzberg 1975). This impact would be even greater were it not for the large federal funding of technological developments.

Values.   Just as technology shapes values, values directly and indirectly influence technological developments.

Values espoused in the political process may affect the volume and focus of public and private sector R&D programs. In this way, values affect the scope and direction of the military and nuclear development programs. Changing values get institutionalized in governmental policies and structures (e.g., the National Environmental Protection Act) and in the requirement that governmental agencies perform technological assessments and thus influence technological developments.

Demographics and Life-styles.   Demographics and life-styles, in part through their impact on social values and the political and regulatory arenas, may also influence the nature and direction of technological development.

> For example, the aging of the population has led to an upsurge of interest in the problems of the aging. One manifestation of this concern has been the commitment of large amounts of public and private scientific research to studying the health issues peculiar to the aged.

Forecasting Methods

An appreciation of the driving forces as previously discussed helps one to understand in which direction specific technological changes may proceed. As also noted, however, technological change sometimes evolves largely autonomously and discontinuously. Thus, from the perspective of an individual firm, many typical forecasting methods such as trend extrapolation (which largely assumes that the future is determined by the past) are not very useful in predicting when technological discoveries will be made or when they may be commercialized.

A number of qualitative techniques employing experts are often used in preparing technological forecasts. These techniques do not provide a detailed procedure or single forecast; they only define possible boundaries within which the future may lie. We briefly outline a few examples of these techniques.

Logistic and S-Curve Approaches.   The frequently used S-curve approach implies a slow start, a steep growth, and then a plateau (just as in the life cycle curve). The curve is a characteristic form of many technological developments. It is broadly applicable to a performance characteristic—for example, speed of transformation as shown in Figure 8.1. In this particular case, the upper limit of the curve can be recognized as the natural limit on transportation speed. The differing curves represent discontinuous innovation. In most cases, predicting the point at which one finds oneself on the curve is difficult and relies on judgments of experts.

Morphological Research Methods.   In a true sense, morphological research is not a forecasting methodology but rather concerns itself with the development and practical application of basic methods to discover hidden opportunities in technological change. The method involves identifying all parameters of a problem and constructing an array of all possible correlations. Table 8.3 illustrates a morphological analysis of building bricks: each row is a separate parameter, and

**Table 8.3 Morphological Analysis:
an Example in the Case of Building Bricks**

		1	2	3	4	5
A	Material	Natural clay	Metal	Plastic	Waste materials	Figures
B	Forming process	Extrude	Mold	Press	—	—
C	Bonding process	Heat	Chemical	Molecular	—	—
D	Properties	Opacity	Thermal insulation	Elasticity	Aesthetic	—
E	Form	Rectangular	Spherical	Interlocking	Cube	—

Known technology: A1, B1, C1, D2, E1—thermal insulation brick

Suggestion: A3, B2, C2, D1, E2—opaque spherical plastic brick

Wells, Gordon S.C. "Forecasting Technological Innovation" in Taylor and Sparkes, (eds.) *Corporate Strategy and Planning*, Surrey, England: Wm. Heinemann Ltd., 1977. Reprinted by permission of William Heinemann Limited.

columns represent different parameter values. Both the search for new technologies and their chances of materializing are calculated from the morphological box. Despite its simplicity, morphological analysis has been found to be a powerful tool in the search for new technologies.

Delphi Forecasting. Delphi forecasting is a popularly employed forecasting tool in the technology arena. It involves polling a panel of experts a number of times. The experts do not meet face to face so that their judgments will not be subject to social influences. (This technique is discussed in more detail in Chapter 13.)

Relevance Trees. The relevance tree method seeks to assess the desirability of future goals and to select those areas of technology whose development is necessary to achieve the goals. These technologies are then singled out for further investigation. A sample relevance tree is presented in Figure 8.2, which starts with the desired objective of military and scientific preeminence (level 1) and suggests technologies that need development (level 3).

Each of the preceding techniques requires some form of expert judgment. Morphological and relevance tree methods focus on creating new solutions and are thus representative of techniques that attempt to capture autonomous evolution (inventive techniques as discussed in Chapter 13), whereas S curves and Delphi are attempts at forecasting the specifics of technological innovation and diffusion.

Assessing and Projecting Technological Change

The complexity and uncertainties inherent in technological change, as discussed earlier, as well as the innumerable predictions of tech-

**Figure 8.2   Relevance Tree Analysis:
an Example in The Case of Military/Scientific Technology**

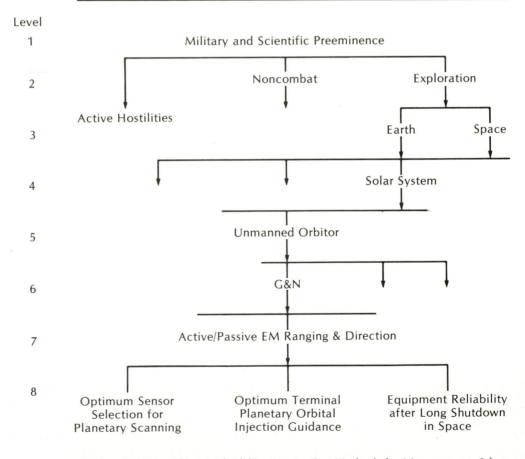

Source: Wheelwright & Makridakis. *Forecasting Methods for Management,* 3d ed., 1980.

nology that did not come to pass, suggest that extreme caution is required in efforts to assess and forecast technological developments. The following set of questions is typically at the heart of most efforts to forecast technological change.

What Is the Relevant Technology?

This question compels a careful consideration of the focal technology. For example, fiber optics, lasers, and semiconductors embrace a variety of (related) technologies. Thus, the analyst might tackle broad or narrow technological assessments in these domains.

In What Stage Is the Technology's Evolution?

As noted earlier, the assessment and forecasting tasks are different across the phases of invention, innovation, and diffusion. For example, assessing and forecasting the likelihood of a discontinuous innovation is different from assessing and forecasting its implications, that is, its acceptance and diffusion. As the innovation unfolds, the uncertainties associated with it are reduced.

What Are the Time Spans Over Which the Technology Will Unfold?

This is a critical forecasting question. It compels a specification of the evolutionary path of the technology, without which deriving meaningful strategy implications would be impossible.

What Forces Are Likely to Impede or Facilitate the Technology's Evolution?

Judgments about the temporal unfolding of technological changes can often be sharpened by considering the forces that drive them. Political, regulatory, economic, and social forces must all be considered. The extent to which these forces conflict or reinforce each other should be especially emphasized.

What Resources Are Available to Those Supporting or Impeding the Technological Change?

This question serves to assess the commitment and intensity of the forces driving the change.

How Is the New Technology Superior to the Old?

In the early stages of technological change, the question of its potential superiority is often unclear, whereas in the advanced stages such superiority (or lack of it) is easier to assess.

What Forces Will Impact the Adoption of the Technological Change?

Inventions sometimes don't evolve into innovations, and innovations diffuse at considerably different rates. Thus, one must consider not only the forces driving technological change but also the forces that specifically impact whether and how the new technological developments will displace the old. A large part of the consideration here are the barriers to adoption that may exist within the adopting organization.

Who Bears the Costs and Benefits of the Technological Change?

Technological change is not neutral in its impacts: some people may benefit, and others may lose. Industries negatively affected by technological change often use political and regulatory means to offset the impact. Neighborhood effects must also be taken into account; that is, those who benefit from technology do not necessarily absorb all its costs.

ASSESSMENT: DERIVING IMPLICATIONS

As we have continually stressed in this book, assessing and forecasting technological change, irrespective of the techniques employed, is not the end in itself; the purpose is to derive strategy-relevant implications. Technological change can impact almost every aspect of a firm's strategy.

In the case of technology, assessment is discussed at two levels: (1) implications for other environmental segments and (2) implications for firms' strategy development.

Implications for Other Macroenvironmental Segments

Two critical reasons exist for highlighting the implications of technology for other environmental segments. First, as the engine of progress, technology heavily impacts the social, economic, and political segments. Second, more than for any other environmental segment, technological change brings forth secondary and tertiary consequences.

As noted in the other segment chapters, technology has pervasive impacts on each environmental segment. Some theorists, such as Ogburn (1955), have proposed that sociocultural arrangements are often derivative of technological developments. Others have noted that economic performance of a society is integrally tied to its level of technological development. Although the proposed causal connections are not unidirectional (i.e., the other segments also affect technology), the critical point is the pervasive and direct influence of technological change on other environmental segments.

Second, technology often produces secondary and tertiary consequences. Hence, assessment should specifically include higher-order consequences, especially when environmental analysis is conducted for long-term purposes. Although such higher-order consequences are elaborated in Chapter 11, note that these consequences, in the case of technological change, offer significant avenues for growth and niches for firms in mature industries. In short, the influence of technological changes on the other segments brings in its turn implications for business strategy; thus, these influences need to be traced.

Implications for Business Strategy

At a broad level, technological change can affect whole industries in three ways: it can rejuvenate an industry, obsolete existing industries, or bring into being totally new industries. Consider the following examples:

- The watch industry has been dramatically rejuvenated (with some segments being obsoleted in the process) by the evolution through mechanical, electronic, quartz, and digital technologies. The advent of personal computers as a potent substitute for personal calculators has rendered the latter almost obsolete.

Further, technological change is a potent force in the reconfiguring of industry boundaries; it may broaden or narrow generally accepted industry boundaries. For example:

- Advances in information technologies have rendered old conceptions of the financial services industry obsolete: insurance firms, banks, and brokerage houses can now all be interconnected to provide new financial services, thus blurring long-held distinctions among the services offered by these industries.

Partly as a consequence of its impact on whole industries, technological change can have a significant impact on the prevailing business definition of individual firms. Firms may find themselves in a different business due to technological changes that they or others have effected. Consider the following example:

- Many U.S. firms have found themselves having to reconfigure their business definitions due to the success of Japanese firms in miniaturizing products, in part through technological advances. This is the position that Xerox found itself in its copier business. Because Japanese firms introduced smaller-sized copiers, Xerox found itself selling to different customers with different needs through different distribution channels and competing of different bases (price was much more important).

Technological change is often one of the important factors giving rise to product substitution and product differentiation. For example:

- Plastics have replaced many uses of steel, word processors have replaced typewriters, and microwave ovens are now frequently substituted for conventional ovens.

- In videotape recorders, firms have sought to differentiate their products through the introduction of technologically based features: longer recording time, longer advanced time setting, sharper picture reproduction, clearer sound, and so on.

The prior examples suggest that technological change is a dominant force in shaping competitive dynamics in many industries. It influences industry boundaries and structure, product substitution and differentiation, and the price and quality relationships between products.

Another important point is that technological change in the form of process (as opposed to product) and materials innovations may contribute to many of the impacts noted earlier. For example:

■ Process innovations such as automation, robotics, and CAD/CAM (computer-aided design/computer-aided manufacturing) have bestowed cost and quality advantages on many firms. Japanese automobile manufacturers have gained a significant competitive edge on their U.S. competitors through the adroit use of this form of technological change.

Much of the preceding discussion is in the context of single-business firms. Technological change, however, may also have multiple impacts specific to the diversified firm.

■ For example, technological change can create new synergies across businesses or obsolete existing ones. Advances in telecommunication and computer technologies have made new synergies possible across businesses dealing with computers, television sets, and communications.

A critical implication of the prior observation is the need to consider technology as a factor in developing portfolios at the corporate level, a point elaborated in Chapter 12.

SUMMARY

Technology lies at the heart of many environmental changes. These changes manifest in the form of new products, processes, and materials. Such changes affect other environmental segments and have direct implication for strategies both at the business-unit and corporate levels.

9

The Political Milieu

Political and regulatory change have long been of concern to business managers. In the last two decades, however, these changes have been so extensive that hardly any facet of the management of large corporations has remained untouched. This chapter addresses analysis of the political milieu. The next chapter addresses the regulatory milieu. Together they make up the political segment of the macroenvironment.

Defining the Political Environment

The political milieu may be broadly defined as the arena within which different interest groups compete for attention and resources to advance their own values, interests, and goals. These groups seek power and influence over one another so that their wishes may prevail. Concern with the political environment thus requires us to address interactions among individuals, organizations, and institutions.

The political environment may be viewed as including the executive and legislative arms of government, and a vast array of interest groups in society at large. Regulatory institutions also directly participate in the processes involved in the political arena, though discussion of these is left to the next chapter.

POLITICAL CHANGE: THE IMPORTANCE OF INTEREST GROUPS

Competition among interest groups resides at the heart of the political process. This is especially true if we adopt a broad definition of an interest group as any collection of individuals, loosely connected groupings, and institutions that temporarily bind together to achieve common purposes. Many different types of interest groups participate in the political arena. A number of dimensions capture the key characteristics of interest groups:

- *Degree of organization:* the degree to which the members of the interest group are organized and coordinated
- *Resource capability:* access to such resources as finances, personnel, information, and decision centers
- *Extent of influence:* the geographic or demographic scope of influence
- *Nature of interests:* which may vary from highly specific or single-issue concerns to broad-based concerns that may include a number of issues
- *Temporal duration:* which may vary from long-standing to spanning a short term
- *Degree of manifestation:* which may vary from latent to manifest
- *Bases of influence:* which may vary from credibility and moral persuasion to ability to invoke sanctions or withhold resources

Consider the following examples:

■ Some groups may be well organized, well financed, and dedicated to specific aims—for example, the NRA (the National Rifle Association). At the other extreme are the many local and community groups that may concentrate on local issues, that are organized to varying degrees, that are typically not well financed but also committed to specific aims, such as church-based groups and local activist groups. Some of the most involved participants in the political process are associations and organizations representing the interests of professional and functional groups—for example, the AMA (the American Medical Association).

■ Many interest groups are amalgams of loosely to tightly coordinated individual groups or collections of individuals—for example, consumers, environmentalists, women, trade unions. Some interest groups arise around specific issues such as taxes, foreign aliens, or particular business decisions (e.g., closing a plant). Many business-related interest groups participate in the political arena—for example, corporate PACs (political action committees), NAM (the National Association of Manufacturers), chambers of commerce, the Business Roundtable, and industry and trade associations.

Interest groups may be viewed as competing in two separate though related arenas: within and outside legislatures. Outside of legislatures, interest groups may compete for attention in such diverse arenas as the streets (through mass demonstrations), the media, or the courts. Actions outside of the legislature are often designed to influence the agenda and decisions within the legislature.

Recent Political Change

As in the other environmental segments, delineating all the political change that has occurred in the last few decades or is currently taking place is not possible. The following represents some of the most significant recent political change:

- *Rise in the number of interest groups:* A dominant feature of the political arena in the United States in the past few decades has been a startling increase in the number of interest groups. As noted in a recent newspaper headline, "there is a group for every cause".

- *Rise in the activism of interest groups:* A greater number of interest groups are increasingly prone to take actions intended to capture public attention. Farmers, unions, women, and gay rights groups engage in mass rallies. Consumer and environmental groups and groups supporting candidates in the electoral process send out mass mailings to millions of people. Many groups are expert at getting access to the media.

- *Escalation of single-interest groups:* Many of the interest groups that have appeared on the political horizon in the last two decades are dedicated to a single issue or cause: the pro-life and pro-choice groups, the antinuclear groups, women's groups supporting equal rights, senior citizens' groups devoted to the protection of their social security income. These groups are not easily distracted from their goals.

- *Rise in the diversity of issues in the political arena:* Given the increase in the number of interest groups, it should not be surprising to discover that an increasingly broader array of issues now find their way into the political process, both within and outside the legislature.

- *More intense and protracted political conflict:* In part because of the increase in the number of interest groups and their commitment to their goals, many more conflicts among more groups now dot the political landscape than previously. Some political conflicts drag on for many years: the Equal Rights Amendment, the nuclear arms issue, and the abortion issue are examples.

- *Greater potential for interest groups to affect the political system:* It is increasingly easy for interest groups to impact the political system—to gain attention for their cause, to make public their plight or gripes, to link with other groups as a means of building support for their cause.

Perhaps the major consequence for corporations of the preceding political changes is the upsurge in claimants they confront, that is, groups external to the firm that can directly or indirectly place a demand for something due from the organization. Such is the prevalence of claimants that managing the corporation is now often spoken of as "the management of stakeholders." Claims are placed upon the corporation by community groups, church groups, unions, consumers, government agencies, and elected political representatives.

SCANNING

The political segment occasionally brings up discrete issues of immediate concern. More often, however, it takes a number of years for social and political concerns to crystallize into recognizable issues. The lead times involved are, therefore, long: it may take five to ten years for an issue to reach the legislative process and materialize into some kind of law or regulation. Thus, during scanning, picking up early warning signals of emerging issues is theoretically possible. Yet, a number of data-related issues need to be tackled to render detection of signals feasible.

For scanning and monitoring purposes, it is useful to divide the political arena into two related segments: outside and inside the legislature. The evolution of the patterns of events in the social and political milieus outside the legislature largely shapes the agenda of issues within the legislature. To facilitate a discussion of scanning and monitoring the political milieu outside the legislature, a brief depiction of the early stages of the process of social and political change—that is, how social or political issues emerge—is required. Consider the following:

■ The process of social and political change invariably begins with aberrant and apparently random and unrelated events that when aggregated over time manifest meaningful patterns. For example, the first signals of the current legislative battle over the proper means to support the farming community through its economic difficulties can be traced back to a number of early indicators: statements by farm leaders that fiscal conditions in farming were deteriorating; statements by community and banking representatives that farmers would need financial help in the not too distant future; occasional farm foreclosures; a depression in farm prices; a continued downturn in aggregate farm income; and policy statements of the executive arm of government that it would not provide extensive amounts of money to buttress any segment of the economy that could not survive on its own under the free flow of market forces. As farming conditions worsened, observers and participants in the farming community began to articulate their concerns more frequently. These concerns began to get more play in various media, and political representatives began to espouse the cause of farmers. The airing of the problems being confronted by farmers both within and outside the farming community gave rise to the emergence of interest groups or organizations that institutionalized the means to further articulate and publicize the concerns of farmers and to advocate change.

Scanning the political arena outside of the legislature thus requires coverage of the actions and statements of a diverse array of political actors. Thinking of scanning the political arena in terms of primary and secondary data sources is useful. Primary data sources include public opinion leaders and elites (e.g., previous and current government officeholders, leading members of the judiciary, media personalities), social critics (e.g., well-known journalists, essayists, book authors), experts on specific issues (e.g., leading authorities in relevant professions and disciplines), sociopolitical action groups (i.e., groups that grow up around causes such as abortion, civil rights, social security, right to bear guns), community groups, political party representatives, corporate PACs (political action committees), futures-oriented research establishments (e.g., the Hudson Institute, the Institute for the Future), public policy research centers (e.g., the Committee for Economic Development, Brookings Institution, the American Enterprise Institute), government-sponsored research (presidential commissions, congressional research reports), academia (university-sponsored studies, preeminent scholars), and those immediately and potentially affected by an emerging political issue (e.g., victims such as farmers in the previous example).

Secondary sources for scanning the behavior and opinions of the preceding political actors are equally diverse and scattered. Many types of journals, magazines, and papers exist, such as daily newspapers; weekly general interest publications (e.g., *Time, Newsweek, U.S. News & World Report*); specialized scientific, technical, professional, industry, and trade publications; newsletters and other publications (e.g., *Scientific American, Science, Electronic News*); popular intellectual magazines (e.g., *Harpers,* the *New Yorker,* the *Atlantic*); broad-issue-related publications (e.g., consumer reports, environmental studies, nuclear documents); and highly specialized publications on politics (e.g., *Politics and Elections*). Governmental documents are also a rich source of data—for example, public hearings on specific topics, congressional hearings, and publicly available submissions requested by various governmental agencies from interested public parties such as those likely to be affected by governmental actions. Public opinion polls conducted by many different types of organizations provide up-to-date attitudinal data. Many specialized publications provide data pertaining to specific issues—for example, governmental statistical documents, economic studies conducted by many different types of organizations, and the publications put out by social action and community groups.

Many of the prior actors and data sources are also relevant for scanning the political process within the legislature. Scanning within the legislature, however, is much more focused than scanning the political process external to it. Some of the actors and their actions and opinions are readily manifest: bills introduced by individual members of the legislature, and statements and speeches made by individual members inside and outside of the legislature. Specific data sources exist for scanning (and monitoring) actions and statements within the legislature, such as the *Federal Register,* committee hearing reports, and media reports of legislative activity.

Some political actors and their behavior and opinions, such as the actions and statements of lobbyists, are not so readily manifest. Lobbyists, however, are often willing to provide statements of their positions on specific issues; their viewpoints are also frequently found in some of the data sources noted earlier.

Precursors of Political Change

Because of the long lead times from the first signs of social concern to the emergence of a political or public policy issue and the multiplicity of data sources, detecting early warning signals or precursors of political change is almost always possible. All of the data sources noted previously may provide the raw material for the detection of signals of potential political change. The following is a partial list of indicators running from the early to the later stages of political change:

Statements or opinions expressed by social critics, leading experts, social activists, affected individuals and groups, research institutes and universities, and public policy think tanks

The emergence of advocates and spokespersons around various aspects of the issue

The emergence of interest groups that are often initially loose coalitions of like-minded individuals

The emergence of full-time advocates or champions of the issue or cause

Movement from local groups to state, regional, and national groups

Statements and involvement of political party representatives

Propositions and amendments placed on the ballot in local, county, and state elections

Election results

Pronouncements and proposed policy changes by various arms of the executive branch of government

Bills proposed in the legislature and the progress of those bills through the legislature

Two points deserve special emphasis in the context of scanning the political environment and especially detecting and assessing precursors of political change. First, political change occurs at an exponential rate; that is, change initially takes place at a slow, almost imperceptible rate, and then as the concerns of a few grow to become the interests of many, the rate at which the issue grows and sustains public attention speeds up considerably. Thus, detecting signals of potential political change is both possible and essential.

Second, the emphasis should be upon threshold signals or indicators of potential political change. The focus should be on events that may provide momentum to an emerging political change or become a catalyst for further significant change.

MONITORING

Discussing the monitoring of political change from the vantage points of outside and within the legislature is also useful. Monitoring is more difficult outside the legislature. It involves tracking the evolution and dissemination of ideas and values throughout segments of society: following the appearance of significant individuals and interest groups who add their voice in support of or in opposition to emerging political causes or issues; following the evolutionary path of key events that may signal major steps forward or backward for the political cause or issue. The types of indicators tracked and the data sources used are those already discussed in the context of scanning political change.

Tracking political change outside of the legislature exemplifies the key features of monitoring. The analyst is required to draw patterns out of what initially may appear to be disparate and unrelated events or indicators of potential change. For example, in the early stages of an emerging political concern, the analyst may have only a few key indicators to suggest that a new issue might be forming: the actions of a few unconnected local communities, the statements of a few social activists, or visionary opinions of a leading politician. As the analyst searches through the data sources noted earlier, and also probably engages in discussions with other analysts of the political arena, he or she is confronted with the task of identifying what trends are apparent, to what extent a pattern is evident, what the connections are that constitute the pattern, and what the alleged pattern signifies regarding likely further political change. These are acts of intuition or perception on the part of the analyst. The data do not speak for themselves; the analyst must infuse them with meaning. The creation of this meaning, however, is what allows the analyst to see beyond isolated and seemingly unrelated data points. Discerning the likely emergence of a local or regional social movement cannot occur without the analyst's weaving linkages into the data that are not self-evident.

Tracking the evolution of the political process within the legislature is in many respects much more straightforward. The analyst can follow developments in the legislature along reasonably clear and preordained paths. The legislative process is built around a series of steps in the fashioning, introduction, assessment, and approval or rejection of bills, amendments to bills, and resolutions. These paths are depicted in Figure 9.1. Note that the lead times for bills or even amendments to pass through any legislature may extend from months to years. Thus, the analyst typically has a considerable amount of time to track and assess developments in and around the legislature.

Identifying and tracking indicators in the political arena requires a certain degree of creativity and inventiveness on the part of the environmental analyst. The process is not nearly as straightforward as it is in the demographic and economic arenas. The major problem is that the analyst may not be able to tell a priori what the relevant indicators of potential political change may be. For example, public polling has occasionally proved to be an unreliable indicator of election results, yet election results may signify that a change has already occurred in the political mood of a particular geographic region. Thus, in scanning and monitoring the political arena, the analyst must always be alert for new signals or indicators of emergent or potential change—that is, indicators that the analyst may not have previously been aware of or to which he or she paid little attention. Moreover, as noted previously, the analyst must derive what change may be signaled by the indicators.

FORECASTING

In part because of the increased instability and turbulence in the political arena as discussed earlier and its importance as a dominant driving force in environmental change, political forecasting has received a great deal of systematic attention in the last decade. Some key insights into understanding and forecasting the political environ-

Figure 9.1   The Stages Through Which a Bill Passes Before It Becomes Law

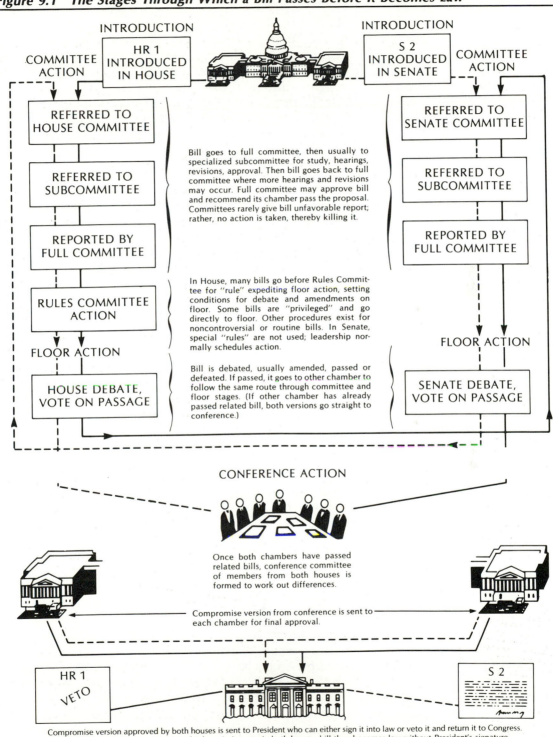

INTRODUCTION

HR 1 INTRODUCED IN HOUSE

INTRODUCTION

S 2 INTRODUCED IN SENATE

COMMITTEE ACTION

COMMITTEE ACTION

REFERRED TO HOUSE COMMITTEE

REFERRED TO SENATE COMMITTEE

REFERRED TO SUBCOMMITTEE

REFERRED TO SUBCOMMITTEE

Bill goes to full committee, then usually to specialized subcommittee for study, hearings, revisions, approval. Then bill goes back to full committee where more hearings and revisions may occur. Full committee may approve bill and recommend its chamber pass the proposal. Committees rarely give bill unfavorable report; rather, no action is taken, thereby killing it.

REPORTED BY FULL COMMITTEE

REPORTED BY FULL COMMITTEE

RULES COMMITTEE ACTION

In House, many bills go before Rules Committee for "rule" expediting floor action, setting conditions for debate and amendments on floor. Some bills are "privileged" and go directly to floor. Other procedures exist for noncontroversial or routine bills. In Senate, special "rules" are not used; leadership normally schedules action.

FLOOR ACTION

FLOOR ACTION

Bill is debated, usually amended, passed or defeated. If passed, it goes to other chamber to follow the same route through committee and floor stages. (If other chamber has already passed related bill, both versions go straight to conference.)

HOUSE DEBATE, VOTE ON PASSAGE

SENATE DEBATE, VOTE ON PASSAGE

CONFERENCE ACTION

Once both chambers have passed related bills, conference committee of members from both houses is formed to work out differences.

Compromise version from conference is sent to each chamber for final approval.

HR 1 VETO

S 2

Compromise version approved by both houses is sent to President who can either sign it into law or veto it and return it to Congress. Congress may override veto by a two-thirds majority vote in both houses; bill then becomes law without President's signature.

ment derived from ongoing political forecasting efforts are noted before we discuss the forces driving political change.

First, *discontinuous and systematic change* are both evident in the political arena. Discontinuities arise in many forms: the election of new public officeholders; the introduction of new policies; the emergence of new political alignments or coalitions; major changes in the positions or viewpoints of interest groups, public officials, or the government. Systematic change is evident in the more evolutionary or continuous nature of much political change—for example, continued gains or decline in the support of political parties or government policies; the increase or decline in support of viewpoints of specific interest groups (e.g., support for the Equal Rights Amendment); the path followed by bills through Congress; the life cycle of many issues: emergence, growth, peak, and decline.

Second, the nature of the forces driving political change is such that *single events* are of much more importance in assessing and projecting political change than other types of environmental change, such as demographic, life-style, and economic change. Election results, presidential pronouncements, legislative votes, mass demonstrations, and local referenda may lead to immediate change or signal future change (or both). These events are often not simply incremental additions to prevailing patterns.

Third, related to the importance of single events is the notion of *thresholds:* as political change unfolds, public awareness, concern, and interest move through thresholds. For example, with regard to the environmental pollution example discussed in Chapter 6, awareness of the issue passed through a threshold when it began to get persistent attention in the media. It then passed through a threshold of public concern when public representatives began to feel the pressure from constituents to take different forms of remedial action. The importance of thresholds is that when they are exceeded, the evolution of political issues may move in unexpected directions and may pick up speed or slow down.

Fourth, political events and trends are typically open to *multiple interpretations.* Their causes and consequences are rarely self-evident. For example, the impact of mass demonstrations (e.g., farmers blocking traffic in many towns to protest low prices) is difficult to project. Different analysts will often make different projections as to the potential consequences of political events.

Fifth, as noted by Ascher and Overholt (1983), although much of the recent attention in political forecasting has been devoted to the development of more sophisticated (i.e., quantitative) forecasting techniques, it has not resulted in noticeably higher quality (i.e., more accurate and insightful projections) than forecasting methods that rely on the forecaster's intuition, judgment, and relevant knowledge.

Ascher and Overholt further note that a major reason is because the complexity and interdependencies characteristic of the political environment do not easily lend themselves to depiction in quantitative forecasting models. Political forecasters, they suggest, must develop methods that can cope with this complexity. These methods must take into account the *forces driving political change and their interrelationships*—a theme we emphasize throughout this book.

Forces Driving Political Change

The forces at play in the political arena itself strongly shape political change. Political outcomes such as getting issues onto society's political agenda, election outcomes, and getting policies established in the legislature are the result of the efforts of interest groups, or more precisely, who wins and loses in the battles waged among and between interest groups.

Yet, equally clear is that a full understanding of current and potential political change cannot be derived simply by examining the political arena alone. Forces in the other environmental segments discussed in this book also contribute to political change. We shall briefly note some of these connections.

Demographics.   The aging of the population has led to many of the concerns of the segment of the population aged fifty and over becoming political issues—social security, health care, and so on. Changes in the ethnic mix in many cities and geographical mobility have greatly contributed to changes in the historical pattern of interest group domination in these cities and thus in election results (e.g., the election of mayors in many cities from minority groups).

Life-Styles.   Life-styles change, through its impact on value change, may influence political change. For example, as individuals' life-styles become more upscale, they manifest higher levels of consumption and leisure, often reflecting higher levels of education and higher-status jobs; their values may become more conservative, resulting in changed voting behavior and support for more conservative interest groups and causes.

Social Values.   As discussed in Chapter 6, political change can be viewed as a direct consequence of value change. Major value change causes political issues: as women's values have changed (e.g., in-

creased importance of careers), women's concerns have become political issues (e.g., the Equal Rights Amendment).

Technology.   Although we may not typically link technological
change and political change, the origins of many political issues such
as environmental pollution, nuclear safety, access to high-quality
health care, and so on can be directly traced back to technological
change. Also, technological change, through its impact on information collection and dissemination, impacts the dynamics of political
change. Technological developments now allow rapid readings of the
political pulse through opinion surveys, and television shapes political opinions through its audiovisual impact.

Regulatory.   Regulatory change almost always has repercussions in
the political arena. New regulations, deregulation, and more or less
commitment to enforcing existing regulations typically lead to the
affected interest groups assuming greater involvement in the political process. For example, business associations and individual firms
greatly intensify their lobbying and public relations efforts when
they perceive negative impacts of pending legislation or changes in
the implementation of existing regulations.

Interrelationships Among the Driving Forces

The ebb and flow of the dynamics of the political process—the battles among interest groups and the clashes among different factions
in the legislature—are indicative of the flux in the forces driving
political change. Rarely will all forces drive political change in the
same direction; sets of forces are typically driving a political issue in
different directions. The previously noted inability of quantitative
forecasting techniques to capture these complex interrelationships
has resulted in their poor performance record in the political arena.

Many issues that have dotted the political landscape in recent
years could be used to illustrate how reinforcing and conflictual
forces shape the evolution of political change: taxes, church-state
relations, capital punishment, consumer protection, workers' rights,
the proper role of government in many aspects of social, economic,
and political life, and so on. We use the issue of taxes for illustration
purposes.

■ Many forces had to coalesce to catapult the tax issue from the periphery
to much closer to center stage in the political arena. The so-called tax
revolt of the late 1970s and early 1980s was one facet of a value shift: the
intensification of antigovernment feelings. This value shift, however, was
in part provoked by economic forces: Inflation pushed many individuals

into higher tax brackets. Life-style concerns were also a factor: individuals at most income levels found it increasingly difficult to maintain their standard of living. The lowering of taxes was viewed as a remedy. Demographic shifts were also involved: many of the leaders of the tax revolt at the local level were older citizens (some of whom had never before been actively involved in any form of political action group) who believed that their tax burden was disproportionately heavy. These and other forces combined to give rise to a political movement in the form of loosely connected interest groups that succeeded in getting tax control or tax-reducing initiatives on the ballot as part of many local, city, county, and state elections.

■ Countervailing forces, however, were equally evident. Indeed, in terms of these initiatives and referenda, the countervailing forces won the day. Other values besides the desire to lessen the sway of the federal government came into play: the need for taxes to support local school systems, transportation systems, and general infrastructure. Also, a ceiling on taxes did not aid the economic interests of many groups who would benefit from the spending of taxes. These and other forces gave rise to many local and community groups that vigorously opposed the tax initiatives.

Assessing and Projecting Political Change

Any effort to forecast future political change must be built upon a solid understanding of current political change. Thus, the assessment of what is currently taking place in the political arena is a sine qua non to developing projections of what is likely to transpire. We emphasize this point because of the lead times that are necessarily involved in almost all political change.

As in the other environmental segments, our emphasis is upon asking the right questions as the cornerstone in the assessment and projection of political change. Because of the linkage between value change and political change, the questions we present here are largely similar to those addressed in the context of assessing and projecting value change:

1. What are the focal political trends or patterns?
2. What are the indicators of the political change?
3. How compatible is the change with other political change?
4. How compatible is the change with current value change?
5. What groups are manifesting and propagating the change?
6. Where is the change in the evolution of the issue?
7. What other groups might support or oppose the change?

8. What resources are available to the protagonists and antagonists of the change?

9. What costs and benefits flow from the change, and to whom do they flow?

10. What forces are driving the political change?

11. What events might most significantly expedite or retard the change?

12. What time pattern is likely as the change unfolds or peters out?

Because of the peculiarities of the political arena, a few of the questions merit brief comments.

Compatibility with other political change (question 3) emphasizes the connectedness among political changes. For example, governmental initiatives tend to appear in clusters: proposals to trim the federal deficit, related efforts to eliminate regulations, and so on. Local and state-sponsored initiatives and referenda such as the previously discussed tax proposals also tend to appear in clusters. Also important is noting that compatibility with some currents of prevailing political sentiments and change is not sufficient to guarantee success for the efforts of the sponsoring interest group or groups.

Change in the evolution of an issue (question 6) raises one important point: issue life cycles. Political issues tend to follow a life cycle in terms of their presence on society's political landscape: they emerge slowly, then become publicly visible as they receive attention from the media, social activists, and political representatives, then evolve into public policy debate in and around the legislature, finally (in many cases) resulting in legislation or actions (or both) by the executive arm of government. Following this sequence, issues rise and fall from society's political agenda.

ASSESSMENT: DERIVING IMPLICATIONS

A concern with the political segment of the macroenvironment reinforces the notion that firms operate within a political economy. For strategists to think only about the competitive context of the marketplace is simply not enough. The economy as a complex of marketplaces is influenced by political forces. Stated differently, a firm is confronted by political demands or claims as well as by economic or market demands. By the word *claims* we mean the demands placed upon a firm by individuals or groups outside of the firm (claimants) who are in a position to directly or indirectly influence the firm.

These individuals and groups are frequently referred to as the firm's stakeholders.

Impact on Strategy

Stakeholders' demands may have direct impact at both the industry and the individual firm levels. In the last few years, for example, many different types of external stakeholders or interest groups have placed demands upon an entire industry or upon individual firms to withdraw products from the marketplace, to not pursue specific types of product development, to augment or limit certain product features, to cease particular forms of advertising and promotion, to take on minority contractors, and to refrain from doing business in various parts of the world.

Many firms have been confronted with product-related demands:

■ During the mid- and late 1970s, the manufacturers of infant formula were besieged by demands from religious groups, health care experts, and local community leaders in many Third World countries to cease promoting infant formula as an alternative to breast feeding. Some of these groups requested the manufacturers to stop entirely the sales of their products in Third World countries.

■ In the late 1970s and early 1980s, biotechnology firms found themselves confronting demands from groups of scientists, scientific and social organizations, and political representatives either to agree to a moratorium of biotechnology research or to desist entirely from this kind of research.

Many stakeholder groups have also focused their efforts on changing the nature and composition of firms' products and services.

■ Credit card companies are currently facing demands from a number of consumer groups and other public interest groups that they lower their interest charges. These groups contend that credit card companies have not lowered the rate of interest they charge in line with other interest rate declines and the decline in the inflation rate.

How firms compete against each other has also been the focus of stakeholder demands:

■ Over the last few years, a number of parent, education, and professional groups have endeavored to inhibit breakfast cereal manufacturers and some childrens' toy manufacturers from advertising their products on television.

■ A number of minority groups and organizations have implemented a well-orchestrated campaign, including product boycotts, protests outside company premises, and direct mail activities, in order to get beer companies to more actively provide distributorships to minorities.

As evidenced in the infant formula example noted previously, many stakeholder groups have taken issue with the foreign operations of many U.S. firms.

■ The demands of student, consumer, labor, religious, and community groups that U.S. firms withdraw from South Africa have received widespread publicity in the last five years.

■ Labor organizations have directed specific demands at many U.S. firms that they close down existing foreign plants or that they not build foreign plants (or both) because these plants are perceived to result in loss of jobs for American workers.

The prior examples indicate the breadth of the strategy implications that can result from stakeholder demands that are directly targeted at industries or individual firms. Stakeholders can also strengthen their direct demands upon industries or individual firms (or both) by working (indirectly) through third parties such as the legislature, regulatory agencies, and the courts.

Developing a Political Strategy

The inevitability of stakeholder demands means that firms have little choice but to develop a political strategy, that is, a set of actions designed to anticipate, respond to, and manage stakeholder demands. The following questions provide an analytical framework to assess the implications of political change for a firm's strategies and to develop an appropriate political strategy.

Who Are the Firm's Current Claimants?

This question requires the firm to identify its stakeholders. For many firms, this question will generate a long list of individuals and groups who have placed claims on the organization: customer groups, social action groups, community groups, labor groups, governmental agencies, church groups, and so on.

What Groups Are Likely to be Future Claimants?

This question forces the organization to go beyond merely projecting political change to identifying what claimants are likely to evolve from that change. Some of these emerging claimants may not be current claimants.

What Are the Claims of These Groups?

Current and future claimants may place an array of diverse and conflictual demands upon an organization. In answering this question, many organizations have been greatly surprised by the extent and variety of the demands they confront.

How Can These Claims Affect the Firm's Current and Potential Strategies?

The purpose of this analysis is not just to identify claimants and their claims but also to determine how they might impact the firm's strategies. Here the firm must ask the types of questions that have been posed in discussing the implications of analysis in the other environmental segments.

How Can the Organization Build Relationships with Claimants to Further Its Strategic Goals?

Analysis of the political environment can also be used by a firm to better anticipate and manage its relationships with claimants. The implication here is that strategic behavior is not confined to the firm's actions in the competitive marketplace but also includes its actions in the political arena.

The previous set of questions deals with the demands of claimants—those in a position to place demands directly and, to a lesser extent, indirectly on the firm. Political analysis, however, may bring up implications that go beyond the demands of claimants. These broader implications stem from the systems view of the macroenvironment as discussed in Chapter 2. For example, political change affects many aspects of the economy, directly impacts regulatory change, and often plays a major role in shaping change in social values. Thus, the indirect impacts need to be investigated for their implications on a firm's strategies.

Linking Political and Product-Market Strategy

Anticipation of and response to political change (in the form of changing stakeholder demands) must be linked to the firm's product-market strategies. Otherwise the two types of strategy may be at odds with each other. Moreover, the benefits of ensuring that the two types of strategy support each other can be enormous. This normally requires that the political strategy be proactive rather than simply a response to political (or other) changes as they occur. For example:

■ Citicorp, one of the major U.S. banking conglomerates, had been trying for years to start full-service banking in a number of states. Under Maryland law, out-of-state banks could only provide credit card services and were barred from advertising and other marketing activities. Recognizing that the state government was the key stakeholder vis-à-vis its goal of extending its product offering in the state of Maryland, Citibank offered to build a major credit card operation in the state that would entail approximately one thousand white-collar jobs and further offered $1 million in cash for the property. As a result, Citibank has become the first out-of-state bank to be allowed to offer certain product options in Maryland.

SUMMARY

Political change can be viewed as the changing nature of claimants or stakeholders and the demands they place, directly and indirectly, upon industries and individual firms. Some of these demands may be temporary; others may be much more long-lived. The prevalence of these demands necessitates that organizations develop and execute political strategies to facilitate and augment their product-market or economic strategies.

10

The Regulatory Milieu

The regulatory segment of the environment receives considerable attention from the business community; yet, it is also frequently not well understood. Who regulates, how they regulate, and how regulatory processes work are questions that many people inside and outside of business find difficult to answer.

Defining the Regulatory Arena

The regulatory environment consists of a body of laws and regulations that directly or indirectly affect the management of business enterprises and of a set of institutions that administer, implement, enforce, and adjudicate these laws and regulations. The regulatory environment is much more focused and organized than the political milieu: the institutional arena is much more clear-cut, and the relevant processes and procedures are much more prescribed. Yet, tremendous heterogeneity exists in the structure, roles, and functions of regulatory agencies and in the means by which they regulate.

Regulatory Institutions

At the national level, almost every federal agency regulates to some extent. Using a broad conception of regulatory activity, a study conducted by the Office of Management and Budget found that regulatory matters of one kind or another were handled by all of the cabinet departments except the State Department. More broadly, in a January 1977 report, the Senate Governmental Affairs Committee defined a (federal) regulatory agency as "one which (1) has decision making authority, (2) establishes standards or guidelines conferring benefits and imposing restrictions on business conduct, (3) operates principally in the sphere of domestic business activity, (4) has its head and/or members appointed by the president . . . and (5) has its legal procedures generally governed by the Administrative Procedure Act."

Within the scope of this broad definition, the composition and functions of regulatory agencies vary widely.

- Some agencies are headed by a single administrator and located within an executive department (such as the Federal Aviation Administration in the Department of Transportation). Other agencies are independent commissions composed of several commissioners and a chairperson that do not report directly to the executive and legislative branches (for example, the Securities and Exchange Commission, the Federal Trade Commission, the Federal Communications Commission, and the Interstate Commerce Commission).

Regulations are not the preserve of federal institutions. Many state, city, and local governmental institutions also issue, administer, enforce, and adjudicate regulations that affect many aspects of business.

The judicial system or courts constitute a separate though integral component of regulatory institutions. The courts are frequently asked to arbitrate in regulatory disputes and may on occasion initiate regulatory processes.

Types of Regulations

Regulations are typically divided into two general categories (Weidenbaum 1981). First, the traditional, or "older," form of regulation: regulation that is usually aimed at specific industries and pursues essentially economic objectives.

- Much of the regulatory activity of the early (i.e., before 1960) independent commissions falls into this broad category—for example, the Food and Drug Administration's regulations pertaining to the food and drug industries, the Federal Energy Regulatory Commission's regulations pertaining to the energy industry, and the Federal Maritime Commission's regulations pertaining to the maritime industry.

The second general category of regulation is the "new" form of regulation: regulation that cuts across industry boundaries and pursues noneconomic or social objectives.

■ This type of regulation pertains to, for example, product specifications, procedures in the work place designed for industrial safety, environmentally acceptable production, acceptable working conditions, pay conditions, and so on. Examples of agencies that administer this type of regulation include the Consumer Product Safety Commission, the Environmental Protection Agency, and the Occupational Safety and Health Administration.

Regulatory Means

Regulatory agencies use a variety of means to regulate: (1) rate making; (2) standard setting—agencies set performance standards that require the achievement of certain goals (e.g., reducing auto emissions, establishing work safety standards) without specifying how they are to be reached; (3) information disclosure requirements—industries are required to provide full disclosure of the dangers or possible problems of a product, rather than banning it entirely; and (4) economic incentives—economic incentives, including taxes and penalties for noncompliance, are used to spur and deter certain business behaviors and activities.

REGULATORY CHANGE

The regulatory arena has been marked by considerable change in the last twenty years. Much regulatory change is continuing to take place, and there is little doubt that it will continue. As we shall see later in this chapter, this change is the consequence of change in the other environmental segments, particularly in the economic and political environments.

Increase in the Volume of Regulations. Regulatory change is perhaps most easily exemplified in the increasing volume of regulations that appear every year. The most frequently noted proxy measure of the annual increase in the volume of regulations is the number of pages in the *Federal Register* —which records the proposal of new regulations on a daily basis—a number that continues to increase every year.

Increase in Social Regulations. The most significant aspect of the increase in the volume of regulations has been the dramatic increase in social regulations. The late 1960s and 1970s were marked by an explosion in the new regulations, both the creation of new sets of regulations and the extension of regulations already in existence.

Creation of New Regulatory Agencies. The rapid explosion of new regulations has resulted in the creation of a stream of new regulatory agencies. For example:

- Seven new agencies were created in the early 1970s, including the Environmental Protection Agency, the Consumer Product Safety Commission, and the Occupational Safety and Health Administration.

Deregulation of Old Regulations. The last decade has seen a continued effort on the part of many interest groups to deregulate many industries—that is, take some of the traditional regulations off the statute books. Some degree of deregulation has occurred in the airline, communications, banking, securities, and transportation industries.

Changing Emphasis in the Implementation of Regulations. As noted earlier, regulatory agencies often have considerable discretion in the implementation and application of regulations. Thus, change can and does take place in the scope of application of regulations, the degree of specification in standards, and the intensity with which regulations are enforced. For example:

- The Antitrust Division of the Justice Department has recently relaxed the criteria by which it chooses to prosecute firms for violation of the antitrust laws. This is much more the case in the context of vertical rather than horizontal mergers. On the other hand, the Securities and Exchange Commission has recently tightened the criteria used to determine whether it should investigate the existence of insider trading. A number of agencies have recently changed the specifications in the standards previously imposed as part of the implementation of particular regulations. The Consumer Product Safety Commission has issued new standards pertaining to safety with regard to some product types. Also, the intensity with which regulations are enforced may vary from time to time.

Some agencies under the Reagan administration—for example, the Environmental Protection Agency and the Federal Trade Commission—have, by their own admission, relaxed the zeal with which they carry out the enforcement of some regulations.

SCANNING

As in each other environmental segment, scanning in the regulatory segment involves searching for recent and emerging change and for precursors of imminent and longer-term change.

Scanning for recent regulatory change involves focusing upon such action indicators as the adoption of new regulations, proposed modifications to existing regulations, elimination of regulations (deregulation), change in the area of application of regulations, and change in the intensity or commitment of agencies to specific regulations.

Scanning for emergent or imminent regulatory change may involve searching for indicators such as agency initiatives or investigations, congressional mandates (e.g., proposed legislation may mandate the promulgation of new rules), judicial directives (e.g., courts are often asked to enforce rulemaking deadlines or requirements), public petitions (in which petitioners try to show that a factual situation exists that justifies, or even requires, rulemaking under a particular statute), other agencies' actions or initiatives, agencies' advisory committee proposals, and internal agency studies and activities.

Scanning for longer-term regulatory change involves scanning and monitoring the other environmental segments as discussed in previous segment chapters. This is a topic to which we shall return in discussing precursors of regulatory change.

Many key secondary sources of data for scanning recent and emerging regulatory change reside within the regulatory arena: the *Federal Register;* the varied published outputs of each regulatory agency, such as reports to congressional committees; notice of hearings; and responses to external requests for information (these are discussed in much more detail under "monitoring"). The process of scanning, however, is greatly facilitated by the existence of a large number of governmental and nongovernmental services and organizations that specialize in tracking and analyzing regulatory activity. Many of these organizations issue regular reports and analyses of what is happening in the regulatory arena. Some of these entities address the regulatory arena in general (e.g., the *Congressional Quarterly Weekly Report,* the *Digest of Public General Bills*), while others focus their efforts upon specific types of regulation (taxation, environmental protection, and so on) or industries (securities, communications, transportation, and so on). Secondary data sources outside the regulatory arena include industry and trade press (these publications typically carry reports and analyses of regulatory activity pertaining to particular industries), the publications of professional associations (e.g., the American Marketing Association), and an almost endless number of weekly, monthly, quarterly, semiannual and annual newsletters, journals, and magazines that specialize in political and regulatory affairs or give them extensive coverage. Many of these publications also specialize in particular types of regulations or industry contexts.

Precursors of Regulatory Change

Regulatory change is usually the end product of change in the other environmental segments, particularly the social, political, and economic environments. Thus, precursors of longer-term regulatory change can be found outside the regulatory arena before laws and regulations are enacted by the political process or before regulatory agencies enact change on their own initiative.

Since laws and regulations are the product of the political environment, the most immediate precursors of much regulatory change can be found in the political arena, especially in the legislative process. Careful scanning and monitoring of the legislative process indicates potential regulatory change in the form of proposed new regulations, deregulation, or modification of existing regulations. The indicators or signals that serve as precursors are the action points and issues in the legislative process discussed in the previous chapter, such as proposed legislation, committee hearings, and so on. The executive branch's participation in the political process also often offers indicators of likely regulatory change: statements by the president or other senior officials indicating the administration's attitude toward regulation in general or specific pieces of regulation, and statements and actions of departments indicating the need for regulatory change.

Because activity in the legislative process is consequent to political activity outside the legislature, early warning signals of potential regulatory change can be gleaned by scanning and monitoring the initial phases of the political process: the emergence of social action groups, the positions of elite groups or opinion leaders, the emergence of coalitions among interest groups, and so on. Indeed, the introduction of new regulations or the withdrawal of existing regulations is often a stated goal of many groups participating in the political process.

As noted in the discussion of political change, the importance of single events as indicators of potential regulatory change also needs to be emphasized. Scanning efforts need to be attuned to the search for these events or happenings. For example:

■ Some technology-related events have initiated or spurred regulatory activity: the sale of technology to unfriendly foreign governments, revelations about industrial espionage on the part of some firms, product failures, and so on. Major political events may also signal potential regulatory change: election results, major policy announcements, and mass political demonstrations.

It follows from the prior discussion that the data sources for scanning for precursors or early signals of regulatory change reside primarily outside of the regulatory arena. The indicators of social, political, technological, and economic change as discussed in the previous environmental segment chapters may also be viewed as indicators of potential regulatory change at a later time. The data sources for scanning recent and current regulatory change, noted earlier, may be viewed as sources of precursors or signals of more immediate or imminent regulatory change. As we shall see in the discussion of monitoring, the decision-making process within regulatory agencies can be tracked and used to generate indicators of regulatory change.

MONITORING

Monitoring regulatory change involves tracking (1) indicators or precursors of potential regulatory change that reside outside the regulatory arena and (2) the regulatory (i.e., decision-making) process within regulatory agencies.

Monitoring the early indicators of potential regulatory change largely involves monitoring events and trends in the other environmental segments, with particular attention to the political process. Since these have been discussed in previous chapters, we devote our attention to monitoring the regulatory process within regulatory agencies.

For monitoring purposes, the decision-making process within regulatory agencies can be viewed as two sequential sets of activities: quasi-legislative (or rulemaking) and quasi-judicial (or adjudicatory) processes or functions. For example:

■ When the Civil Aeronautics Board (CAB) promulgated a rule asserting its primary jurisdiction over airspace for both civil and military purposes, it was exercising its quasi-legislative or rulemaking power. When it decided which of several commercial airlines should be awarded a specific airline route, it was exercising quasi-judicial or adjudicatory power. Similarly, the Federal Communications Commission is engaged in rulemaking when it establishes criteria to evaluate competing claims for a television license, and it is exercising its adjudicatory function when it chooses among claims and awards a license.

These rulemaking and adjudicatory functions greatly facilitate monitoring because the 1946 Administrative Procedure Act (APA) requires agencies to follow a strict format with regard to their administration in terms of notice, hearings, procedures, evidence, oral argument, and formal judicial decision. More recently, specific congressional mandates, as part of legislative packages and executive orders imposing procedural requirements on rulemaking by executive branch agencies, go far beyond the procedures required by the APA.

Because of the variety of procedural requirements imposed on agencies by congressional statutes and executive orders, generalization about these procedures must be treated with caution. However, the different procedures involved in regulatory decision-making processes are commonly characterized as formal rulemaking, informal rulemaking, formal adjudication, and informal adjudication.

Formal rulemaking is much less widely used than informal rulemaking. It applies mostly to rate-making cases and other narrow categories of regulatory proceedings. Formal rulemaking is triggered by a statute other than the APA that requires rules to be made on the record after opportunity for an agency hearing. If formal rulemaking is required, then the rulemaking proceedings must be conducted following the trial-type or adversary procedures set forth in sections 556 and 557 of the APA. Table 10.1 summarizes the key characteristics of formal rulemaking.

Informal or "notice and comment" rulemaking follows a different procedure, as shown in Figure 10.1. The "notice and comment" label derives from the requirements for (1) publication of a notice of

**Table 10.1   Some Key Characteristics
of Formal, or "On-the-Record," Rulemaking**

1.   Regulatory agency must support its proposed rule with substantial evidence in an exclusive rulemaking record.

2.   The agency must hold an oral hearing presided over by agency members or an administrative law judge.

3.   The parties to the rulemaking must be allowed to submit rebuttal evidence and conduct such cross-examination as may be required for a full and true disclosure of the facts.

4.   There must be no ex parte communication with the decision maker.

5.   The parties to the rulemaking must be allowed to submit proposed findings and conclusions and present exceptions to the initial or recommended decisions of subordinate agency employees or to tentative agency decisions.

proposed rulemaking in the *Federal Register,* (2) opportunity for public participation in the rulemaking by submission of written comments, and (3) publication of a final rule and accompanying statement of basis and purpose in the *Federal Register* not less than thirty days before its effective date. We stress that these requirements are the procedural floor below which an agency may not go in prescribing procedures for a particular rulemaking.

The impact of executive orders and congressional mandates on regulatory rulemaking is shown in Figures 10.2 and 10.3, respectively. The steps or procedures imposed on regulatory agencies as shown in these figures provide a basis for monitoring agencies' efforts to introduce and establish new rules.

FORECASTING

Forces Driving Regulatory Change

Evident from the previous discussion of scanning and monitoring is that in forecasting short-term and medium-term regulatory change,

Figure 10.1   Rulemaking Under Section 553 of the APA and the Regulatory Flexibility Act *

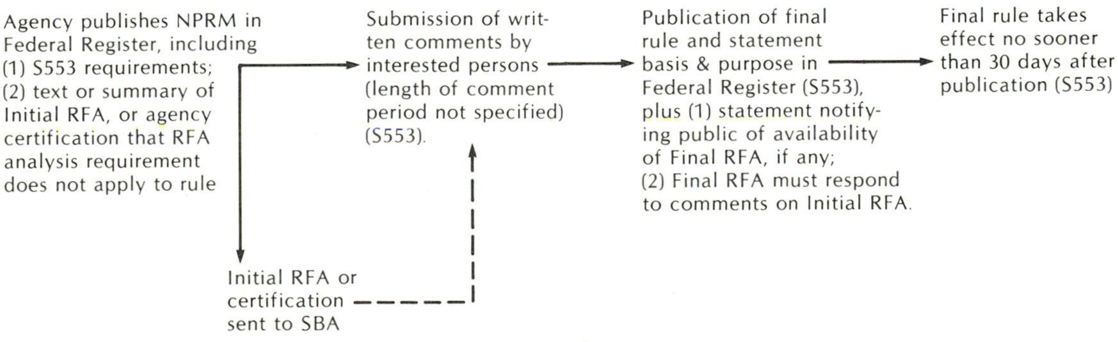

Agency publishes NPRM in Federal Register, including (1) S553 requirements; (2) text or summary of Initial RFA, or agency certification that RFA analysis requirement does not apply to rule

Submission of written comments by interested persons (length of comment period not specified) (S553).

Publication of final rule and statement basis & purpose in Federal Register (S553), plus (1) statement notifying public of availability of Final RFA, if any; (2) Final RFA must respond to comments on Initial RFA.

Final rule takes effect no sooner than 30 days after publication (S553)

Initial RFA or certification sent to SBA

Notes: NPRM = notice of proposed rulemaking: F.R. = Federal Register;
IRIA = initial regulatory impact analysis; FRIA = final regulatory impact analysis;
OMB = Office of Management and Budget.

*Chart shows normal pathway for rulemaking under these statutes. Options available if exceptions apply to the rulemaking are not included.

*Figure 10.2 Rulemaking Under Executive
Order No. 12,291 and Section 553 of the APA* [1]

1. For major rule, agency submits NPRM and IRIA to OMB sixty days before F.R. publication. For nonmajor rule, to OMB ten days before publication. → [Agency must refrain from publishing NPRM for sixty days, if major, or ten days, if nonmajor, or until OMB review completed.] → 2. NPRM published, including (1) S553 requirements; (2) major/nonmajor determination, with reasons; (3) summary or text of IRIA for major rule. → 3. Period for receipt of written comments (length not specified) (S553). →

4. Agency takes final action. For final rule, must be "substantial support" in record for factual conclusions (E.O.). → 5. For major rule, agency submits rule and FRIA to OMB thirty days before F.R. publication. For nonmajor rule, to OMB ten days before publication. → [Agency must refrain from publishing rule for thirty days, if major, or ten days, if nonmajor, or until OMB review completed.] → 6. Publication of final rule, with concise statement of basis and purpose (S553). If major rule must include FRIA or notice of availability. → 7. Rule takes effect no sooner than thirty days after publication (S553).

Notes: NPRM = notice of proposed rulemaking; F.R. = Federal Register; IRIA = initial regulatory impact analysis; FRIA = final regulatory impact analysis; OMB = Office of Management and Budget.

[1] Chart shows normal pathway for rulemaking under these laws. Options available if exceptions apply to rulemaking are not included.

*Figure 10.3 Rulemaking Subject to the Paperwork
Reduction Act and Section 553 of the APA* [1]

1. Agency submits collection of information requirements in rule to OMB for review not later than day NPRM is published. → 2. NPRM published in F.R., including S553 requirements; notice that OMB paperwork review requested and that public may submit paperwork comments to OMB desk officer. → 3. Opportunity for submission of written comments (S553). OMB has sixty days to file paperwork comments or lose right to disapprove requirements. OMB comments must be placed in rulemaking record.

→ 4. Agency takes final action. Final rule must be published in F.R. with concise statement of basis and purpose (S553); must include response to OMB paperwork comments. → 5. Rule takes effect no sooner than thirty days after publication (S553). However, collection of information requirements may be disapproved by OMB within sixty days after publication.[2] OMB can disapprove if agency response to paperwork comments if "unreasonable" and OMB finds collection of information requirement "unnecessary" for agency functions.

Notes: NPRM = notice of proposed rulemaking; F.R. = Federal Register; OMB = Office of Management and Budget.

[1] Chart shows normal pathway for rulemaking under these statutes. Options available if exceptions apply to rulemaking are not included.

[2] However, OMB approval of collection of information requirements will usually be obtained prior to publication.

the forces operating within the regulatory and political arenas are critical. For short-term regulatory change, regulatory forces such as the commitment of key units and personnel within the relevant agency, recent regulatory actions by the relevant agency or other agencies, and decisions emanating from the judicial system indicate likely regulatory actions.

Note also that other forces affecting shorter-run regulatory change may also be revealed in the procedures inherent in the regulatory arena: the positions of interest groups as evidenced in submissions as part of the rulemaking and adjudication procedures; position statements by the executive branch representatives; and opinions and positions of the legislative branch as part of the oversight process, as part of representations to individual agencies, or as simply the views of members of the legislature.

Change in the regulatory arena, however, does not occur autonomously; it is heavily influenced by forces in the other environmental segments, particularly the political arena.

Politics. The political arena in the form of social movements and legislative change provides much of the impetus for regulatory change, as we have emphasized throughout this chapter.

Values. Value change, as we have noted in previous chapters, provides much of the impetus for political change and thus regulatory change.

Demographics and Life-Styles. Demographic and life-style change may also spur regulatory change. The aging of the population has contributed to a major increase in regulatory concern with the welfare and protection of senior citizens.

Economics. Economic change also contributes to change in regulations. Structural change has led to a number of new regulatory initiatives. For example, merger and takeover booms have given rise to regulations to control such activity.

Assessing and Projecting Regulatory Change

The following are some key questions an analyst should ask in assessing and projecting regulatory change.

What Is the Nature of the Regulatory Change?

Specifying the type of regulatory change involved is important. Whether it is the addition or deletion of a regulatory agency, the creation of a set of regulations, or the abolishment of a set of regulations, change in existing rules or rulemaking procedures, change in standards, or change in the commitment of agencies to enforce rules or standards affects the timing of change, its scope, and implications for an individual firm or industry.

Is the Change Congruent With Other Regulatory Change?

This question compels consideration of whether the change is an isolated regulatory trend or pattern, or whether it is consistent with other ongoing regulatory change. To the extent that the latter is true, the change is more likely to occur. For example, patterns of deregulation that began under the Carter presidency have been accelerated and extended under the Reagan presidency. Frequently, changes initiated or anticipated within an individual agency may be in line with change already implemented by the agency. For example, some rule changes that some observers speculate the FCC (Federal Communications Commission) will initiate seem to be consistent with recent changes introduced by the agency. Where the potential change represents a break from previous regulatory trends (e.g., a relaxation of rules that had previously been stringently enforced or changes in the criteria applied in the adjudication process), the remaining questions in this section need to be examined especially carefully to assess the forces driving the change.

Who Supports or Opposes the Change?

As noted previously, regulatory change is part of larger sociopolitical change in society. As such, the political forces or interest groups supporting or inhibiting the change need to be carefully assessed. Rarely will general agreement exist in the political milieu as to the desired scope and direction of regulatory change. The following are some key questions to ask in attempting to assess the political dynamics around regulatory change:

1.   What is the position of the executive? The initiative for some regulatory change emanates from the executive branch of government. Particularly important is discerning the level of support or opposition of the president or relevant governmental department for specific regulatory changes.

2.   What is the position of the relevant congressional committees and key representatives? These legislative entities can bring much pressure to bear on regulatory agencies, often (as noted earlier) compelling them to take specific actions.

3.   What groups outside of the legislative and regulatory arenas support and oppose the change? Which interest groups are pushing for change or opposing it, and to what extent are these interests represented in the legislature and executive arm of government?

   ■ For example, some social and political-action-oriented groups, such as some women's and minority groups, now find themselves pushing for regulatory change or maintenance of the status quo, but find that they now have less support in the legislative and executive branches of government than in previous years.

4. What is the position of the courts? The courts may initiate change, enforce regulations, or be used by participants in the regulatory change process to advance or protect their interests.

What Key Events Have Propelled or Might Propel the Change?

Regulatory change often receives major impetus from single events or episodes. For example:

■ Public tragedies or scares (e.g., failure of a nuclear plant, pollution spills, unanticipated side effects of drugs) give rise to social pressure for regulation. Presidential announcements, election results, the appointment of new agency personnel (e.g., new commissioners or agency heads), and judicial decisions are other examples.

What Is the Relevant Agency's Position?

The momentum for regulatory change is sometimes created by the relevant regulatory agency itself. Even if it is not, the agency must carry out the intent of the enabling legislation or judicial directive. Thus, assessing the commitment of the agency to anticipated or emerging regulations is important.

What Is the Relevant Time Line?

Implicit in much of the prior discussion is the time line inherent in regulatory change. Detection of early warning signals or precursors in other environmental segments to actual regulatory change may entail a period of five to ten years. On the other hand, forecasting change over the next year can be accomplished with a lot more certainty: the signals are much clearer, since the driving forces are much more evident.

Consideration of these questions provides the inputs to forming projections of likely regulatory change. In line with the discussion in other segment chapters, the intent of projecting regulatory change is to develop likely scenarios of change so that its impact of strategy development can be detected and managed.

ASSESSMENT: DERIVING IMPLICATIONS

The pervasive impact of the regulatory arena on industries and firms has been given wide prominence in recent years. These impacts arise from both the body of regulations and the regulatory institutions. Three key themes need to be emphasized in this regard. First, regulations and actions of regulatory agencies affect corporate, business, and functional levels of strategy. Second, though regulatory developments are often viewed as a threat to organizations or as constraints on managements' prerogatives, the regulatory arena, like any other segment, may constitute opportunities as well as threats for any organization. Third, influencing regulatory agencies and regulations is part of the political strategies pursued by firms.

Impact on Strategy

Regulations and regulatory changes affect key industry variables: its boundaries, structure, and general expectations, and hence, business-unit strategies.

Regulatory change could affect many of the forces shaping industry structure in myriad ways. Three key areas deserve mention. First, they could influence entry barriers directly or indirectly.

■ Direct influence is probably easily exemplified by such factors as patent protections and expiration. Indirect influence is exemplified in the case of pharmaceutical firms who have to go through a stringent set of product-testing requirements with the FDA (Federal Drug Administration) before they can launch new products. This may take five to seven years, thereby serving as an entry barrier to many new-product-based firms.

Second, regulatory change can influence product features and markets. For example:

■ Some firms have had to pull products off the market when they were deemed unsafe by the Consumer Product Safety Commission. Many children's toys have suffered this fate.

■ The ICC (Interstate Commerce Commission) imposes restrictions of the flow of goods across state lines. The FCC (Federal Communications Commission) places limits on the number of geographic markets that firms owning television stations can serve.

Third, regulatory change may also affect the rules of the game in the competitive arena. For example:

■ With regard to price competition, firms are prohibited from colluding to fix prices under a variety of regulations enforced by the FTC (Federal Trade Commission) and a variety of regulations pertaining to fair trade pricing. With regard to nonprice competition, a long list of regulations pertain to how firms may compete against each other in advertising (e.g., truth in advertising), warranties (e.g., warranties must meet certain conditions), and so on.

The influence of regulatory change on industry boundaries has been visible in recent years, especially in the wake of deregulation. When viewed in conjunction with technological change, regulatory change often brings about the merging of industry boundaries.

■ A recent example is the change taking place in the banking industry. Traditionally, banking, insurance, and brokerage businesses were deemed separate industries. In the wake of regulatory and technological changes, however, these traditional industry definitions have given way to a new definition: financial services industry.

Finally, the degree of certainty or uncertainty in the regulatory arena has a lot of influence on the general expectations about the industry and volatility in such expectations.

Industry-level factors affect most competitors. In turn, they affect business-level strategies of the firm. Given the plethora of examples provided in this chapter, this is a point that will not be dwelt on. Highlighting the influence on corporate-level and functional strategies is crucial, however.

At the corporate level, regulations may affect patterns of diversification.

■ Market dominance is prohibited for many firms because of the antitrust statutes, which are enforced by the Antitrust Division of the Justice Department. The pursuit of growth goals through mergers and acquisitions must also be sanctioned by the Justice Department and the FTC (Federal Trade Commission) in many instances. Even firms' profitability goals may be influenced by regulations.

Similarly, regulations permeate and often dramatically impact how an organization carries out its various functions (e.g., marketing, manufacturing, human resources, and finance). For example:

■ Human resource management is affected by regulations emanating from the Equal Employment Opportunity Commission, the Occupational Safety and Health Administration, the National Labor Relations Board, and the Labor Department's Employment Standards Administration. In other words, the internal operations of any firm are not immune to regulatory impact.

The types of linkages noted earlier between strategic management and regulatory change can be summarized in the following questions. The questions may refer to current or anticipated change.

1. How will the change affect product choice?
   Our current products
   Products we may wish to offer

2. How will the change affect market choice?
   Our current markets
   New markets

3. How will the change affect modes of competition?
   How we compete now

How we may wish to compete

4. How will the change affect patterns of diversification and profit-ability goals?

Current goals
Future goals

5. How will the change affect operations?

Which aspects of current operations
Which aspects of future operations
How can these operations impacts affect the strategy issues not-ed in 1–4

Strategic Action: Creating Opportunities Out of Regulations

Regulatory change frequently gives rise to myriad product-market opportunities. Consider the following examples:

■ The creation of environmental protection regulations in the past fifteen years has led to a multibillion dollar industry in pollution controls and other means of cleaning and protecting the physical environment. Deregulation opens up many product and market opportunities, as witnessed by the change in the banking, communications, airline, and transportation industries in the past five years. Some firms have taken advantage of this change; others have been hurt by it, in part through their inaction.

Firms need not and do not simply wait for regulations to happen and then respond; they anticipate them and take proactive action. Even after regulations do take place, firms can still take proactive action: they can turn them into opportunities. For example:

■ A few banks were ready to take immediate action as soon as some regulations inhibiting interstate banking were removed.

■ Many firms have exploited consumer protection regulations to advertise to consumers that they have gone further than the regulations require to develop an enhanced image in consumers' minds. These firms viewed these regulations as opportunities rather than as threats.

Finally, regulatory change often provides avenues for taking action against competitors: erecting entry barriers or delaying entry or competitive moves, signaling, and in some cases gathering competitive intelligence.

■ In the judicial arena, patent suits are often filed either to prevent entry or to delay entry. Lawsuits often serve as signaling devices. Firms sometimes file suit against competitors to gather competitive intelligence, especially in cases in which technology is highly protected or data about market share movements are difficult to obtain.

The key issue to note here is that the regulatory arena provides many opportunities in the form of new product-market choices, competitive moves, and signaling. These regulations need not be considered only as constraints on managerial discretion.

Political Action in the Regulatory Arena

In keeping with the potential for proactive actions in the marketplace, many firms enact highly activist political strategies toward regulatory agencies and regulatory issues. In other words, firms do not merely react to the rules, standards, and norms promulgated by regulatory agencies. They seek to shape the rules, standards, and norms as they are being created by agencies; they seek to replace rules, standards, and norms they dislike, and to retain rules, standards, and norms they favor; and finally, they seek to have these interpreted in ways they prefer.

To attain these goals, firms participate in the regulatory process in all the phases shown in Figures 10.1 through 10.3 and discussed under "Monitoring." For example:

■ Many firms have resorted to the courts to challenge and change regulations and to compel agencies to enforce existing regulations. Zenith Corporation has engaged in a fifteen-year-long battle in the courts to bring Japanese firms to task for violating "dumping" regulations (i.e., selling television sets in the U.S. market below cost).

These activities are part of political strategies that come into play in the political segment in general. (For a more detailed discussion, see the MacMillan and Jones volume in this series.)

SUMMARY

The regulatory arena is more structured and focused than the political arena: it is easier to scan and monitor. This chapter briefly discussed some of the major forms of regulatory change and the processes involved in the regulatory arena. Finally, the chapter outlined how firms can create opportunities in the regulatory arena, in addition to its influence on various levels of strategies.

11

Integration of Environmental Segments

In the previous seven chapters, we outlined an approach to the analysis of the major segments of the macroenvironment: demographics, life-styles, social values, technology, the economy, politics, and regulation. In this chapter, we provide a framework of analysis so that the outputs of analysis of the individual environmental segments may be integrated. The purpose of this integration is to identify the issues pertaining to the macroenvironment that need to be addressed by an organization during strategy formulation and implementation.

In line with the terminology developed in Chapter 3, this chapter begins our treatment of the assessment phase in environmental analysis. The identification and assessment of issues is the focus of this chapter. The next chapter is concerned with the integration of environmental analysis into strategy analysis.

The scheme of this chapter is as follows. First, we consider the objectives of integrating analysis across environmental segments and the reasons why this integration is important. Second, we introduce the key ideas that guide the discussion in this chapter. Third, we present a framework for integrating across environmental segments. Finally, we present a set of key questions that need to be addressed by firms engaged in this analysis.

OBJECTIVES OF INTEGRATING
ANALYSIS ACROSS ENVIRONMENTAL SEGMENTS

The following are the four major objectives in integrating the analysis conducted within the environmental segments.

1.   To identify issues generated by the discernible trends and patterns in each segment. Analysis of the segments often reveals a multitude of trends and patterns. From the perspective of a firm, however, trends and patterns assume importance only to the extent that they affect the strategies of the firm as it interacts with its many stakeholders and publics. That is, trends and patterns assume importance when they have implications for the strategic actions of the firm; by themselves they have relatively little significance, though they may be intrinsically interesting.

2.   To discover relationships among trends and patterns across various environmental segments. As noted in the discussion of the individual environmental segments, often trends and patterns in different segments that may appear disparate and unconnected may over time join together to generate critical issues for an organization. Some of these joint effects may come about by the actions of agents in the environment, but they may also be brought about by the actions of a firm. They therefore present opportunities and threats that may be missed if the different environmental segments are treated in isolation of each other.

3.   To distinguish between trends and patterns that have current and future implications. Trends and patterns have different life spans. Some may have implications for the current operating environment of the organization, whereas others may necessitate action at some point in the future.

4.   To keep environmental analysis manageable. Any organization's capacity to identify and assess issues is constrained by its resources and limited managerial time. If the organization attempts to handle too many issues, it can become bogged down in the analysis, with the result that organizational action becomes much less likely. Identifying the few key issues that need to be tackled is considerably more difficult than generating a whole host of issues (King and Cleland 1978). Such identification requires a fairly exhaustive analysis and screening of discernible trends and patterns.

CONCEPTUAL NOTIONS UNDERLYING INTEGRATION

A number of key conceptual notions underlie and facilitate integration across the environmental segments.

A General Sequence of Analysis

The general sequence of analysis that underlies the identification of issues within and across environmental segments can be portrayed as follows:

Trends ———▶ Patterns ———▶ Issues

Analysis of each environmental segment yields a number of discernible and emerging trends and patterns. A number of trends within a specific segment or across segments may be interpreted as constituting a pattern.

These trends and patterns are related in a hierarchic fashion, as shown in Figure 11.1 and as illustrated in the following example:

■ The life-styles arena has a number of distinct trends: (1) increasing numbers of people are engaged in athletic activities (e.g., jogging, tennis); (2) increasing numbers of people are attending fitness classes; (3) the number of people who smoke is declining; (4) increasing numbers of consumers are switching to diet foods and drinks. Together, the trends portray a pattern: increased health consciousness in a large segment of the population.

Note that as one moves from trends to patterns, the environmental changes become imbued with meaning as trends that may have appeared unrelated suddenly fall into place as parts of a coherent pattern. This is even more so the case as trends across environmental segments are connected. For example:

■ Connections among trends in the political, regulatory, and economic segments of the environment create patterns that may suggest change in the political economy (as opposed to the more narrow economy). Thus, we often speak of a more or less regulated economy.

Also, as we have previously noted, trends provide concrete indices to measure the evolution of patterns over time.

The patterns revealed in the various environmental segments and their interrelationships provide the basis for determining the key

**Figure 11.1 Analytic Hierarchy
Relationship between Trends and Patterns**

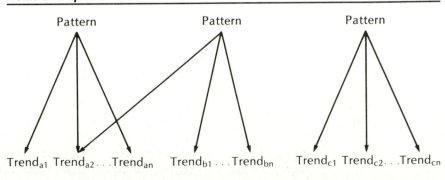

Figure 11.2 Issues: The Interaction of Patterns and Organizational Context

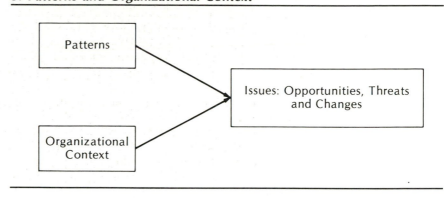

issues to be addressed by the firm. These patterns suggest various issues for the firm depending upon its context. Thus, issues lie at the intersection of environmental patterns and organizational context, as shown in Figure 11.2 and as illustrated in the following example:

■ The pattern of health consciousness noted earlier may suggest different issues for different firms depending upon their context—that is, the business they are in, the strategies they are pursuing, their goals, and their resources. It may open up product development opportunities for frozen food manufacturers, growth opportunities for fitness centers, and may portend legislative pressures for cigarette manufacturers. It may not be important at all for garment manufacturers or automobile makers.

In line with the terminology presented in Chapter 3, identifying trends and patterns reflects the outside-in element of environmental analysis, whereas moving from patterns to issues is essentially an inside-out process.

The Time Frame of Patterns

Patterns of environmental change evolve over time. Patterns exhibit a life cycle, as shown in Table 11.1. In the nascent stage, these patterns are in the embryonic state and will often come into effect only by the actions of various environmental actors or by the firm itself. In this stage, predictability of the development of these patterns is low. As the life cycle moves into the emergent stage, the pattern has come into effect, though the growth rate is difficult to assess and may be under the control of various environmental agents. Once the pattern enters the evolution stage, its evolution is relatively more

Table 11.1 Phases in the Evolution of Patterns

	Stage of Life Cycle			
	Nascent	*Emerging*	*Evolving*	*Stabilizing/ declining*
State	Embryonic	Has emerged	Diffusion	Normal/ac-cepted
Sources of Uncertainty	Forces driving the pattern	Speed of evolution	Relatively cer-tain	
Action Points	Description/ facilitation of emergence	Speed of evolution	Adaptation to pattern	
Implica-tions	Need careful monitoring and further scan-ning	Needs moni-toring	Needs fore-casting	Normal part of doing business
Time Frame of Issues Gen-erated	Long-term	Medium-term	Short-term and current	Current

predictable unless strategic surprises take place. In the fourth stage, or stabilization period, the pattern is accepted as a normal part of the environment.

A critical point here is that the stages in the life cycle of patterns have temporal implications for organizational issues. Identification of nascent patterns generally suggests issues that provide a relatively long time for resolution. The issues generated by emergent patterns will generally need to be tackled in the medium term. Issues created by the identification of patterns in their later stages, or "surprises," may require resolution in the immediate or short-term period.

Interrelationships Among Environmental Segments

As suggested throughout this book, patterns in each environmental segment are invariably related to those in other segments. The inter-relationships among patterns across segments can be discussed from four vantage points.

First, as noted in each of the segment chapters, the forces that drive the evolution of patterns in one segment are often located in other segments. These causal factors need to be understood to monitor and forecast the evolution of a pattern. Analysis of patterns in one segment often sheds light on these forces, and tracking of these forces is facilitated by inputs from other segments.

Second, patterns in one segment may reinforce or decrease the impact of patterns in another segment or in the environment in general. Useful in understanding these linkages is the development

Figure 11.3 Cross-Pattern Impact Matrix:
An Illustration in the Context of Health Care

	Pattern 1 Increasing Health Con-sciousness	Pattern 2 Increasing Cost of Health Care	Pattern 3 Increasing Po-litical Activism	Pattern 4 Research and Technology Advances
Pattern 1 Increasing Health Con-sciousness		May cause health care cost to increase fur-ther	Jointly, may in-crease regulatory pressures in the health field	May accelerate commitment to research to prevent/cure diseases such as cancer
Pattern 2 Increasing Cost of Health Care	May dampen diffusion of health con-sciousness		May cause cost control to be key focus of po-litical activity	May result in channeling of R&D funds into cost contain-ment rather than into find-ing cures for diseases
Pattern 3 Increasing Po-litical Activism	May facilitate diffusion of health con-sciousness as a result of attempt to mobilize polit-ical action	May focus atten-tion on physi-cians', hospitals', and insurance costs, thus facili-tating cost con-tainment		May cause ef-forts to control research and technology de-velopments via regulation
Pattern 4 Research and Technology Advances	Technology de-velopments may heighten health consciousness by increasing awareness of choices	Technology de-velopments may bring down health care costs	Technology de-velopments may give rise to pro-tagonists and an-tagonists	

of a cross-pattern impact matrix, as shown in Figure 11.3. These matrices array into columns and rows the patterns revealed from various segments, so that the analyst can make judgments about the effect of one pattern on another. Further, judgments are also required as to whether two or more patterns jointly lead to a third, as yet undiscovered, pattern. Consider the following examples:

> ■ Patterns in the technology segment suggest that laser technology is increasingly being adopted by hospitals for surgical purposes. A pattern in the economic segment suggests continuing increases in health costs. Many patterns in the life-style and value segments suggest increasing health care consciousness and interest in preventive medicine. These patterns may spur the adoption of laser technology, as it is expected to reduce hospital care costs and greatly facilitate diagnostic tests as an element in preventive medicine.

> ■ Patterns in the life-style and value segments suggest increasing health consciousness on the part of many groups in the population. In conjunction with increased consumer activism in the political segment, these patterns may give rise to a pattern of increased demand for regulation.

In the laser technology example, an existing pattern (the adoption of lasers) is reinforced by a pattern from another segment, whereas in the second example, the two patterns (health consciousness and consumer activism) jointly result in a third pattern, which may not have been discovered or fully understood during analysis of individual segments.

Third, patterns should be analyzed for second-order consequences. These consequences are neither direct nor immediate; rather, they are chains of effects (which have often been described as phenomena analogous to atomic reactions). Second-order consequences may be best illustrated by the problems created by the missionary-induced replacement of stone axes as the primary cutting tools of the Australian Yir Yorunt aborigines:

> ■ Stone axes played important functions in Yir Yorunt life beyond that of cutting wood. The men owned the stone axes, which were symbols of masculinity and respect for elders. The missionaries had distributed the steel axes to men, women and children without discrimination. But the older men, having less trust of missionaries, were not as likely to accept the steel axes. Soon elders of the tribe once highly respected were forced to borrow steel axes from women and younger men. The previous status relationships were thoroughly upset. (Bauer 1969, 15)

Cross-pattern impact matrices may also be constructed to identify potential second-order consequences. This necessitates specifying the conditions under which patterns emerging in one segment may create a chain of effects in other segments.

STEPS INVOLVED IN INTEGRATING SEGMENT ANALYSIS

As illustrated in Figure 11.4, three major steps are involved in the integration of patterns across segments. The basic inputs or raw material for this analysis are the trends and patterns identified in each environmental segment; the outputs of the analysis are strategic issues for the organization. Each of the steps in the analysis is discussed in some detail.

Identification of Patterns Within and Across Segments

The first step in the process is to discern some meaningful patterns across environmental segments from the discrete trends and patterns unearthed from the analysis of each environmental segment. At least three important reasons exist for aggregating environmental segment-specific trends and patterns into meaningful cross-segment patterns. First, drawing meaning from segment-specific trends, taken in isolation from one another, is often difficult; the trends need to

Figure 11.4 Key Steps in Integration of Analysis Across Segments

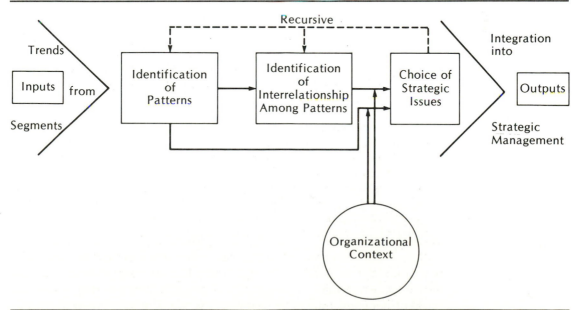

be related to each other so that the analyst does not miss the forest for the trees.

Second, meaningful aggregation of segment-specific trends and patterns into cross-segment patterns reduces the sheer amount of information that needs to handled by the analyst.

Third, cross-segment patterns often facilitate the derivation of action implications far beyond those triggered by segment-specific trends and patterns. A case in point: the megatrends identified by Naisbitt (1982) are the product of integrating the myriad of specific individual trends occurring in the United States. The usefulness of the book derives primarily from the aggregation of these trends into meaningful patterns—ten, in Naisbitt's case—which render relatively unrelated trends into a coherent whole.

The identification of patterns (segment-specific and cross-segment) from trends is an inductive process (Dutton, Fahey, and Narayanan 1983). This inductive process begins in and is facilitated by the scanning phase, as the analyst begins to conceive gestalts of trends taking place or emerging in each environmental segment and as the analyst becomes immersed in the wide variety of data pertaining to each segment. This requires the analyst to be imaginative and sometimes speculative, especially concerning long-term patterns.

Two errors are likely to creep in during the identification of patterns. First, the analyst will quite likely miss a pattern. This could occur because of inadequate scanning: as environmental analysis becomes more inside-out, the errors of omission are likely to be greater. Alternately, this could be a failure of perception and imagination; that is, the analyst may not spend sufficient time reflecting upon the disparate trends and patterns and relating them to one another. The second error is one of commission: the analyst may have invented patterns that have no factual grounding or are fads likely to disappear in the short run. The possibility of these two errors can never be completely eliminated in any environmental analysis. Organizations need to continually ask questions concerning the completeness, surrealism, and linkages among segment-specific trends and patterns in the identified or hypothesized cross-segment patterns.

More specifically, the patterns that are identified or conjectured should be carefully analyzed in order to answer three specific questions.

What Are the Specific Trends That Constitute or Suggest a Pattern?

Delineating a pattern in specific terms is important if it is to be useful for deriving action implications. Hence, each pattern must be described in terms of the specific trends that constitute it. Such a breakdown also enables the analyst to judge whether the patterns are likely to be enduring or faddish, and to continue further monitoring where necessary.

What Forces Drive the Evolution of a Pattern?

Projection of the evolution of patterns is facilitated by recognizing the forces that inhibit or facilitate such evolution. Although trends are indicators that suggest a pattern, they do not explain the reasons why such a pattern exists or may come to be. Typically, as noted in previous chapters, the forces that drive the evolution of patterns in one environmental segment are located in the other segments. The early recognition of these forces not only enables prediction of pattern evolution but also facilitates consideration of interrelationships across the segments. Further, these forces may need continual monitoring in the future, especially for patterns in the early stages of development.

Where Does the Pattern Lie in its Stage of Development?

Judging whether the pattern is nascent, emerging, or already well developed is always important. To do this, the analyst will have to predict the probable evolution of the pattern. Such prediction is necessary to classify the patterns into those that generate short-, medium, and long-run issues for the organization.

Interrelationships among Patterns

The next step in the analysis is to consider the interrelationships among patterns identified in the various segments. As noted in the discussion of the environmental segments, patterns in one segment may reinforce, conflict with, or be unrelated to patterns in other segments. Two steps are involved in this stage of the analysis.

The first step is to consider the secondary consequences of patterns for the other environmental segments. Using impact matrices of the kind presented in Figure 11.3 is useful for considering the impact of each pattern on the other segments. Some of these patterns will be the driving force for the evolution of prospective patterns in the other segments. For example, an emerging computer technology may have implications for life-styles (e.g., allowing more people to choose their place of work) or prospective regulations (e.g., the potential for computer fraud or the invasion of privacy). These secondary consequences are typically contingent upon conditions created by the actions of environmental agents or the firm itself. Thus, in assessing these consequences, three crucial questions need to be posed:

1. What are the possible and likely secondary consequences of a pattern on the other environmental segments?

2. What conditions need to occur for the secondary consequences to ensue?

3. What actions are likely to engender these conditions?

Analysis of the secondary consequences and conditions leading up to them is necessary for the determination of organizational actions, but they also suggest specific conditions that need to be further monitored.

The second step is to consider the mutual impacts among patterns. As noted earlier, the patterns often reinforce or conflict with each other and sometimes generate other patterns not discovered earlier. Cross-impact matrices, as discussed previously, may be constructed to determine the effects of patterns on one another. Considerable skill is required in constructing these matrices, as it is important to specify not only the nature of the impacts but also the forces driving them.

In addition to cross-impact matrices, which are most useful in the short and medium term, scenarios built around alternative futures can be constructed for consideration of the long term. As we shall see in Chapter 13, scenarios bring visible patterns into coherence, thus facilitating the derivation of action implications.

Choice of Strategic Issues

As we have emphasized previously, not all patterns triggered by environmental analysis are worthy of systematic attention. From the perspective of linking environmental analysis and strategic management, the critical question is, What are the likely positive or negative impacts of environmental patterns on the firm's strategies? This question compels the linking of environmental patterns and the organization's context. It represents a transition from a predominantly outside-in orientation to a largely inside-out perspective. Those patterns that are judged to be already impacting the organization's strategies or to possess the potential to do so are deemed to be issues for the organization.

Emphasis must be placed here upon the judgment required to identify issues, that is, to determine which patterns are affecting or will affect the organization. Judgment involves assessing and prioritizing patterns against the following four criteria.

How Might the Pattern Impact the Organization?

The intent behind the first criterion is to determine whether the pattern has or will impact the organization. This question forces members of the organization to make a preliminary assessment as to whether the pattern is likely to evolve into an issue: Does it have relevance given the organization's current and anticipated context? Those patterns that are assessed to have potential relevance to the organization are then subjected to the other three criteria.

What Is the Likely Evolution of the Pattern?

Any assessment of how the pattern will impact the organization presumes some depiction of the future evolution of the pattern. For example, it is difficult to assess the impact of any technological pattern without implicitly projecting the future path of the evolution of the technology: When will the scientific discovery result in innovations? What innovations must occur before commercializable products emerge? How long will it take the new technology to diffuse and displace the old?

How Great Will the Eventual Impact Be on the Organization?

Issues can then be conveniently arrayed on a probability-impact matrix, with a separate matrix being prepared for each of the three planning periods: near-term, medium-term, and long-term. Although the scoring system for this assessment of probability and impact can be simple or complex, a general categorizing of high, medium, or low is usually sufficient. The merits of the matrix display are that it provides a comprehensive, at-a-glance array of issues, orders them in a manner that facilitates discussion and planning, and places them in time frames appropriate to the allocation of resources and management attention.

When Is the Issue Likely to Peak?

The temporal dimension is implicit in any probability-impact matrix. However, explicitly considering the time horizons for issues is important for two reasons. First, the general state of knowledge pertaining to issues differs from those of current importance to those of long-term significance. The organization knows very little about an issue in its early stages of evolution: what forces are driving the issue, how quickly the issue will evolve, and what its implications are likely to be. The organization merely senses that certain existing or potential patterns may represent a possible threat or opportunity. On the other hand, in the later stages of issue evolution, the organization will have a much clearer picture of the forces driving the issue and its implications.

Second, the kind of action responses an organization takes depends upon the time frame. In the long run, where the organization's uncertainty about an issue is highest, the primary response may be to develop among senior management awareness of the potential issue and its possible implications for the organization. Action may take the form of continued scanning and monitoring as well as an assessment of the organization's capability to anticipate and respond to the issue.

In the medium term, the organization has to identify and assess specific strategic action responses: product-market strategy responses such as new products, product modifications, search for new markets or extension of existing markets, modification in modes of competition in the marketplace; and political strategy responses such as lobbying the legislative branch of government, making presentations to legislative committees, developing alignments with social action and community groups, and effecting corporate advocacy positions through public relations and advertising. Both product-market and political strategies may require responses at the level of organizational structure and resource allocation.

In the short term, direct action responses are always required. The organization has a pretty good understanding of the issue's implications and what actions it should take.

In summary, the temporal dimension of an array of issues is of primary importance. Unless issues are considered along the three time horizons, strategy implications of issues will not likely be completely thought through. Stated differently, unless multiple time horizons are invoked, the full benefits of environmental analysis will not be reaped.

Some Comments on the Process

As we have repeatedly noted in this chapter, the derivation of issues from a long enumeration of trends and patterns cannot be reduced to a simple set of operating routines. It requires that analysts bring to bear their intuition, creativity, knowledge base, and judgment during each step in the analysis outlined in this chapter. The process is largely inductive: just as analysts must infer patterns from trends, so must they induce issues from patterns. As we noted in the discussion of scanning, monitoring, and forecasting in Chapter 3, the process also has a deductive element: the picture of the environment in analysts' minds influences what data they search for, how they interpret or make sense of the data, and what inferences they draw.

Because the process is so heavily inductive, it is imperative that the analyst ask the right questions. A series of questions that ought to be asked at each stage of the analysis is provided in Table 11.2. The intent of these questions is to help guide the analyst through the process.

Also, the process of moving from trends to patterns to issues is recursive; that is, during each step in the analysis as depicted in Figure 11.4, specific questions may arise that may necessitate the analyst's return to a previous step (note the reverse arrows in Figure

Table 11.2 Key Questions in Analysis Across Environmental Segments

	Identification of Patterns	Interrelationship Among Patterns	Choice of Strategic Issues
Generic Questions	1. What are the alternative patterns in each segment? 2. What specific trends constitute a pattern? 3. What forces drive evolution?	1. What are the secondary consequences of each pattern? 2. How do the patterns impact each other? 3. What megatrends do these patterns reveal?	1. How do we array the patterns into time horizons? 2. What is the probability of their unfolding? 3. What is the magnitude of impact?
Tools	Process is intuitive	Cross-pattern impact matrices Scenarios	Probability-impact matrices for each time horizon
Recursiveness	What forces require further monitoring?	Conditions that trigger secondary consequences need monitoring Megatrends for scanning	
Checkpoints	Are we aware of all patterns? Are some of the patterns fads or fantasies?		Have we considered the details of the impact?

11.4). In short, the process of identifying issues is just another example of the recursive rather than linear nature of environmental analysis.

SUMMARY

Integration of analysis across the segments of the macroenvironment provides the firm with a holistic view of the macroenvironment it faces and the analytical framework within which to identify the key issues that need resolution. This step is vital, as it provides much of the backdrop against which strategies are formulated.

12

Integrating Environmental
Analysis into Strategic Management

In this chapter, we highlight how environmental analysis may be integrated into strategic management. The major purpose of integration is to derive strategic action implications from issues identified during environmental analysis. Three points need to be kept in mind regarding integration. First, environmental analysis, though often intrinsically interesting, is useful only to the extent that it results in strategy-related insights and actions. Second, the integration does not just happen—it is *made to happen.* The specific linkages to various kinds of actions need to be thought through and not left to evolve in a happenstance manner. Third, integration needs to take place for short-, medium-, as well as long-run dimensions of strategic action.

The scheme of the chapter is as follows. First, we note the role of environmental analysis in strategic management; this is a recapitulation of the themes of the book. Second, we highlight the content interface between environmental analysis and strategy formulation. Third, we point out some strategic decision process-level implications, and finally we touch upon its implications for organizational design.

THE ROLE OF ENVIRONMENTAL ANALYSIS

Environmental analysis provides one basic type of intelligence out of which strategy is formulated. Thus, environmental analysis needs to *precede* strategy formulation and should permeate the *thinking* of those involved in strategic decision making. This sets many of the basic premises (assumptions) around which current and future actions of the firm are to be assessed.

Three points need to be highlighted here. First, environmental analysis is not a substitute for industry and competitor analysis. Current action domains represent the industry or industries in which the firm is functioning. These industries and the competitors within them need to be analyzed in their own terms, in addition to environmental analysis. However, some of the forces that drive the evolution of industries reside in the macroenvironment and are, therefore, highlighted by environmental analysis.

Second, environmental analysis alerts organizations to potential action domains available to an organization or worthy of exploration. These are often not comprehensively covered during strategy formulation without attendant macroenvironmental analysis. This aspect renders it different from a predominantly inside-out focus.

Finally, note that during integration, the responses and actions by the firm may range from changes in strategy to decisions to conduct further environmental analysis.

The treatment in this chapter is an elaboration of the theoretical overview presented in Chapter 2. Readers are referred to Figure 2.4 in that chapter for the underlying framework.

CONTENT INTERFACE BETWEEN ENVIRONMENTAL ANALYSIS AND STRATEGY FORMULATION

The implications of environmental analysis outputs for economic or product-market strategy need to be assessed at three levels: (1) at the corporate level, where product-market decisions—that is, decisions to enter, withdraw, or remain in an industry—are usually the focus; (2) at the business level, where the focus is how to compete within an industry; and (3) at the functional level, where operational decisions are the concern (Hofer and Schendel 1978). Implications for political strategy also need to be derived. Given the pervasiveness of business strategy, we discuss this level first and in greater detail, and then point out implications for functional- and corporate-level strategies. We then discuss linkages between environmental analysis and political strategy.

Business-Level Strategy

Macroenvironmental analysis presents one set of critical intelligence inputs into the formulation of business strategy—that is, strategy at the level of a single-business firm or of a business unit in a multibusiness firm. For a comprehensive strategy analysis at this level, environmental analysis outputs need to be assessed for their implications for the industry and competitor environment (see Figure 12.1).

Industry and Competitor Environment. Changes in the macroenvironment may affect (1) the boundaries of the industry; (2) the forces shaping industry structure, such as suppliers, customers, rivalry, product substitution, and entry barriers; (3) strategic groups; (4) the key success factors; and (5) the general expectations within the industry. These elements provide the competitive context within which business strategy is formulated.

First, and of perhaps the greatest importance, is the impact of environmental change on the survival of an industry or specific industry segments. Environmental change can sometimes have more sudden and significant impact on *industry* (segment) *boundaries,* and thus survivability, than the structural and competitive forces within the industry. Consider the following example:

■ In recent years, regulatory changes have transformed the boundaries of such industries as financial services, telecommunications, and airlines.

Figure 12.1 Linking Environmental Analysis and Business Strategy

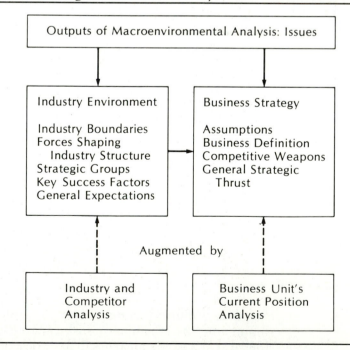

New competitors have been allowed to enter each of these industries. They now offer more products or services than previously. Indeed, defining what precisely is meant by the financial services or telecommunications industries is difficult because the scope of the products and services offered is changing so quickly.

Economic progress can be viewed as one long history of technological change contributing to shifting industry boundaries. For example, technological advances underlying frozen foods and personal computers have irrevocably altered our conceptions of the food and computer industries.

Second, environmental trends directly influence *the forces shaping the industry structure.* The forces may be conveniently summarized as suppliers, consumers, new entrants, and substitutes. Consider the following:

■ Technological developments often change the competitive dynamics of suppliers; they may leapfrog and obsolete each other's products. Microprocessors and semiconductors are highly visible examples. Sometimes technological advances lead to the emergence of a new type of supplier. Computer-aided manufacturing improvement techniques have been initiated by a small number of firms over the last two to three years as a means to effect efficiencies in firms' manufacturing operations and to enhance product quality.

■ Changes in social values and life-style can exert a significant impact on customers' behavior and sometimes do so rather swiftly. The rise and subsequent decline of jeans in general, and designer jeans in particular, amply illustrates the sensitivity of many markets to the tastes, preferences, and propensities of major segments of customers. The rapid rise and subsequent decline of the bowling industry is another example of where customers succumbed to other leisure activities and the product did not fit the life-styles of the younger generation.

■ Changes in life-styles, such as an increasing tendency for people to move from suburbs to urban areas, changes in work patterns, dual-career families, and later marriages, have contributed to condominiums replacing single-family homes for many individuals and couples. This movement also received impetus from and was reinforced by regulatory factors: rent controls in many cities and prohibitions on building more apartment complexes.

■ Technological obsolescence (process technology) has reduced entry barriers in the steel industry, inviting competition (for the larger manufacturers) from smaller, more profitable firms. Political and regulatory shifts have eliminated some entry barriers in financial markets: banks are threatened by competition from other banks, financial institutions, and nonbank firms.

As seen in the previous examples, environmental changes can affect (1) the number, type, and location of suppliers; (2) the products, supply costs, and competitive dynamics of suppliers; (3) the size, characteristics, and behavior of a firm's customers; (4) rate and trends in product substitution; and (5) change in entry barriers.

Third, environmental changes have differential impact on various *strategic groups* within the industry. Changes, to the extent that they affect customers' preferences, suppliers' capabilities, substitute products, and so on, could potentially enlarge or decimate the product-market arenas in which different strategic groups operate. Perhaps more important, environmental changes may afford opportunities for firms in a specific strategic group to overcome mobility barriers—that is, the barriers inhibiting a firm from moving from one strategic group to another. For example, deregulation of the airline industry in the late 1970s had adverse impacts on longer-haul firms relative to shorter ones, thus facilitating restructuring of the routes of larger airlines and the capturing of these by smaller airlines.

Fourth, environmental change can potentially affect the *key success factors* in almost any industry segment. Consider the following example:

■ In the late 1970s, a major success factor in the motel/restaurant industry—location—was impacted by environmental change. A number of motel chains were traditionally located near highways due to the continually increasing volume of highway traffic. With gasoline becoming increasingly expensive, however, some motel chains decided to employ nonhighway sites based on their assessment that the potential of highway locations was likely to decline considerably due to decreased automobile travel.

At a minimum, environmental changes need to be assessed with respect to their impact on key success factors such as relative cost positions, product quality and functionality, image, reputation, and resource requirements for major product-market segments.

Fifth, perhaps the prior discussion can be summarized by noting that environmental changes potentially affect *general expectations about an industry* and of firms within it. These general expectations are important, as they may have an impact on the level of investment funds into the industry and on the stock price behavior of the firms within it.

Similarly, firms that have not had to contend with major competitive battles may be completely misled if they do not carefully assess implications of environmental change. Their prior general expectations may no longer be valid. For instance, after the deregulation of the telecommunications industry, many telephone companies discovered that their assessments of competitors' responses shaped by past behavior were no longer valid.

In summary, forces in the macroenvironment can impact industry structure and, therefore, the choice and implementation of business-level strategy. The implications of macroenvironmental trends need to be assessed for each of the industry elements noted earlier. In this context, it is convenient to develop issue-impact matrices tracing the influence of environmental issues on each of the industry factors. Unlike the case of integration across segments (Chapter 11), these issue-impact matrices detail the effect of each one of a selected set of environmental issues on industry-level factors. The matrix displays of the type shown in Table 12.1 facilitate assessments of these impacts. These assessments should include not only the general direction of change but also its *timing* and *intensity*. Such assessments form much of the industry backdrop against which business strategies are formulated.

Impact on Business-Unit Strategy. Together with industry and competitor analysis, environmental analysis outputs need to be assessed for their impact on business-unit strategy, with respect to (1) business definition, (2) assumptions, and (3) general strategic thrust. These assessments are likely to be medium- and short-term oriented.

In broad terms, strategy formulation at the business or corporate levels includes a *definition of the business* and positioning of the business in an industry. Definition and positioning are inevitably affected by industry structure; macroenvironmental trends, as they affect industry structure, open up opportunities and threats for business strategy. Each of the three elements of business definition suggested by Abell (1980) can be affected by environmental change: What customers does business serve? What customer needs are satisfied? What technologies are employed to satisfy these customer needs? Consider the following examples:

■ Demographic change has altered the *served* or *target customer base* of many businesses. Insurance firms are now focusing upon the elderly market. Life-style change has also influenced the customer base of many businesses. The emergence of health maintenance and physical fitness as major life-style trends has expanded the base of potential customers for many leisure, health care, and food businesses.

■ Customers' needs or wants satisfied by a business's offerings may also be affected by environmental change. The aging of the population has altered the needs and wants satisfied by many industries: health care, education, financial services, transportation, and food. Life-style change also impacts needs and wants: the emergence of yuppies has exacerbated some needs and dissipated others.

■ Technological change critically affects the dimension of business, that is, the technologies employed to satisfy customer needs. For example, advances in the electronics industry and their application to automobiles have prompted auto manufacturers to develop a competency in electronics.

Thus, any given business definition needs to be evaluated in the context of environmental change. Each of the three key elements in a business definition may be directly or indirectly affected by change in any of the environmental segments discussed in this book.

Some pivotal *assumptions* always underlie a firm's strategy—for example, industry assumptions such as actions of suppliers, competitive responses, the likelihood of new entrants, or the market penetration of substitute products. The success or failure of a strategy is often determined by the veracity of these assumptions. Assumptions about the macroenvironment, however, may also critically influence strategy success.

Table 12.1 Implications of Environmental Analysis for Industry Structure and Business-Unit Strategy

Industry Elements	Key Question	Opportunities	Problems	Domain of Action
Boundaries	How do environmental issues impact industry boundaries?	What are potentials generated for boundary expansion?	What are the threats to current boundaries?	What actions would enable boundary shrinkage?
Forces Shaping Structure	How do issues affect new entrants, substitutes, customers, suppliers, and competition?	What are the potentials generated by impact of forces shaping structure?	What are the threats to current forces?	What actions could exploit the opportunities and hinder the threats?
Strategic Groups	How do environmental issues impact strategic groups?	How do environmental analysis issues open up (1) new strategic groups and (2) new ways of creating strategic groups?	What are the threats to existing strategic groups and strategic group definition?	What potential actions could facilitate new strategic groups or inhibit threats to existing ones?
Key Success Factors	How are environmental factors likely to affect key success factors?	What are the potential key success factors generated?	Which key success factors now existing are rendered obsolete?	How should one exploit potential success factors or get ready for obsolescence of new ones?
General Expectations	How are environmental factors likely to affect attractiveness of industry?	How does it generate potential for enhancing general expectations?	How does it generate threats to current expectations?	What is the implication for general strategic thrusts?

The merits of identifying the pivotal environmental assumptions are threefold. First, it forces a thorough assessment of environmental change, culminating in the major environmental assumptions that will serve to inform strategy analysis. Second, it facilitates sensitivity analysis, the extent to which strategy options are vulnerable to change in specific environmental factors. Third, it frequently serves to heighten awareness of environmental change and its importance to strategic management.

Finally, the *general strategic thrust* of the firm or its business units, such as share building or share maintaining, is built around assumptions about the industry. As we have noted, these assumptions are influenced by changes in the environment. Environmental analysis often signals the need for changes in strategic thrust by opening up pathways to gain market share or by rendering share-maintaining strategies obsolete.

Functional-Level Strategy

Macroenvironmental change has implications for the functional-level strategies of an organization, over and beyond the business strategy. Consider the following examples:

- Advances in telecommunications and computer applications have made it possible for marketing specialists to much more precisely segment and target customers. This is leading to changes in the implementation of marketing research, advertising, and distribution.

- Changes in demographics, life-styles, values, and technology have created a set of customers who are much more sophisticated than their predecessors in terms of the information they demand on products and how they use it. Partly as a consequence, some firms are retraining or revamping their sales force to meet the "new" customer.

- In the early seventies, as a result of general expectations regarding work hours, many organizations introduced flextime and alternative work schedules. In the late seventies, due to the increase in women in the work force, some organizations have created child-care centers.

As illustrated in the previous examples, macroenvironmental change often necessitates changes in how various functional strategies are performed. Traditionally, these functional changes are regarded as operating issues within the context of strategic management. Environmental changes offer opportunities for enhancing the operating capabilities of firms, as well as rendering some capabilities obsolete. Such enhancement of capabilities often accumulates over time, and these capabilities may become distinctive competencies that firms can wield to their advantage. The process is highlighted by Peters and Waterman (1982) in their discussion of the importance of incremental adaptation. An important point is that macroenvironmental trends affect not only business-level strategy but also the operating capabilities of businesses.

Corporate-Level Strategy

Corporate-level strategy focuses on questions related to business portfolio, including patterns of diversification and risk-return issues. Macroenvironmental impacts also need to be explicitly considered at the corporate strategy level. These impacts are likely to be medium- and long-term. Consider the following examples:

■ A diversified consumer products organization, which has grown in the past by acquisitions and mergers, has recently been confronted by macroenvironmental forecasts that suggest low growth in its major business segments. Senior-level executives are worried that the current business portfolio portends low growth for the firm. They are debating whether the conventional patterns of diversification should be reviewed to enhance the growth potential or whether the goal of maintaining the firm's historic growth rate should be abandoned.

■ Confronted by forecasts of tight capital markets (i.e., a decline in potentially available resources), another large firm, which has financed its growth by a mixture of debt and equity, has decided to consider joint ventures as a major means of creating future growth. Further, the firm is considering the potential divestiture of some of its existing operations.

■ Confronted by predictions that technological changes in microelectronics will unify products and generate demand for new services, one firm is reconsidering its approach to portfolio assessment: it is moving its emphasis from unrelated toward related products.

Macroenvironmental impacts need to be assessed *separately* for each one of the corporation's business units. In addition, however, they have implications for the corporate-level strategy, as shown by the previous examples.

At the level of corporate strategy, environmental impacts on three key issues need to be considered: (1) patterns of diversification, (2) portfolio planning, and (3) risk-return trade-offs.

Patterns of Diversification.   Environment influences patterns of diversification in at least three modes. First, firms differ in the synergies they try to exploit across their businesses. These synergies could be upset or enhanced by macroenvironmental change. Second, different patterns of diversification manifest different vulnerabilities (see Table 12.2). Macroenvironmental change may amplify these vulnerabilities. Third, macroenvironmental trends may open up or close out existing patterns of diversification. This is particularly so

Table 12.2   Vulnerabilities in Diversification Patterns

Patterns of Diversification	Vulnerability
Horizontal diversification	All businesses share the general economic environment
Vertical integration	Markets
Technology-related concentric diversification	Key technology synergy
Conglomerate diversification	Society and general economy

when the pattern of diversification is not conglomerate. For example, regulatory changes in the fifties rendered impossible vertical (forward) integration for the "Big Five" movie houses, resulting in their divestiture of theaters. Similarly, technological and regulatory changes are opening up pathways for diversification in the financial services industry.

Portfolio Planning.   Macroenvironmental trends have important implications for the *bases* of portfolio planning. Typical portfolio approaches focus on businesses' competitive advantages within an existing industry, constrained by the internal financial resources of the firm. Ansoff (1975) notes that macroenvironmental trends may necessitate portfolio planning based on such bases as resources or technology.

Environmental analyses are also particularly important for planning potential future portfolios. Product portfolio approaches are useful for portfolio planning *within* the existing set of businesses or, at best, for pointing the direction of search for additional businesses. The specific businesses to be targeted need to be considered in the light of macroenvironmental forecasts and predictions.

Risk-Return Trade-Offs.   Political, economic, technological, and demographic shifts impact the returns and risks of existing and planned portfolios.

■ In a conglomorate firm, the accepted macroenvironmental trends suggested a persistent level of high inflation in the economy. One of the consequent considerations was that additional investments in any business unit should be justified not only by competitive position but also by returns in excess of the forecasted rate of inflation.

■ In a technology-related firm, a technology study suggested obsolescence of some key technologies within the next decade. As a result, the firm is searching for methods of converting existing technology so as to retain competitive advantage in their existing markets.

It is important to consider environmental impacts on each of these characteristics of corporate-level strategy. A set of questions is presented in Table 12.3 to facilitate this consideration.

Political Strategy

In addition to economic or product-market strategies, firms often use political strategies to support their competitive strategies. (For a

Table 12.3 Assessing Implications of Environmental Analysis for Corporate Strategy

		KEY QUESTIONS			
Macroenvironmental Segments	Patterns of Diversification	Portfolio Planning			Risk-Return Trade-offs
		Attractiveness of Current Business	*Bases of Portfolio*	*Potential Future Portfolio*	
Demographics Life-styles Social Values Economy Technology Politics Regulation	How do environmental trends provide opportunity for future synergy?	Are environmental trends taking place in areas of key vulnerabilities?	How do the trends affect the attractiveness of existing business?	Which bases are rendered obsolete by environmental trends?	What new opportunities are unearthed by environmental analysis?	How do environmental trends reduce or increase (1) the risks and returns of existing business and (2) the risks and returns of portfolios?
	How do they impact existing synergies?	What potential new vulnerabilities will be brought forth by environmental trends?		What different bases should be considered in current and future portfolio planning?	How should these be incorporated in designing future portfolios?	
	How could existing synergies be better utilized to exploit opportunities provided?					

detailed discussion of political strategy, see the MacMillan and Jones volume in this series.) By the term *political strategy,* we mean a set of actions designed to influence actors in the external arena of the firm. Environmental change has implications for political strategy. These implications may be discussed at two levels: (1) stakeholders and (2) political strategies.

Impact on Stakeholders and Their Demands. The firm's stakeholders are those groups who can directly or indirectly place demands on the organization. Environmental change, however, can affect the firm's stakeholders and their demands—and, thus, the firm's requisite political strategy—in a variety of ways. First, it can give rise to new stakeholders, who frequently place new types of demands on the firm, can cause the demands of existing stakeholders to change, or can increase the intensity of existing demands. For example:

- Changes in social values have given rise to many new stakeholders: consumerist, environmentalist, and minority groups. Many minority groups have placed demands on large corporations for greater employment, greater access to supplier business, and not to do business in some foreign countries.

- Downturns in local economic conditions have given rise to many local activist groups who demand that corporations generate more employment and who protest vigorously when plant closings or layoffs are announced.

Second, differing degrees of connectedness exist among potential and current stakeholders. These often take the form of networks or coalitions. The glue that holds networks and coalitions unravels under environmental impacts; new coalitions and networks are often created by such changes. These changes differentially affect organizations.

- The petroleum-producing countries' (OPEC) decision to exert their market power sent shocks throughout the economic systems of many countries. More recently, due to increases in energy production, OPEC influence has waned, and many describe the coalition as highly unstable. Such changes have affected many organizations ranging from international banks to state governments (e.g., Texas).

Political strategies of firms are anchored in stakeholders and networks; as these change under environmental changes, political strategies will need to be refashioned.

Impact on Political Tactics. Through its impact on stakeholders and their demands, environmental change affects the political tactics (i.e., actions and moves) used by firms. It impacts the objects of the tactics (i.e., the focus of the tactics), the nature of the tactics (i.e., what tactics are employed), the intent of the tactics, and the timing of tactics. Consider the following scenario:

■ When issues in the public policy arena crystallize in the form of proposed legislation, corporations often engage in a flurry of political activity to support or oppose the proposed legislation. They lobby public representatives, make presentations to legislative committees, develop position papers for public consumption, engage in media advocacy, and encourage senior executives to give speeches to interested or affected social groups. If some form of the legislation comes to pass, the focus of the political activity switches to the relevant regulatory agencies. The intent is to influence the implementation, enforcement, and adjudication of the regulations. The tactics most often switch from actions to shape and sway public opinion to actions to influence those involved in managing the implementation of the regulations. In their efforts to influence regulatory agencies, many firms prefer more direct contact than in their efforts to influence the legislative process. For example, senior executives appear before the relevant regulatory panels rather than rely on trade or industry associations.

The impact of environmental change on the *timing* of political tactics merits special emphasis. If firms initiate political actions too far ahead of or behind environmental change, they are likely to be less successful. For example:

■ Many corporate PACs (political action committees) have become involved in social or political issues after they have been shaped by other interest groups in society.

In summary, environmental changes must be assessed to identify their impact on firms' stakeholders and their demands so that the effectiveness of political strategy can be enhanced. A set of questions to guide this analysis is provided in Table 12.4.

PROCESS–LEVEL INTEGRATION INTO STRATEGY FORMULATION AND IMPLEMENTATION

Two process linkages need to be considered here. The first is at the level of long-term decision making orientation, and the second is at the level of strategic decision making.

Decision Making Orientation

At the broadest process level, the linkages to strategic management ensue from awareness of the kind of developments taking place or having the potential to unfold in the environment. External awareness *conditions* the strategic thinking of top management.

**Table 12.4 Assessing Implications
of Environmental Analysis for Political Strategy**

Key Questions	Gaining in Importance	Reducing in Importance	Newer Ones
How do environmental changes affect stakeholders?	Which stakeholders gain in importance?	Which reduce in importance?	Are new stakeholders suggested?
How do environmental changes affect networks?	Which parts of the networks are coming into prominence; or which parts can be activated by the firm?	Which parts will be rendered passive by environmental change or can be rendered passive by the firm, given environmental change?	What are the potential new entrants that may come in or be brought into the network?
How do environmental changes affect tactics?	What tactics are rendered effective and legitimate?	What tactics lose effectiveness or are rendered legitimate?	What other new tactics can be formed and/or combined?
How does environmental change affect timing?	For what actions is timing most important?	For what actions is timing least important?	

■ Royal Dutch Shell has been a frequently cited firm in the area of environmental analysis. Pierre Wack, who headed these efforts for a number of years, notes that a primary task of his environmental analysis group was to change the *thinking* of the top management.

■ The American Medical Association has had an active environmental analysis group for some time. In one of its publications, it notes that the focus of environmental analysis is to determine the types of services that will be required of the organization in ten to fifteen years, and *more generally,* to identify the kinds of questions policymakers should now be asking themselves about the future.

At this level, the linkages lead to changes in top management's *long-term* vision of the future, and to policy questions for further analysis. Participation in the development of scenarios and other environmental analysis techniques is particularly useful for conditioning strategic thinking.

Strategic Decision Making

Strategic decision making may be viewed as consisting of a sequence of steps: diagnosis, alternative development, evaluation and choice, planning and implementation, and finally, evaluation of results. Table 12.5 provides a set of questions to be posed at each stage of strategic decision making to guide the development of linkages to environmental analysis.

At the *diagnosis* stage, environmental analysis provides an important set of inputs into understanding the forces that drive or constrain industries or product-markets, critical assumptions, and business definition relevance. These inputs help to explain change in the industry forces and also help to anticipate likely change in these forces. Similarly, the inputs provide one means of assessing the continued relevance of a given business definition. A central thrust of this book is that environmental analysis provides an important means of diagnosing the external conditions and forces that shape organizational performance.

In the *alternative development* stage, strategy options are developed and considered within the context of threats, opportunities, and constraints identified during product-market, industry, and environmental analysis. An important point is that strategy options—that is,

Table 12.5 Implications of Environmental Analysis for Strategic Decision Making

	Stage of Decision			
Diagnosis	*Alternative Development*	*Evaluation and Choice*	*Planning and Implementation*	*Evaluation of Results*
Assumptions	Threats	Consistency with environmental analysis	Contingency plans	Environmental assumptions
Cause-effect relationships	Opportunities		Triggers for analysis	Triggers for environmental analysis
Constraints				
—Are the assumptions justified in environmental analysis? —What does environmental analysis offer as forces that drive or constrain the outcomes?	—Do alternatives address threats and opportunities presented by the environmental analysis? —Does environmental analysis provide any alternatives not considered? New technologies? Market segments? New product ideas?	—Does the chosen alternate adequately address the threats and opportunities?	—Are contingency plans developed to cover the variability in environmental forecasts? —Does implementation suggest further environmental analysis?	—What was the role of environment and the environmental analysis on outcomes? —Are the deviations in results from expected performance due to unforeseen contingencies? —Does it suggest further environmental analysis?

product-market opportunities—may stem from environmental analysis. The many examples of the impact of environmental change on organizations' strategies discussed in this book suggest the pervasive significance of environmental change as a source of strategy options.

In the *evaluation and choice* stage, one of the criteria for the evaluation of strategy options should be *consistency* with the outputs of environmental analysis. In many organizations, strategy options are too frequently evaluated primarily in the context of industry change, with comparatively little reference to the content of environmental change. Yet, if the chosen strategic options are not consistent with changes in the macroenvironment, the chances of strategic success are obviously lessened.

In the *planning and implementation* stage, there is an ongoing interplay between strategy implementation and environmental analysis. *Contingency plans* are anchored in the variability of environmental forecasts; thus, environmental monitoring serves as an input to implementation. Alternate courses of action may have to be pursued depending upon what transpires or is anticipated in the technological, regulatory, and life-styles arenas, and so on. Conversely, issues that arise during implementation serve as *triggers* for further environmental analysis.

Finally, in the *evaluation of results*, we return to the themes raised in the diagnosis stage. Environmental assumptions (in retrospect) and their fallibility should be considered as *explanations* for results. A key question here is the extent to which unanticipated environmental happenings contributed to deviations from expected results. Strategic performance or results will often serve as *triggers* for further environmental analysis.

The preceding linkages do not evolve naturally. Rather, specific questions must be explicitly posed at each stage of strategic decision making in order for these linkages to be developed.

ORGANIZATIONAL IMPLICATIONS

The linkages of environment (and, therefore, of environmental analysis) to organizational structure and process may be discussed at two levels: level of business unit and level of corporate-business-unit linkages.

At the Business-Unit Level

Specific changes in organizational structure and processes at the level of a single-business firm or a business unit may be triggered by environmental forecasts. Consider the following examples:

■ Due to the expectation that CAD/CAM and robotics will play an increasing role in the manufacture of an industrial good, one firm recently decided on major organizational changes for the future. It noted the decline of blue-collar workers, the need for intellectual personnel for controlling the operations, and different styles of supervision appropriate for the anticipated labor force. The firm notes that increased delegation will be necessary, and with it, a greater degree of consultative leadership.

■ As a result of demographic and life-style shifts, a consumer products firm noted that what was once a national market for its product is now increasingly fragmented, with local competition an important threat to the firm. To meet these environmental changes, the firm has decided to create regional divisions for fast adaptation to local markets.

The previous examples are illustrative of how environmental changes are linked to organizational changes. In the case of the industrial products firm, technological changes are driving the organization from a machine bureaucracy to an organic form. In the case of the second firm, the social changes necessitated regional divisionalization.

Typically, the environmental changes affect the bases of differentiation and integration in a business unit. The questions that should be posed are as follows:

1. Do environmental forecasts and attendant strategy implications affect the *bases* of differentiation? Do they require addition, deletion, or modification of functions?
2. What do these changes imply for issues related to coordination or integration?

At the Corporate Level

Environmental changes have implications for organizational structure and process at the corporate level.

■ In a telecommunications firm, environmental analysis revealed that technological change was an important uncertainty confronting the firm and that the firm's technological competency was low in the light of these developments and uncertainties. The firm has decided to create a corporate unit to track new technologies and to develop in-house capability.

■ Demographic, life-style, and economic changes have increased the number and sophistication of individuals engaged in total financial planning. Many brokerage houses and banks used to specialize around a traditional conception of business lines: investment, securities, trusts, and so on. Recently, some of these financial services firms have introduced a team concept: individuals drawn from different business lines are in charge of providing a range of services to clients.

■ Technological and regulatory changes in electronics are predicted to unify a number of product-markets that were once separate: television, telephone, and computers are a few. Some firms are considering whether the bases for creating strategic business areas are appropriate in light of this environmental development.

As can be seen from the previous examples, environmental changes often necessitate (1) addition or deletion of new functions at the corporate level, (2) reconsidering the linkages between corporate and business-unit relationships, and (3) changing the bases for designing strategic business units. In the first example, environmental analysis alerted the firm to adding a function at the corporate level. In the second, the financial "supermarkets" are discovering the need for increased control from the corporate level. In the third case, the bases of strategic business-unit design are being reconsidered.

Thus, with respect to linking environmental analysis to the corporate level, three specific questions must be posed:

1. Do the environmental analysis outputs suggest strengthening or deleting functions at the corporate level?
2. Do they necessitate reconsidering the linkages between corporate and business units?
3. Do they indicate different bases for creating strategic business units?

SUMMARY

Linking environmental analysis and strategy formulation is the key analytical step that ensures that strategy development is not an exclusively inside-out process. Linkages between environmental analysis and the formulation of strategy do not evolve automatically but have to be developed. These linkages need to be developed for various levels of strategy as well as for various time horizons.

13

Environmental Analysis Techniques

This chapter presents an overview of the techniques often used in environmental analysis. Given the wide array of techniques, the discussion is brief, though some integrative forecasting methods are presented in some detail. The scheme of the chapter is as follows. First, some key conceptual ideas are presented to place various methods and techniques in perspective so that their potential, limitations, and problems in utilization can be understood. Second, we address a number of methods and techniques from the viewpoint of their utility in analyzing various environmental segments. Third, we detail some forecasting methods that are useful for integrating forecasts from various segments. Scenarios are especially emphasized because of their wide applicability and popularity as an environmental analysis technique. Finally, we touch upon some of the common problems encountered in applying environmental analysis techniques and suggest ways of dealing with them.

CONCEPTUAL NOTIONS FOR DISCUSSING TECHNIQUES

As emphasized in earlier chapters, scanning, monitoring, and forecasting activities involve data gathering and analysis about the relevant environment. The term *relevant environment* was defined as the parts of the macroenvironment to which the analyst pays attention, and is therefore guided by a framework, such as the one presented in this book.

Distinguishing between frameworks, data-gathering methods, and forecasting techniques is important. *Frameworks* are content-specific; they direct analysts' attention to issues or areas they should focus on and provide them with the constructs to look at the environment.

They also sometimes provide some of the relationships among concepts, often basing these on the theoretical bases developed from past experience. Frameworks thus specify a structure for data collection and point the direction to data sources. *Data-gathering methods* specify data sources and the methods of data collection. *Forecasting techniques* are procedures for transforming data to yield answers to the questions posed by analysts, in a manner consistent with the available data and the relationships suggested by the framework. Typically, forecasting techniques serve three functions: (1) to verify hunches or intuitive judgments, (2) to answer "what-if" questions, and (3) to facilitate the forecasting of trends, events, and patterns.

These relationships are sketched in Figure 13.1. Frameworks provide the lenses through which analysts can or will view the relevant environment. The data-gathering techniques provide the mechanisms by which the relevant environment is detailed. Hence, the techniques depend on the nature of the relevant environment or especially for our purposes, the environmental segments under consideration. These details, which include a description of current and potential patterns in various segments, and a sketch of their historical evolution, feed into forecasting techniques where projections or alternative futures are generated.

Two critical observations are in order with respect to Figure 13.1. First, frameworks, data, and constructed reality stand in a lexicographic relationship to each other: That is, data assume a framework, whereas the constructed reality assumes both data and a framework. The implication here is that the projections or alternative futures that are the outputs of forecasting techniques are only as good as the underlying data and conception of the macroenvironment (that is, the relevant environment) invoked by the analyst. Second, the transformation of the "real world" into "constructed reality" involves a series of microdecisions (Mackenzie and Barron 1971), each of which influences the correspondence between the two. The correspondence is never perfect, though during the process of linking environmental analysis into strategy formulation, analysts often focus on constructed reality. A general understanding of these microdecisions is important to keep the projections or alternative futures in proper perspective.

TECHNIQUES AND ENVIRONMENTAL SEGMENTS

To consider their utility for analyzing various environmental segments, classifying data-gathering and forecasting techniques according to their generic characteristics is useful.

Data-gathering Methods

Data-gathering methods may be represented along three key dimensions: (1) source of data, (2) nature of data, and (3) temporal dimension.

Figure 13.1 Conceptual Notions for Discussing Techniques

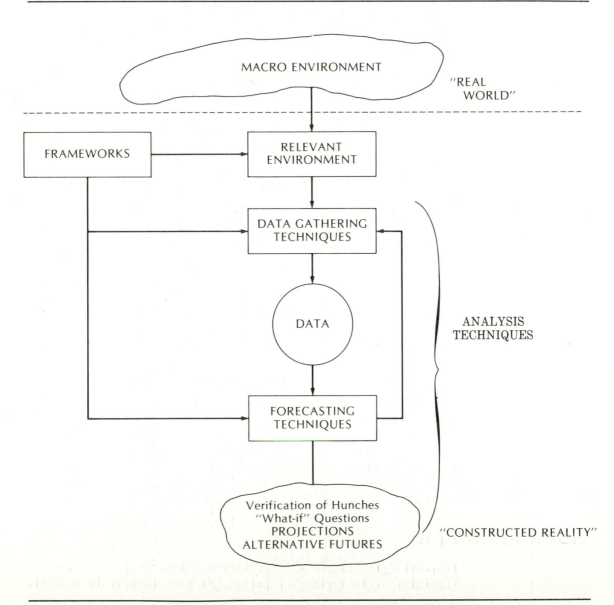

Source of Data.   Data sources may be either primary or secondary. Primary sources are sources of data tapped by an organization or by agencies hired by it, with a specific purpose in mind. Such sources tend to be individuals and include randomly sampled populations and expert panels. Secondary sources are sources of data gathered by various agencies for general purposes and are typically available to most organizations. Competitive informational advantages primarily accrue to a firm from primary sources; such sources are often necessary for detection of life-styles, technological developments, and political changes.

Nature of Data.   The data may be quantitative, qualitative, or inferential. The first two categories are self-explanatory. The word *inferential* is used to describe data that are arrived at as a result of drawing conclusions from various data sources. For example, social values are often not directly manifest or measurable, but need to be inferred from the behavior and words of individuals. Note that in environmental analysis, all types of data are necessary, though their relative importance will vary from segment to segment.

Temporal Dimension.   The temporal dimension refers to whether the data are collected on an ad hoc, periodic, or real-time and continuous basis. The temporal dimension is highly dependent on the nature of the segment. Thus, in the political segment, which is most turbulent, events need to be tracked often on a continuous basis, whereas in the demographic segment, such tracking needs to be done only on a periodic basis. Ad hoc data collection is often necessitated when strategic surprises confront a firm, irrespective of the segment.

A critical observation is in order with respect to the data-gathering methods. Organizations often have archives of data collected from previous or ongoing (or both) data-gathering efforts. These data are valuable; however, purposeful environmental analysis must always start with the questions: What data do we want? and Where and how can we find this data? This is especially so during the scanning and monitoring phases. Stated differently, the design of the data collection phase should precede choice of data-gathering techniques and should not be guided by existing data alone. Such design is contingent on the scanning efforts, which to some extent breed purposefulness into systemic data collection methods, as noted in Chapter 3.

These data form the grist for the forecasting mill. A classification of forecasting methods is presented before their relative utility for various environmental segments is discussed.

Forecasting Techniques

Forecasting techniques for environmental analysis may be classified according to the underlying perspective that informs the analysis:

what assumptions the technique makes about the future and how the technique aids analysis. Following Jantsch (1973), techniques may be classified into three categories: (1) deterministic, (2) adaptive, and (3) inventive.

Deterministic Techniques. Deterministic techniques assume that the future can be completely known from the past, provided that the analyst has at hand a model of the underlying causes. These techniques presume that the macroenvironment is a closed system. The appropriateness and usefulness of deterministic techniques stem from three sources. First, some elements of the environment behave in a relatively deterministic way. For example, the demographic segment, because of its relatively slow evolution, is particularly amenable to deterministic techniques. Other elements may be viewed somewhat deterministically over the short run. Second, because of the appearance of certainty, the outputs of deterministic techniques are easier in many cases to interpret than other techniques. Third, deterministic techniques are generally relatively simple.

Deterministic techniques, however, also possess some severe limitations. First the ability of these techniques to accurately capture the future is often limited; it is particularly suspect in the face of major structural and discontinuous change in the macroenvironment. Second, these techniques invoke a closed view of the future; thus, they do not provide for consideration of various options by firms interested in changing the future or the environment.

Adaptive Techniques. Adaptive techniques do not assume that the future is knowable. Rather, they are oriented toward creating descriptions of how the future is unfolding. They focus on signs that do not "determine" the future but reveal the process of change that is taking place. These techniques are built around abstractions of the world developed by the analyst; usually, they account for a number of factors (not a single factor) in the abstraction or model. Adaptive techniques thus employ a more open view of the environment: they take the structure of developmental change as given but take into account the flexibility that firms have in adapting to various contingencies.

The appropriateness and usefulness of adaptive techniques stem from their capacity to consider the futurity of current decisions—that is, the manner in which current decisions of different environmental factors as well as the firm itself will affect the future that will confront the firm. These techniques emphasize the need to understand the current environment as a prerequisite to anticipating the future environment. Their successful utilization, however, requires considerable skill, time, and effort.

Inventive Techniques.   Inventive techniques are especially oriented toward an open future. They emphasize how a firm can "redesign"
its future and the environment. They place a lot more emphasis on
speculative or conjectural approaches to considering the environment. In these techniques, the analyst is guided by the intentions of
the firm, and analysis is oriented toward creating pathways (products as in technology or strategies as in scenarios) to the intended
future. These techniques, therefore, assist in exploration of the spectrum of possibilities for inventing new products, technologies, markets, and strategies.

The advantages of inventive techniques are that they open up new
ways of thinking about the environment. They force individuals to
go beyond conventional ways of thinking, to identify their assumptions, and to look at different combinations of relationships among
given variables. The disadvantages are that many of the outputs of
these analyses are conjectural in nature and may not be of immediate practical relevance. Also, application of these techniques has
primarily been in the technological sector and may be useful only for
firms with a high level of resources.

A major characteristic of these forecasting techniques is their
large number and variability. They range from traditional market
research techniques such as the use of focus groups and value
profiles to more complex techniques such as scenarios and cross-
impact matrices. Their relative utility for different environmental
segments varies—a point to which we now turn.

Relative Utility of Techniques for Various Environmental Segments

Table 13.1 presents the relative utility of data-gathering and forecasting techniques for analyzing various environmental segments. As
shown, quantitative data are primarily available for the demographic and economic segments; for these segments abundant data are
also available from secondary sources on a real-time basis. In the
case of technology, quantitative data at an aggregative level are available (e.g., expenditures on R&D across industry segments), but data
on specific technologies need to be gathered actively for managerial
analysis. For the remaining segments (life-styles, social values, political, and regulatory), data are essentially qualitative, and in the case
of social values they are inferential.

These differences in the nature of data across environmental segments are reflected in the forecasting techniques employed in each
segment. Except in the case of demographics (e.g., logistic equation
models) and the economic segment (e.g., econometric models), environmental forecasting techniques rely primarily on systematically

Table 13.1 Environmental Analysis Techniques

	Social			Political			
Data-gathering Methods	Demographics	Life-styles	Social-values	Political Milieu	Regulatory	Economic	Technological
Type of sources	Primarily quantitative / Secondary sources	Quantitative and qualitative / Secondary and primary	Inferential/qualitative / Primary and secondary	Real-time personal / Qualitative	Historical/real-time / Primary and secondary / Qualitative	Historical/real-time / Secondary / Quantitative	Mostly primary/qualitative / Secondary sources for later stages
Techniques	Market research techniques	Focus groups / In-depth interviews / Panels	In-depth interviews / Panels / Content analysis	Content analysis of speeches / Lobbying / Opinion leaders	Content analysis of legislation / Regulatory opinions / Expert opinion	Outputs of models	Expert panels / Interviews with experts
Forecasting Methods[1] Techniques	Simulation (A) / Logistic equation models (M) / Transition matrices (M) / Geographic mobility models (A-M)	Life-style (M) profiling / Probability-diffusion matrices (A)	Analytical (A) / Value profile / Social pressures, priority analysis (A)	Event history analysis / Political risk analysis (M) / Networks (M)	Network analysis (M)	World and industrial dynamics (A-M) / Econometric models (A-M) / Input-output analysis (M) / Simulation models (A) / Trend extrapolation (M) / Time-series analysis (M)	Historical analysis (M) / Probability-diffusion matrices (A-M) / Morphological methods (I) / Delphi (A) / Relevance trees (I) / Logistic curves
Characteristic	Generally robust	Variable in robustness	Very variable	Weak in robustness	Moderately robust	Robust in terms of direction of change	Variable/inventive

← Sociopolitical forecasting → (spanning Social-values through Economic)

Integrative forecasting methods
←——— Scenarios, delphi, cross impact matrices (A-I) (A) ———→

[1]M = mechanistic
A = adaptive
I = inventive

processing individuals' judgments around qualitative data. As such, these latter techniques are not very robust; that is, their precision in forecasts is variable.

Table 13.1 also notes a number of techniques that may be used for any segment; in addition, these techniques are often useful for integrating analysis across segments, as discussed in Chapter 11. These techniques are dealt with in some detail in the next section.

Two specific comments are in order with respect to these techniques. First, quantitative data-based techniques are not necessarily superior in their accuracy for long-run environmental analysis. To cite one example, and as noted in Chapter 7, the performance of econometric models is far from perfect in accurately predicting economic trends. Second, techniques are not mutually exclusive at the point of application; many techniques rely on others for data inputs. For example, scenarios often rely on trend extrapolation for data inputs. The issue of how to go about structuring the analysis is often left to the creativity of the analyst. The sequencing of these techniques is often determined by the kinds of questions posed, the resources of the firm, and the importance of the questions to the decision maker.

SELECTED FORECASTING TECHNIQUES

In this section, we detail three widely used techniques for environmental analysis: (1) Delphi forecasting, (2) Cross-impact matrices, and (3) Scenarios. These techniques are useful not only for a number of environmental segments but also for integrating analysis across segments, as was noted earlier. We pay particular attention to scenarios because of their widespread use and applicability.

Delphi Forecasting

The Delphi technique was developed to allow a number of experts to interact with each other in the process of analyzing some specific aspects of the current and future environment. It is intended as a technique to enable experts to contribute to each other's understanding and to refine their opinions as a result of interaction with each other.

A Delphi analysis typically involves a number of steps:

1. Each expert is asked to make an initial prediction.
2. The predictions are then tabulated and clarified by a neutral investigator.

3. The output of the second step is fed back to the experts, and they are then asked to make a second round of predictions based on the information provided to them; that is, they are asked to review their earlier predictions in light of the predictions of other experts. The process of making predictions and then receiving feedback may go on for several rounds.

The Delphi technique can involve both quantitative and qualitative data. This is because Delphi is applicable to any segment of the environment and could be used to forecast and assess almost any aspect of any environmental segment. For example, Delphi analysis has frequently been conducted in the technology arena. Delphis have also been conducted in the social, political, and regulatory arenas.

The Delphi technique can be and often is used to identify and assess the underlying causes or forces driving the environmental change under investigation. Experts can be asked to provide the rationales supporting their predictions or assessments. These rationales can then be provided to other experts for their review and critique. Thus, the output is not just a set of predictions but also an identification and assessment of the key underlying forces as determined by the participating experts.

Cross-Impact Matrices

The cross-impact matrix provides a more complex means of assessing and forecasting the future environment than trend extrapolation or Delphi. The matrix is intended to provide a systematic approach to identifying and tracing through chains of effects among several forecasts or elements of the environment that are believed to interact with one another. Thus, the matrix provides a means to identify secondary and tertiary consequences: when one environmental phenomenon that is being forecast affects the likelihood of occurrence or the timing of another, cross-impact matrices allow assessment of these consequences in an explicit manner.

The raw material for a cross-impact matrix is a set of events that are forecast to occur within a specified time period. The analyst must specify not only the time period within which the event is likely to occur but also its probability of occurrence. As shown in Figure 13.2, the events are listed in chronological order of occurrence in rows and columns of a matrix. The cells of the matrix represent the interactions among the events. Note that arraying the interactions in a matrix format is simply a procedural means of assuring that the analyst considers all possible impacts.

The cross-impact matrix serves two major purposes. First, it can be used to check the consistency of the forecasts that go into it (i.e.,

Figure 13.2 Cross-Impact Matrix: An Illustrative Structure

Timing and Probability of Events	Event 1	Event 2	Event 3	Event 4
Event 1 (Prob., Timing)	///			
Event 2 (Prob., Timing)		///		
Event 3 (Prob., Timing)			///	
Event 4 (Prob., Timing)				///

the predictions of events, the likelihood of changes in trends, and relationships among events and trends). If inconsistencies exist, they will become apparent from the anomalies and conflicts that will appear in the results. Second, the matrix can be used to identify key events and trends that will have the greatest impact on the subsequent course of events.

To use the matrix, the analyst begins with the earliest event and assesses whether the event will take place. In either case, the analyst then assesses the impact of this outcome on all later events. The impact of the later events may be to make them more or less probable and to speed up or delay their timing. When this analysis is completed for the first event, the analyst then proceeds to the second event. The analysis continues in this fashion until all events have been examined.

In the same way that a Delphi goes through a number of iterations, or just as multiple scenarios are constructed, going through the cross-impact matrix a number of times is strongly advisable. Each "play" of the matrix generates a different representation of the future involving different cause-effect linkages.

Cross-impact matrices can be developed to explore interactions among events and trends within any individual segment of the environment or across multiple segments.

Scenarios

Scenarios represent hypothetical descriptions of sequences of future events and trends, that is, plausible alternative futures. Although scenarios are less rigorous than cross-impact matrices in identifying cause-effect linkages among environmental events and trends, they nevertheless allow the environmental analyst to explore the possible consequences of a series of complex and interrelated aspects of the environment.

A scenario displays in a dramatic and persuasive fashion a combination of possibilities about the future. A scenario typically includes some trends, patterns, and events, assumptions pertaining to these, conditions in the current environment, and the dynamics that lead from the present state of the environment to some future state.

Uses of Scenarios. Scenarios serve several purposes. First, they provide an opportunity for the environmental analyst to describe or lay out possible blueprints of the future. In so doing, they allow the analyst to examine the future by searching for and postulating linkages among different aspects of the macroenvironment.

Second, they serve as an explicit context for identifying assumptions, clarifying perceptions about the environment, and assessing risks and implications of environmental change.

Third, scenarios often provide a context for using other environmental analysis techniques: they serve as a collection of insights for evaluating, adjusting, and making sense out of more formal analytical techniques such as econometric forecasting and more qualitative techniques such as Delphi and cross-impact matrices.

Generating Scenarios. Developing a scenario can be done in many different ways. The following steps, illustrated in Figure 13.3 and drawn from Mandel (1983), are common to the methodology employed by a number of organizations to generate scenarios.

1. *Identify the strategic decision context.* Scenarios should not be developed in a vacuum; rather, they should lay out alternative plausible futures that will serve as a context within which strategic decisions facing the organization will be made. Stated differently, the content of scenarios should be guided by the organization's current and anticipated strategic decisions. For example, if some strategic decisions are strongly impacted by technological change, some scenarios may be focused upon likely developments in the technology arena and their impacts on the organization.

The purpose of beginning by specifying the decision context is to focus and constrain subsequent steps in generating, refining, and applying the scenarios. Insufficient focus results in scenarios too global and too general to be useful. Inadequate specification of the decision context can lead to too many scenarios, or to scenarios that become unnecessarily complex and irrelevant.

2. *Identify key industry, competitive, and organizational forces.*
The first step can be further refined when we remember that strategic decisions are impacted by the industry, competitive, and organizational context within which they are made. As noted throughout this book (and as emphasized in the next chapter), these industry, competitive, and organizational forces are influenced by broader macroenvironmental forces. Thus, scenarios should be geared to identifying the macroenvironmental forces that impact the relevant environment within the industry.

3. *Identify key macroenvironmental forces.* In this step, the challenge is to identify the forces in the macroenvironment that will

Figure 13.3 Steps in Scenario Development

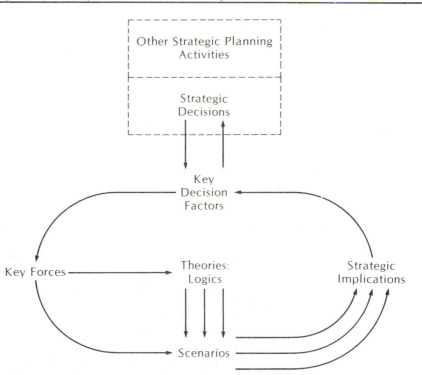

Adapted from Thomas F. Mandel "Future Scenarios and Their Uses in Corporate Strategy" in The Strategic Management Handbook, Kenneth J. Albert, Ed., McGraw-Hill, 1983. Reproduced with permission.

impact the forces in the industry and organizational context. This largely involves the analysis element—identifying the driving forces—that we have discussed in each segment chapter (Chapters 4– 10). Much of this effort involves developing a qualitative model of the most significant forces driving change within the industry. Again, as we have noted in many places previously, no simple routines or rules of thumb can be invoked to perform this task. Rather, the analyst must draw upon personal intuition, expertise, and knowledge to identify the relevant environmental forces.

4. *Analyze key forces.* This step also draws upon the analysis previously discussed in the segment chapters. The intent here is to develop an understanding of the interrelationships among the macroenvironmental forces identified in the previous step: To what extent are the forces reinforcing, conflictual, or disjointed? By identifying forces that tend to reinforce each other or are conflictual, the number of scenarios that are created in the next step may be considerably reduced.

5. *Develop scenario logics.* This step is the core of the scenario process. It involves building a scenario around a set of relationships among the macroenvironmental forces noted in the previous step. By the word *logic,* we mean the rationales or glue that holds the story line in the scenario together. The logic provides the explanations for how the elements in the scenario fit together.

Creating a scenario logic involves careful consideration of the relevant environmental forces, the relationships among them, their impact on the firm's industry, competitive, and organizational context, and the focal strategic decisions.

Again, note that no simple rules of thumb are available to aid in the selection of scenario logics. Various individuals, provided with the same set of data (i.e., environmental trends, patterns, and events), might arrive at different scenarios because they might impose different logics on the data. The operative logics stem in part from individuals' own cognitive models of the world, experience, and background. The great merit of developing a scenario, however, is that each individual or group working on a scenario must lay bare their logic, thus exposing it to critique by others.

Creating a small number of logics (i.e., different scenarios) is usually useful. Different logics identify different linkages among the macroenvironmental forces, different assumptions, and possibly different scenario outcomes. These differences help to sharpen the insight into the relationships among the scenario's elements. The most difficult part of selecting scenario logics is to incorporate the dominant environmental forces in consistent ways without creating too many scenarios or different logics.

The primary output of this step is skeletal scenarios. This implies relatively simple causal statements that show the logic linking the key environmental forces.

6. *Elaborate the scenarios.* This step combines the outputs of the two previous steps. The skeletal scenarios may be elaborated in varying degrees of detail, depending on the knowledge base of the scenarios' users and providers. Scenarios can range from simple descriptions or summaries of the major environmental forces and the logics connecting them to highly complex and detailed analyses of the interactions of the environmental forces and their impact on the decision variables.

7. *Implications for strategic decisions.* Since the purpose of environmental analysis is not knowledge about the environment for its own sake but rather information that is useful in strategic decision making, the implications of alternate scenarios for the relevant decision context must be clearly identified. Thus, the purpose of this step is to move from the outside-in perspective of the previous four steps to an inside-out perspective: What do the scenarios imply for the decision context of the organization?

A number of applications of scenarios have recently been reported—for example, in product planning (Morris 1982) and in creating end-century scenarios (Martin and Mason 1982). Zenter (1982), after reviewing fifteen applications, notes that scenarios have been used to describe situations ranging in scale from global forecasting to that of individual market contexts. Klein and Linneman (1981), after intensive study of eight case histories, conclude that the technique is adopted as a result of an increasingly turbulent environment. They also note that scenarios are intricate, expensive, and time-consuming.

Avoiding Common Mistakes in the Use of Environmental Analysis Techniques

Using the right techniques is not sufficient; they must be used correctly. Often it is not the techniques themselves per se that lead to problems but rather how they are used. The intent of this section is to identify some common problems in the use of environmental analysis techniques and to suggest ways of dealing with them.

Do Not Substitute Forecasts for Reality. All too often a forecast is viewed as the representation of the future. Because some picture of the future environment is captured in a forecast (e.g., a scenario), this does not mean that it will come to pass. Rather, forecasts should be regarded as nothing more than possible alternative futures.

Create Alternative Possible Futures. The mind-set that erroneously seeks the one true picture of the future can best be handled by creating a number of alternative representations of the future—for example, multiple scenarios. Each representation of the future can be used to indicate different cause-effect relationships among environmental variables, different assumptions, and different key events and their consequences.

View the Future as a Set of Assumptions. The notion of alternative futures emphasizes that the future can best be viewed as a set of assumptions. The output of environmental analysis is really assumptions about what will happen in the environment over some specified time period. An emphasis upon depictions of the future as assumptions not only serves to lessen the likelihood that forecasts will be substituted for reality but also serves to heighten awareness among analysts that environmental analysis is a continuing activity.

Recycle Through Techniques. The exigencies surrounding environmental analysis—time constraints on those involved, the need for instant information—create pressures to short-circuit the analysis process. One consequence is that analysts may go through an analysis routine or technique only once or as quickly as possible. Much learning is lost, however, if analysts do not go through the steps in the technique a number of times using different assumptions, testing different causal relationships, and so on. Relatedly, recycling through the techniques is necessary to test for consistency in the connections implied among environmental events and trends. Indeed, this is a prerequisite to the establishment of alternative possible or plausible futures.

Search for Causal Processes. Recycling through techniques, by itself, is not sufficient. The emphasis must be upon the search for causal processes—that is, the forces driving environmental change. Environmental analysis in many organizations often stops at describing the current or anticipated environment. Building upon our discussion of driving forces in each of the segment chapters, environmental analysis techniques can be oriented to the identification of driving forces. Cross-impact matrices, Delphi forecasting, scenarios, and other techniques can all be used to seek out the forces driving change. This orientation is essential if we accept the maxim that the future cannot be told from the past.

Identify Key Events and Their Consequences. An essential element of insightful environmental analysis is the need to focus on major events and their consequences; this is a central part of the search for causal processes. This focus tends to sharpen analysts' sensitivity to linkages among environmental trends and patterns because not just the event but also its consequences are important. For example, as noted in Chapters 9 and 10, political and regulatory events typically lead to ramifications in the other segments. Postulating what these consequences are likely to be leads to the identification of the linkages that are at the core of the task in environmental analysis.

Develop an Integrated Analytical Approach. A major handicap in the efforts of many organizations engaged in environmental analysis is overemphasis upon quantitative data and underemphasis upon qualitative data. Quantitative data do not speak for themselves: numbers must be interpreted, and statistics must be imbued with meaning. The point here is that the nonquantified or nonquantifiable is often crucial in creating meaning out of the quantitative data. For example, in the political arena, electoral results are easily quantified, yet to assess the implications of these results requires an understanding of the political process and its interactions with other environmental segments. Stated differently, the rationale underlying any environmental assessment or forecast always goes beyond mere numbers or statistics; the quantitative and the qualitative must be integrated.

Use Forecasts as Early Warning Systems. Many of the previous points—create alternative possible futures, view the future as a set of assumptions, search for causal processes—suggest that environmental forecasts can be used to identify indicators that should be used to monitor change. In this way, environmental analysis directly serves as an input to monitoring and, to a lesser extent, scanning. Thus, forecasts and forecasting provide a feedback loop to the earlier stages of environmental analysis; they are not just ends in themselves, as all too frequently happens in many organizations.

SUMMARY

This chapter briefly discussed some key environmental analysis techniques. It especially emphasized the distinctions between frameworks and techniques and between data gathering and analysis. Environmental analysis techniques require multiple forms of judgment on the part of analysts. Techniques serve to facilitate and explicate analysts' thought processes.

14

Managing Environmental Analysis

In the preceding chapters, we discussed the mechanisms of conducting environmental analysis. We highlighted the role of judgment in many phases of the process of environmental analysis: what data to scan, what indicators are relevant, what interpretations or inferences to draw from the data, what strategic implications flow from the data. In short, environmental analysis is much more an art than a science; it cannot be reduced to the application of a collection of mechanical rules. The role of judgment renders environmental analysis susceptible to influence by organization-related factors. As conceived and implemented in organizations, environmental analysis therefore needs to be conceptualized as more than an analytical activity so that its full potential can be realized.

Environmental analysis is an activity that requires people, resources, and time. Someone in the organization must spend the time to do the requisite analytical tasks involved in environmental analysis. Resources beyond people are often required: money to fund data collection, to buy outside analysis capability, or to support internal analysis efforts. Much managerial time is often consumed in organizing to carry out the analytical tasks inherent in environmental analysis: deciding who should do what in collecting, analyzing, and interpreting data; establishing scanning and monitoring roles and overseeing their implementation; and creating the organizational processes such as task forces, ad hoc teams, or working groups required to effect these tasks.

The importance of the need to manage environmental analysis cannot be overemphasized. Almost all the studies dealing with environmental analysis in large organizations (Fahey, King, and Narayanan 1981; Diffenbach 1982; Stubbardt 1982; Lenz and Engledow 1986) suggest that the management of environmental analysis often dominates the technical or analytical factors as a determinant of the quality and effectiveness of environmental analysis.

In this chapter, we focus on managing environmental analysis—the organizational issues that need to be resolved for the potential of environmental analysis to be realized. The scheme of the chapter is as follows. First, we present the framework for organizing the discussion of issues related to the management of environmental analysis in organizations. Second, we present some of the issues and problems usually encountered during environmental analysis, and point out how these issues and problems are related to organizational factors. Third, we consider some alternative solutions to these problems. Note, however, that our discussion is confined to environmental analysis in relatively large organizations. These organizations usually have the need and the resources to establish internal environmental analysis capability and to procure help externally if needed.

ORGANIZING FRAMEWORK FOR DISCUSSION

A framework around which our discussion is conducted is presented in Figure 14.1. Four factors are considered in the framework: (1) structure, (2) culture, (3) politics, and (4) managerial processes.

■ *Structure* refers to the organizational design for environmental analysis: the role of individuals as they relate to the mechanics of doing environmental analysis (operating structure); mechanisms

Figure 14.1   A Framework for Considering Managerial Issues

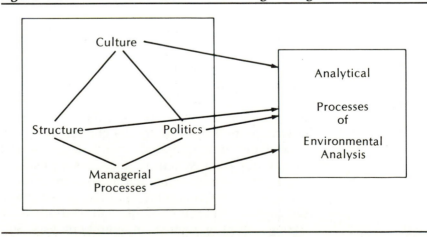

to link outputs of environmental analysis to other activities; and the role of environmental analysis activity within the overall organizational structure.

- *Culture* refers to the beliefs, norms, and behavioral patterns held as valid by members of the organization.
- *Politics* refers to influence patterns employed by individuals in organizations in the pursuit of their own self-interests—for example, the efforts of individuals to steer analytical processes and decision making in directions they deem important.
- *Managerial processes* refer to the dynamics of managing environmental analysis.

These organizational factors influence the analytical tasks—scanning, monitoring, forecasting, and assessment—involved in environmental analysis as delineated in Chapter 3. Illustrations of these influences are presented next to highlight the role of organizational factors. This discussion is woven around the key issues that need to be resolved during management of environmental analysis.

ISSUES IN ENVIRONMENTAL ANALYSIS

The analytical tasks involved in environmental analysis, noted previously, suggest that the process of analysis is not entirely deductive but necessarily relies on intuitions, judgments, and sometimes the conjectures of organizational members. Table 14.1 shows the major issues that crop up during environmental analysis and the role of organizational factors in spawning these issues. These linkages are described in greater detail next.

Conception of the Environment

The conception of the environment in the minds of key decision makers and ways of relating to the environment often act as a strong hindrance to effective environmental analysis. Thinking about the environment is a messy process. The scope of the analytical tasks in environmental analysis can be challenging, as revealed by the complexity and interconnectedness of the segments that may need attention. Consequently, putting these issues aside because the environment appears too formidable is convenient at one level. At another level, it is easy to discount potential environmental impacts based on the current capabilities of the organization. Either approach acts as a strong inhibition to environmental analysis. Such beliefs on the part

Table 14.1   Influence of Organizational Factors on Analytical Tasks in Environmental Analysis

Analytical Task	Organizational Factors				
	Cultural	*Structural*	*Political*	*Process*	*Life Cycle*
Definition of Environment Inadequate conception	Operating culture	(1) Remoteness of environmental analysis from strategy formulation (2) Lack of expertise	Vested interests opposed	Staffing of low competence	Early introduction
Inadequate frame of reference					
Definition of Segments Inadequate appreciation of uncertainties	Search for certainty	Inadequate linkage	Entrenched interests	Lack of educating key people	Start-up phase
Scanning and Monitoring Early convergence	Bias toward action	Lack of diversity	Support for preconceived notions	Reward systems	Learning
Inadequate time for reflection					
Forecasting Kinds of analytical techniques	Quantitative emphasis	Overly specialized units		Lack of education	Learning
Assessment Inadequate linkage Inadequate follow-up		Absence of linkage mechanisms	Window dressing	Inability to institutionalize	Middle
Routinization	All				late phase

of top management often manifest themselves in the treatment of environmental analysis as an afterthought and as a symbol of progressiveness in management style without any real impact on decision making or by not engaging in environmental analysis at all.

A number of potential reasons may explain why this problem often exists in organizations. Culturally, the organization may be dominated by an operating orientation as opposed to a strategic orientation; thus, the problems of today displace the possible concerns of tomorrow. Alternatively, environmental analysis may have low credibility at the top levels of management. Politically, environmental analysis has the potential to redistribute resources within the organization. Politically motivated vested interests may prevent consideration of environmental issues, lest it endanger their power position or resource base. Structurally, the individuals, units, or groups may be located well away from the organizational centers of strategy formulation and implementation and thus have little real influence on the process. On the process side, individuals performing environmental analysis may be perceived as having low competence or not providing inputs into strategy formulation perceived as relevant by key decision makers.

Frames of Reference

Closely related to inadequate conception of the environment are the frames of reference brought to bear when doing environmental analysis. In much of this book, we note the importance of integrating outside-in and inside-out approaches to environmental analysis; unfortunately, this is much easier said than done in organizations. Much of the organization's attention is focused on the interface between the organization and its immediate task environment. The macroenvironment is viewed as far from the immediate concerns of management; moreover, its impact is often indirect and delayed. Thus, the pull toward inside-out analysis is great; outside-in analysis may be invoked when the organization finds itself in the midst of a crisis. At first glance, this may appear to be a failure of analysis; however, the basis for this failure may lie in the nature of the organization's functioning.

Cultural forces such as an operating orientation at the top levels of management, absence of structures for doing outside-in analysis, and political factors that inhibit search for new avenues of business development often engender a predominantly, if not exclusively, inside-out orientation. Alternatively, those entrusted with responsibility for environmental analysis may view their task as providing only analyses relevant to the task environment (e.g., market research) and thus may be distorting the intent of the analysis.

The two problems noted earlier—inadequate conception of the environment and distorted frame of reference—tend to appear in organizations with no prior history of engaging in environmental analysis or which have just introduced it as a part of the strategic planning process.

Kinds of Uncertainties

A third problem that emanates from a lack of understanding of the macroenvironment is a low level of appreciation of the kinds of uncertainties involved in environmental analysis. Environmental segments differ in terms of their uncertainties. For example, demographic trends are relatively predictable in the short term, whereas technological change and political change can produce surprises even in the short term. Thus, the kinds of analytical issues are different across segments. In a similar vein, the time frames of impacts are also different. Despite these differences, the tendency to treat uncertainties as though they are similar is indeed great amid the push and pull of organizational life.

Furthermore, involvement in the task environment, which is relatively certain in the short run, predisposes managers to look for certainties that do not exist in the macroenvironment. Projections and forecasts, for example, are tentative statements about alternative futures; yet, often the tendency is to treat them as "real" statements about the future. This tendency not only misses the point of forecasting but also often results in disappointment and loss of faith in environmental analysis, as the forecasts turn out to be much off the mark.

Structural, process, and political factors may underlie this problem. Structurally, where linkage mechanisms between environmental analysis and strategic analysis are weak, the understanding of these uncertainties and their implications is less likely to be widespread in the organization. On the process side, exclusive focus on the outputs of environmental analysis without attendant appreciation of the importance of involvement in the process often leads to misunderstanding the role of different uncertainties. Finally, entrenched interests can always play up the differences as a means of ridiculing environmental analysis itself.

The following are some problems and issues related to the various stages of environmental analysis.

Early Convergence during Scanning

We have noted that the early stage of environmental analysis—scanning—requires the analyst to reserve judgment and postpone drawing conclusions; rather, the focus is on general surveillance of the environment. Data at this stage are filled with "noise." Sufficient time and attention should be paid to developing an understanding of the environment. This is made difficult in many organizations because of the incessant pressure to get something done. Managers are called upon to be decisive; reserving judgment is equated by others as indecisive. These forces all too often result in early or premature convergence in the initial scanning stage. Unless these forces are thwarted, the potential is high that important pockets of information will be missed during this stage, rendering further stages of analysis shaky with regard to data, potential conclusions, and implications.

In addition to the bias toward action, other strong cultural norms are frequently operating that can inhibit the nurturing of ambiguity. Particularly important in the scanning phase is searching out data that are contradictory to existing beliefs; operant norms often inhibit this process. Structurally, if environmental analysis is staffed with people who are homogeneous in their orientation, alternative perspectives are not likely to be represented. Reward systems that are short-run in focus and time frames too short for the process of scanning could also contribute to the lack of representation of alternative perspectives. Politically, early convergence often reflects political interests that seek environmental analysis to support preconceived conclusions.

Inadequate Time for Reflection

Beyond early convergence during scanning, a related but broader issue is common in environmental analysis: analysts may find themselves with inadequate time for reflection in the process of drawing inferences, which is a central component of monitoring, forecasting, and assessment. Note again that the data do not yield inferences; analysts must exercise their creative and intuitive capacities to weave inferences from the data. This requires that time be devoted to reflection. Reflection requires a certain organizational milieu; many of the structural, process, and political impediments to effective environmental analysis already noted may inhibit the emergence and maintenance of this milieu.

Inadequate Appreciation of the Kinds of Analytic Techniques

As discussed in Chapter 13, analytic techniques involved in environmental analysis vary widely in terms of data requirements, data characteristics, and nature of outputs. Two different issues emerge here. First, many organizations rely heavily on highly quantitative techniques. This provides an appearance of precision and results in a tendency to accept the outputs as definitive statements. This tendency is common in organizational cultures where there is heavy emphasis on analysis, where there are overly specialized environmental analysis units that have poor linkages to strategy analysis groups or the operating organization.

Second, at the other end of the spectrum, some techniques may be completely neglected. This robs monitoring and forecasting of much of their vigor. This is likely to take place when on the process side there has been a failure to educate the various key organizational actors of the scope and potential utility of the various techniques. Alternatively, some of the outputs are debunked without examination, purely to avoid unsettling analyses that may dilute the base of entrenched political interests.

Inadequate Linkage Between Environmental Analysis and Strategy Analysis

Perhaps the most significant problem in many organizations is inadequate linkage between environmental analysis and strategy analysis: the outputs of environmental analysis are weakly or not at all linked to further stages in strategy formulation. This manifests itself in several ways: uncertainties postulated by environmental analysis are neglected; weak signals are not further pursued; operating assumptions from the past continue to shape strategy formulation; and no specific action plans emanate from environmental analysis. The effects of such inadequate linkage are often not immediately clear. Over the long run, however, organizations typically face foreseen crises and continue to be driven by short-term issues.

Although several factors may inhibit adequate linkage, structural factors are perhaps the most important in effecting adequate linkage. Isolated environmental analysis units, staffed by individuals with high technical expertise, often develop into "fortune tellers," with their own language and their own agenda and objectives, and as a consequence, lose touch with the needs of the organization. Not surprising, then, is that the outputs of environmental analysis are not seen as action relevant, and the value of the process to those engaged in strategy analysis is lost. On the process side, the absence of linkage could emanate from not tailoring the outputs of environmental analysis to planning cycles, and lack of continual exchange of information between environmental analysis units and those engaged in strategy analysis. Communication becomes important not only to educate individuals to the differing kinds of environmental uncertainties but also to underscore that environmental analysis addresses different time frames. Political factors such as the top management's view of environmental analysis as merely window dressing can also inhibit these linkages.

Inadequate Follow-up

An equally compelling drawback in many organizations is inadequate follow-up of actions based on environmental analysis. As we have noted, environmental assumptions should permeate various stages of strategy formulation and implementation. To be effective, environmental analysis should not be viewed as a one-time event but as an ongoing process. The scanning, monitoring, forecasting, and assessment phases are closely intertwined; each stage may trigger issues or trends that need further fine-grained analysis. Inadequate follow-up is likely to occur in cultures where planning is not ingrained and where environmental analysis is done primarily on an ad hoc basis to develop action plans to avert crises.

Routinization of Environmental Analysis

Where environmental analysis units are part of an ongoing organization, and especially where they have been in existence for some period of time, the routinization of environmental analysis is a great possibility; that is, the organization continues with environmental analysis based on an inappropriate and often earlier view of the environment. Critical issues with regard to the definition of the environment and the delineation of segments are neglected; the organization relies heavily on indicators and data bases of previously identified issues and concerns. As we have noted, however, environmental segments often change, and the rate of change changes. For example, social or regulatory issues often play themselves out and bring new ones in their wake. As routinization of analysis reaches an advanced stage, environmental analysis becomes increasingly irrelevant.

Structural, process, and political factors play a role in the routinization of environmental analysis. If the structure is highly formalized and environmental analysis units have relatively low interaction with operating management or the outside world, then routinization is likely to occur. Alternatively, managerial failure to infuse variety into environmental analysis by bringing in new blood and perspectives or by rotating individuals may induce routinization. Finally, top management, through stylized reports and highly formalized structures, may induce routinization.

ORGANIZATIONAL PREREQUISITES

The previous discussion of some key problems in environmental analysis should sensitize readers to the inevitable role of organizational factors. In this section, we briefly consider some of the organizational prerequisites and approaches to managing environmental analysis in general, and the problems noted earlier in particular. The discussion is organized around cultural, political, structural, and process factors.

Cultural-Political Prerequisites

Some key cultural-political prerequisites are involved in getting environmental analysis initiated, sustained, and integrated into the strategic management process in organizations. These prerequisites are necessary for maintaining and reinforcing the legitimacy, visibility, and credibility of environmental analysis.

Top Management Commitment. Top management plays a key role in shaping the culture of an organization; without top management commitment, environmental analysis is not likely to be initiated or sustained in organizations. The term *commitment* means more than the allocation of resources; it also means a propensity to highlight the importance of environmental analysis. Top management involvement in environmental analysis sends a major signal to the organization.

An Environmental Analysis Champion. Environmental analysis especially in its early stages, requires a credible champion to make it visible within the organization. Ideally, the champion should be able to wield significant influence in the organization. The role of the champion is important because not all members of the top management can pay continual attention to environmental analysis issues, given the demands on their time. Additionally, the champion's role is to nurture environmental analysis efforts; this includes granting political "refuge" to those engaged in environmental analysis who are likely to be viewed with suspicion in the organization until that time when environmental analysis becomes ingrained as part of the culture.

The Sustenance of Ambiguity. A key role for top management in general and for the environmental analysis champion in particular is to create and sustain a sufficient level of ambiguity in the process of doing environmental analysis. This implies an ability to live with uncertain information and uncertain interpretations, and to downplay expectations of certainty, often demanded by the operating sectors of the organization. This also involves legitimizing analyses that challenge the status quo through such processes as devil's advocacy or institutionalizing dialectical processes (Mason and Mittroff 1983). Further, individuals engaged in these analyses should be shielded from norms of conformity and should be encouraged to think openly and creatively.

Interfaces into Strategic Management.   Commitment to environmental analysis at the operating levels in the organization needs to be generated primarily by highlighting the role of environmental analysis in strategy analysis and particularly the need to weave environmental assumptions into strategy analysis. This could be accomplished by having senior line management ask environmentally related questions in strategy presentations and making environmental analysis a formal part of analysis in strategy decisions, strategy development, and implementation.

Structural Prerequisites

Structural prerequisites are important because they delineate allocation of tasks and responsibilities for doing environmental analysis, and impact the quality of environmental analysis outputs and their usefulness for strategic analysis. Five key issues in this area are discussed.

Multiple Structural Mechanisms.   A wide number of choices are available to an organization with respect to structural mechanisms to facilitate doing environmental analysis. At the simplest level, an organization could rely on outside agencies to provide it with the requisite analysis; at the other end of the spectrum, an organization may have a unit devoted entirely to doing environmental analysis. To some extent, the structural mechanism employed defines the scope of environmental analysis: the skills and biases represented in the structure determine which segments are attended to and which are omitted.

An important point is that most organizations use multiple structural mechanisms for environmental analysis. What structure is used depends on the purpose of the analysis and the amount of resources available. Outside agencies are often relied upon for routine data provision (e.g., economic data) or sophisticated data analysis and forecasts (e.g., technological and political issues). Ad hoc teams are frequently assembled to identify and assess strategic issues. Task forces involved in strategic activities such as new product development or diversification may include environmental analysis representatives. More generally, environmental analysis units can serve multiple functions in ongoing strategic planning processes. Where the intent is to institutionalize environmental analysis, these structural mechanisms should be considered as complementary and not mutually exclusive.

Linkage Mechanisms.   Without linkage mechanisms, environmental analysis is not likely to be integrated into strategic analysis. The driving forces behind the creation and maintenance of these linkages are the notions that involvement in the process of environmental analysis is an important learning experience for organizational members and that environmental factors should be considered in all stages of decision making.

Linkage problems are likely to be acute in the case of reports from outside agencies. Thus, sufficient time must be devoted to understanding the implications of outside agency reports. This may involve getting such reports on the agendas of ad hoc committees, task forces, or regular management meetings. Linkage problems may also arise in the case of environmental analysis units at an advanced stage of expertise. For many reasons, the "experts" may have problems communicating with the rest of the organization. Thus, a useful consideration is rotating individuals through environmental analysis units to partially alleviate these problems. In the case of ad hoc task forces, having an environmental analysis representative may be necessary to help ensure that critical environmental factors are considered during all phases of decision making.

Differentiation Between Corporate and Business-Unit Levels.
In large corporations, environmental analysis is done at both the corporate and business-unit levels. For example, many types of macroenvironmental forecasts (economic and political forecasts) are frequently produced at the corporate level, whereas other types of environmental analysis (e.g., demographic and life-style assessments) are done at the business-unit level. Establishing such differentiation on a rational basis is important. Environmental analysis at the corporate level is frequently germane to a majority or all of the business units, whereas analysis at the business-unit level may have little relevance to other parts of the organization. Thus, where the corporation is composed of diverse business units, a certain degree of decentralization of environmental analysis efforts may be necessary.

The decisions with respect to the prior structural mechanisms may be guided by some principles pertaining to the location of environmental analysis centers and the design of environmental analysis units or task forces.

Location of Environmental Analysis Center. We use the term *analysis center* here to emphasize that environmental analysis may be conducted within many different structural mechanisms: environmental analysis units, ad hoc teams, task forces, outside agencies, or as a part of the activity of other organizational entities such as market research or R&D groups. Irrespective of the structural mechanism employed, in attempting to assure linkage, it is important to locate environmental analysis as proximate as possible to strategy analysis so that its outputs are useful for and utilized in strategy analysis. Unless there is close interaction between the two streams of analysis, the value of both the process and the products of environmental analysis will not be fully realized. Such proximity in location enables those engaged in environmental analysis to (1) portray the outputs in terms meaningful to strategy analysts, (2) fine-tune the process and outputs of environmental analysis so that they correspond to the strategy analysis requirements, thus enhancing the chances that action implications are relevant and meaningful, and (3) help strategy analysts to think through the implications in specific action terms.

Design of Environmental Analysis Units or Task Forces. A final set of considerations involves the design of environmental units or task forces. We noted earlier that heterogeneous viewpoints need to be represented throughout environmental analysis and especially in the early stages so that premature convergence is avoided. This in turn necessitates that design should focus on creating groups with a heterogeneity of perspectives. Diversity should be maintained on specific projects over time. Diversity over time is particularly important for long-standing environmental analysis units so that "groupthink" does not ensue. This may necessitate that new blood with fresh viewpoints be brought in over time to resuscitate what may be an ossified analysis unit.

Managerial Process Considerations

Process considerations involve the dynamics of managing environmental analysis. They influence how environmental analysis gets done and also how it is linked to strategy analysis. We address four major considerations in this area.

Managing the Design Process.   A critical step is managing the process of setting the overarching premises of environmental analysis and how it gets done. First, the premises involve two key issues: (1) that environmental analysis outputs should be included in strategy analysis and (2) that environmental analysis is not a quick fix or panacea for organizational problems. Setting these premises is not an exercise in rational analysis but should be viewed as an educational effort. The key individuals who play a role in strategic analysis need to be educated about the role of environmental analysis. Managing these expectations about the role, scope, and nature of environmental analysis is a key to the success of environmental analysis.

Second, environmental analysis is a function: multiple ways exist for carrying out the function contingent on the circumstances. For example, we noted that multiple structural mechanisms are available for effecting environmental analysis. The choice of these structural mechanisms should be a deliberative process intended to fulfill the function of environmental analysis.

Managing the Internal Process.   Managing the internal dynamics of environmental analysis units or task groups is another important consideration. Although issues germane to managing organizational processes are relevant here, two issues specific to environmental-analysis-related activities deserve mention. First, as previously noted, environmental analysis is characterized by divergent, retroductive, and recursive processes; the analyst is expected to exercise judgment, intuition, and sometimes speculation. This necessitates internal norms different from those in operating cultures. Stated differently, norms of decisiveness, specificity, and consensus are not always functional. In contrast, norms of reflection, ambiguity, and legitimacy of differences in viewpoints need to be nurtured. The tasks of managing are twofold: (1) to reinforce to those engaged in the analysis that such norms, though possibly drastically different from the rest of the organization, are functional and (2) to highlight their functionality to those not involved in environmental analysis. The first task ensures quality of environmental analysis, while the second serves to protect those engaged in environmental analysis from negative political pressures.

Second, managing the time frame of those engaged in environmental analysis is critical. Focusing on the current environment is always easy because data are plentiful and analysis is relatively straightforward. As the time horizon lengthens, however—as we have shown in previous chapters—data become murky and interpretations are much more difficult. Where individuals are rewarded on short-term considerations, the focus will predominantly be on the short term. A necessity, therefore, is to manage the motivational and reward schemes so that individuals are focused not merely on the short term but also on the long term.

Managing Linkages. Like the structural factors, managing the process of linkage is important if environmental analysis is to be useful for strategy analysis. Four key issues need to be considered.

First, and perhaps most important, the environmental analysis outputs should have direct utility to the strategy problems at hand. Thus, the kinds of outputs useful for corporate strategy are likely to be different from those at the business-unit or functional levels. Loss of linkage results when the outputs are mismatched.

Second, and relatedly, environmental analysis outputs should be timed to fit into different planning cycles. We noted earlier that the short-, medium-, and long-term characterization of environmental issues is useful for different planning horizons.

Third, the form of environmental analysis outputs should be carefully considered. Environmental analysis is facilitated by the use of several methodologies and its own jargon. However, environmental outputs are not necessarily intelligible to those not familiar with these methodologies and jargon and thus may be ignored. This is particularly likely to happen with a highly differentiated environmental analysis unit staffed with individuals of unique expertise.

Finally, environmental issues should be given visibility at all stages of strategy analysis. Often the role of the linking person is to make sure that environmental issues are raised at the various stages of decision making.

Evaluation of Environmental Analysis. Of particular importance to organizations where environmental analysis has been in existence as a formalized process is the need to periodically evaluate the performance of environmental analysis. Stated differently, the function of environmental analysis should be audited with a view to assessing its contribution to strategy analysis. For example, at the analytical level, as the environment changes, previously held definitions of the environment will have to be discarded. At the organizational level, structures and processes will have to be changed, given the particular set of circumstances facing the organization. At the cultural-political level, leadership changes may necessitate that environmental analysis will have to redefine itself and renew its legitimacy and utility.

SUMMARY

Environmental analysis as practiced in organizations needs to be conceptualized as more than a set of analytical routines. Cultural, political, structural, and systemic factors influence the quality of environmental analysis as well as how well it is integrated into the strategic management of the organization. These factors vary over the life cycle of environmental analysis and have to be managed in order to realize the full potential of the analysis.

References

Abell, D. F. *Defining the Business: The Starting Point of Strategic Planning.* Englewood Cliffs, N.J.: Prentice-Hall, 1980.

Aguilar, F. J. *Scanning the Business Environment.* New York: Macmillan, 1967.

Aldrich, H. E. *Organizations and Environments.* Englewood Cliffs, N.J.: Prentice-Hall, 1979.

Aldrich, H. E., and S. Mindlin. "Uncertainty and Dependence: Two Perspectives on Environment." In *Organization and Environment,* edited by L. Kerpit pp. 149–70. Beverly Hills, Calif.: Sage, 1978.

Ansoff, I. "Managing Strategic Surprise by Response to Weak Signals." *California Management Review* 18(2) (Winter 1975): 21–33.

———. *Strategic Management.* New York: Halsted Press, 1981.

Argyris, C. *Reasoning, Learning, and Action.* San Francisco: Jossey-Bass, 1982.

Ascher, W., and W. H. Overholt. *Strategic Planning and Forecasting: Political Risk and Economic Opportunity.* New York: Wiley, 1983.

Baier, K., and N. Rescher. *Values and the Future.* New York: Free Press, 1969.

Bartos, Rena. *The Moving Target: What Every Marketer Should Know About Women.* New York: The Free Press, 1982.

Bauer, R. A. *Second-Order Consequences.* Cambridge: MIT Press, 1969.

Bertalanffy, L. V. *General Systems Theory: Foundations, Development, and Applications.* New York: Braziller, 1968.

Brown, J. K. *This Business of Issues: Coping with the Company's Environments.* New York: Conference Board, 1979.

Carson, R. *Silent Spring.* Boston: Houghton Mifflin, 1962.

Cooper, A. C., and D. Schendel. "Strategic Responses to Technological Threats." *Business Horizons* (February 1976): 61–69.

Diffenbach, J. "Corporate Environmental Analysis in Large U.S. Corporations." *Long Range Planning* 16(3) (1983): 107–16.

Dutton, J. E., L. Fahey, and V. K. Narayanan. "Toward Understanding Strategic Issue Diagnosis." *Strategic Management Journal* 4 (1983): 307–23.

Emery, F., and E. Trist. "The Causal Texture of Organizational Environments." *Human Relations* 18 (August 1965): 124–51.

Fahey, L., W. R. King, and V. K. Narayanan. "Environmental Scanning and Forecasting in Strategic Planning: The State of the Art." *Long Range Planning* (April 1981): 32–39.

Freeman, R. E. *Strategic Management of Stakeholders.* Boston: Pitman, 1984.

Galbraith, J. R., and R. K. Kazanjian. *Strategy Implementation: Structure, Systems, and Process.* 2d ed. St. Paul: West, 1986.

Glover, J. "Innovation and Evolution of the Environment." Graduate School of Business, Harvard University, 1966.

Hannan, M. T., and J. H. Freeman. "The Population Ecology of Organizations." *American Journal of Sociology* 82 (1977): 929–64.

Hazard, L. "The Power of Technology: Challenges for Urban Policy." In *Values and the Future,* edited by K. Baier and N. Rescher. New York: Free Press, 1969.

Hofer, C. W. and D. E. Schendel. *Strategy Formulation: Analytical Concepts.* St. Paul: West, 1978.

Jantsch, E. "Forecasting and Systems Approach: A Frame of Reference." *Management Science* 19(2) (1973): 1355–67.

Kelly, P., and M. Kranzberg. *Technological Innovation: A Critical Review of Current Knowledge.* National Science Foundation, February 1975.

King, W. R., and D. I. Cleland. *Strategic Planning and Policy.* New York: Van Nostrand, 1978.

Klein, H. E., and R. E. Linneman. "The Use of Scenarios in Corporate Planning—Eight Case Histories." *Long Range Planning* 14(5) (1981): 69–77.

Kluckhohn, C. "Values and Value-Orientations." *In Toward a General Theory of Action*, edited by T. Parsons and E. A. Shils, pp. 338–433. Cambridge: Harvard University Press, 1962.

Kolde, E. J. *Environment of International Business.* Belmont, Calif.: Kent, 1985.

Lawrence, P., and D. Dyer. *Renewing American Industry.* New York: Free Press, 1983.

Lenz, R. T., and J. L. Engledow. "Environmental Analysis Units and Strategic Decision Making: A Field Study of Selected Leading Edge Corporations." *Strategic Management Journal* (Vol. 7, No. 1, 1986): 69–83.

Leontief, W. "Input-Output Economics." *Scientific American* 1(85) (October 1957): 8.

Little, Arthur D. and Co. "Strategic Management of Technology." Paper presented at the European Forum, 1981.

Lodge, G. *The New American Ideology.* New York: Knopf, 1975.

MacKenzie, K. D., and F. J. Barron. "Analysis of a Decision Making Investigation." *Management Science* 17(4) (December 1970): B226–41.

MacMillan, I. C., and P. E. Jones. *Strategy Formulation: Power and Politics.* 2d ed. St. Paul: West, 1986.

Mandel, T. F. "Future Scenarios and Their Uses in Corporate Strategy." In *The Strategic Management Handbook,* edited by K. Albert, pp. 10–1—10–21. New York: McGraw-Hill, 1983.

Martin, W., and S. Mason. *Learning and Work: The Choices for 1991 and 2001.* Sudbury, Suffolk: Leisure Consultants, 1982.

Meadows, D. H., D. L. Meadows, J. Randers, and W. W. Behrens III. *The Limits to Growth: A Report for the Club of Rome's Project on the Predicament of Mankind.* New York: Universe Books, 1972.

Miles, R. E., and C. C. Snow. *Organizational Strategy, Structure, and Process.* New York: McGraw-Hill, 1978.

Mintzberg, H. *The Structuring of Organizations.* New York: Prentice-Hall, 1979.

Moore, W. L., and M. L. Tushman. "Managing Innovation Over the Product Life Cycle." In *Readings in the Management of Innovation,* edited by M. L. Tushman and W. L. Moore. Boston: Pitman, 1982.

Morris, G. K. "The Uses of Future Research in Product Planning." *Long Range Planning* 15(6) (1982): 67–73.

Naisbitt, J. *Megatrends: Ten New Directions Transforming Our Lives.* New York: Warner Books, 1982.

Narayanan, V. K., and L. Fahey, "Environmental Analysis for Strategy Formulation." In *Strategic Planning and Management Handbook,* edited by W. R. King and D. I. Cleland. New York: Van Nostrand (in press).

Ogburn, W. F., and M. F. Nimkoff. *Technology and the Changing Family.* Boston: Houghton Mifflin, 1955.

Peters, T., and R. Waterman. *In Search of Excellence.* New York: Harper & Row, 1978.

Pfeffer, J., and G. Salancik. *The External Control of Organizations: A Resource Dependence Perspective.* New York: Harper & Row, 1978.

Porter, M. E. *Competitive Strategy.* New York: Free Press, 1980.

Quinn, J. B., and J. A. Mueller. "Transferring, Research Results to Operations." *Harvard Business Review* (January–February 1963).

Rescher, N. "What Is a Value Change? A Framework for Research." In *Values and the Future,* edited by K. Baier and N. Rescher. New York: Free Press, 1969.

Sahal, D. *Patterns of Technological Innvoation.* Reading, Mass.: Addison-Wesley, 1981.

Schnee, J. E. "Government Programs and the Growth of High Technology Industries." *Research Policy* (January 1978): 2–24.

Schon, D. A. "Forecasting and Technological Change." *Daedalus* (Summer 1967): 759–70.

Scott, W. R. *Organizations: Rational, Natural, and Open Systems.* Englewood Cliffs, N.J.: Prentice-Hall, 1981.

Stubbardt, C. "Are Environmental Scanning Units Effective?" *Long Range Planning* 15, (June 1982): 139–145.

Terpstra, V., and K. David. *The Cultural Environment of International Business.* Cincinnati, Ohio: Southwestern, 1985.

Toffler, A. *The Third Wave.* New York: Morrow, 1980.

Vernon, R., and L. T. Wells, Jr. *Economic Environment of International Business.* Englewood Cliffs, N.J.: Prentice-Hall, 1981.

Weick, K. "Middle Range Theories of Social Systems." *Behavioral Science* 19 (November 1974): 375–67.

Weick, K. E. *The Social Psychology of Organizing.* 2d ed. Reading, Mass.: Addison-Wesley, 1979.

Weidenbaum, Murray L. *Business, Government, and the Public* 2d ed. Englewood Cliffs, N. J.: Prentice-Hall, Inc., 1981.

Wells, Gordon S. C. "Forecasting Technological Innovation," in Taylor and Sparkes (Ed.) *Corporate Strategy and Planning*, Surrey England: Wm. Heineman Ltd., 1977.

Wheelwright & Makridakis Forecasting Methods for Management, 3rd Ed. 1980.

Wilson, I. "Forecasting Social and Political Trends." In *Corporate Strategy and Planning*, edited by B. Taylor and J. R. Sparkes. London: Heinemann, 1977.

Zentner, R. D. "Scenarios: Past, Present, and Future." *Long Range Planning*, 15(3) (1982): 12–20.

Index